100 Best Plants
for the Ontario Garden

The Botanical Bones of Great Gardening

STEVE WHYSALL

WHITECAP BOOKS

Edited by Elaine Jones
Proofread by Elizabeth McLean
Cover and interior design by Warren Clark
Color insert design by Susan Greenshields
Research assistance by Loraine Whysall
Cover typeset by Antonia Banyard
Cover photographs by Ryan McNair
Photographs not otherwise credited provided by Horticopia Inc.

Printed and bound in Canada

National Library of Canada Cataloguing in Publication Data

Whysall, Steve, 1950–
100 best plants for the Ontario garden

        Includes index.
        ISBN 1-55110-892-5

        I. Gardening—Ontario. I. Title. II. Title: One hundred best plants
for the Ontario garden.
SB453.C2W483 1999   635.9'09713   C98-911017-6

The publisher acknowledges the support of the Canada Council for the
Arts and the Cultural Services Branch of the Government of British
Columbia for our publishing program. We acknowledge the financial
support of the Government of Canada through the Book Industry
Development Program for our publishing activities.

For more information on this and other Whitecap titles, please visit
our website at www.whitecap.ca

Contents

Thoughts and Thanks

The day I sat down to write this book, my son Joel started a rock band in the garage. A few days later, the band brought home a drummer! As I tried to write about hellebores and euphorbias, Joel and his friends crashed chords on their electric guitars and made the most dreadful racket. They got better, but they were terrible when they started.

My daughter, Aimee, was also graduating from high school around the same time and my youngest son, Peter, was learning to drive and enlisted me to accompany him on numerous nerve-wracking practice trips. So our house and life was a whirl of activity and high spirits. I tell you this because I think some of this raw energy and enthusiasm found its way into this book. So if, while reading about potentilla or hostas, daylilies or maple trees, you suddenly feel the urge to put on some Britpop music and dance around the living room, you are probably subconsciously tuning into all that youthful vitality that was swirling around me at the time of writing this book. That brings me to an important point. When I sit quietly and think what is at the heart and soul of this book, I remember the excitement of being introduced to a marvellous plant for the first time. There was a time when I did not know lady's mantle or daylilies, euphorbias or hardy geraniums, hellebores or salvia, and so on. And I remember very clearly the thrill of discovery, the excitement of being introduced to them for the first time, and the fun of bringing them home and planting them. It is this sense of wonder and pleasure that I hope this book communicates most. If it gets you excited about gardening and if it introduces you to the wonderful world and language of plants, then I feel you have got the best out of this work. My one hope is that you come away with a love of plants and a desire to use them to make a beautiful garden.

Now a special word of thanks to those who made writing this book possible. My wife, Loraine, has been fantastic. It was love at first sight when we met and married back in 1975. She knows me better than anyone . . . and still loves me for all that! Without her patience, intelligence and hard work, I would never have made it through this project. Our children, Joel, Aimee and Peter, were wonderfully supportive and admirably tolerant of the disruption this book brought to their lives. I am also very grateful for the help and information

I got from the following individuals and organizations: Sheridan Nurseries, of Unionville, Ont.; Humber Nurseries, of Brampton, Ont.; Weall and Cullen, of Whitby, Ont.; Picov's Water Garden Centre and Fisheries, of Ajax, Ont.; Specimen Trees, of Pitt Meadows, B.C.; Jacques Amand; The Bulb Specialists, England; Heritage Perennials, of Abbotsford, B.C.; The Perennial Gardens, of Maple Ridge, B.C.

Many gardeners—too many to mention here by name—have played a major role over the years in introducing me to all the beautiful plants mentioned in this book. I know their love of gardening and passion for plants has found its way into the following pages. Every success!

oreword

There are any number of books that suggest perfect plants for the garden but, from our point of view, they all suffer from the same defect: they are written by European gardeners with large estates, or by U.S. writers who live in Virginia or California. Most of the plants they recommend either won't survive here or are unobtainable. This book is different. Its focus is Ontario, and I wish I had thought of it first.

The author now lives in B.C., but gardened for several years in colder regions and knows Ontario's climate and what will grow here. He also consulted with major Ontario nurseries to research the availability of plants and their popularity with the gardening public.

If you designed your garden around a selection of the 100 best plants described in this book, it would be pleasing. However, the author goes much further than this by suggesting plants to use for contrast or harmony, or other plants you could use for similar effect. I certainly found plant combinations that I want to try in my own garden.

Beginning gardeners will appreciate the sections on "Where to plant it" and "How to care for it" given in each plant description. These take the guesswork out of siting and caring for a new plant and enable you to decide on a suitable species for a specific location before you shop. More experienced gardeners will enjoy the "For your collection" section, where the author lists more unusual varieties of plants you might want to consider. In fact, the title *100 Best Plants* is misleading—many, many more than this are included.

This is a book for adventurous gardeners, be they novices or experienced. The wide range of plants described encourages you to plant something different. Remember, hardiness zones are only a guide. There are areas within each zone that are warmer or colder than the average. Also, the hardiness ratings given to plants are not absolute. Often, they are educated guesses and, especially for more unusual plants, may be wrong. Just because you live in Zone 5 doesn't mean you shouldn't try growing plants with a Zone 6 hardiness rating. As a friend of mine puts it, "Never believe a plant isn't hardy until you have killed it three times yourself."

Obviously, I don't agree 100 per cent with Steve's choices. Every gardener has their favorite plants and cannot understand why others don't think as highly of them. However, the majority of the plants he has included in this book would be on my personal list as well.

The upsurge in gardening in recent years, and the ensuing demand for plants, has resulted in some nurseries selling plants that are not particularly suited to the Ontario climate. This book will help gardeners avoid these pitfalls and choose plants that will grow well here.

—Trevor Cole,
author of *The Ontario Gardener*
and *Gardening with Trees and Shrubs*

Before We Begin

What is gardening?

If you're a new gardener, you will undoubtedly feel overwhelmed by the mind-boggling array of gardening information being thrust at you. There are more magazines, books and radio and television shows on gardening than ever before competing for your attention. It is perfectly natural if you feel bombarded and pressured by it all. But gardening is not supposed to be a tense race to acquire knowledge or a difficult project to undertake or a perpetual goal to achieve. It is not something we do with the calculated precision of a mathematician. It is a life-long adventure with nature—creative, playful, intuitive—that often involves a degree of trial and error.

Gardening is all about observation, about looking closely and learning from the physical world around you, noting where the sun shines, where shadows are cast, where frost lingers, where rain puddles, where the wind blows. In gardening, we learn from nature and we find out how to co-operate with nature to grow healthy, beautiful plants. From doing all this, we end up creating lovely gardens that are not only esthetically pleasing but heavenly places in which we can find a deep refreshment for the soul.

Why do we do it?

The question I always love to ask gardeners is, "Why do you do it, what do you get out of gardening?" Some tell me it gives them peace of mind and a deep sense of tranquility to be surrounded by the color and fragrance of beautiful plants.

For them, the garden is a special retreat, an oasis for quiet contemplation in a world frantic with activity. These gardeners enjoy the hard work and physical exercise involved in digging and planting and weeding and doing general garden chores, but their main motivation is to have a beautiful place in which they can rest and relax at the end of the day.

For others, gardening is a creative outlet for their artistic talents. They see the space in their yard as a blank canvas on which they "paint," using plants to create beautiful three-dimensional pictures. They get pleasure out of lovely landscape scenes—not to hang on a wall and look pretty, but tangible, living masterpieces you can actually step into and walk around, where you can touch the trees and smell the flowers. These gardeners like to see what happens when they mix colors and blend the textures of different plants. Most important to them is the artistic satisfaction they derive from creating a picturesque landscape.

Most gardeners are a mixture of these two types—the person looking for a quiet, restful retreat, and the person looking for creative challenge and artistic fulfilment. What about the gardeners who are only interested in growing fruit and vegetables? I tend to think of them more as farmers than gardeners, which is not to say that their enthusiasm, skill and intelligence are less valid or valuable. Their passion for chemical-free, organically grown food is always impressive and their skill at growing fruit and vegetables to perfection is laudable. They have the attitude and vitality we all hope for in large-scale farmers. But I don't think these gardeners are touched by the same spirit as the ones who look to the garden as a place for spiritual and emotional renewal and as a vehicle for artistic expression. Food gardeners are often quite disparaging about ornamental gardeners. "If you can't eat it why grow it?" is the kind of thing they say.

This book is not for them. It is really for gardeners interested in ornamental horticulture, particularly in the beauty of decorative plants and how they can be used to create places for soothing the soul and stimulating the senses.

For me, gardening is a satisfying union of the artistic and the spiritual. It is about working hard to create a place of extraordinary visual and sensory loveliness, a space where you can find spiritual nourishment through a direct and intimate encounter with the transcendent beauty of nature.

Stages of a gardener

Most gardeners go through a series of stages. We start out buying a few annuals to grow in a pot or a window box. Then we hear about perennials—plants that come back every year. This is often when we really get bitten by the gardening bug. Suddenly, the world looks different. There are all these fabulous plants we've never noticed before at the garden center. Then comes plant lust. Lusting after plants is all part of a gardener's natural maturing process. Falling in love with every plant at the local nursery is a stage every new gardener seems to go through. It stems in part from reading and listening to the likes of world-class garden-makers like Beth Chatto, Rosemary Verey, John Brookes, Christopher Lloyd and Penelope Hobhouse. These popular English garden gurus talk with such passion about the beauty of different plants—the color and variation of hosta leaves, the open-faced beauty of a Christmas rose, the enchanting fragrance of old garden roses—it is hard to read one of their books or attend one of their lectures and not want to own every plant mentioned.

The truth is that most of the world's great gardens don't contain every plant going. They don't need to. What they have is a wonderful collection of outstanding plants, arranged in intelligent, practical combinations. Less can indeed be more in the garden when it means restricting your choices to the best of the best. A restrained planting of three or four identical high-quality plants can look infinitely more attractive than a more complicated scheme involving a jumble of different plants of dubious caliber.

Less is more

There are millions of fantastic plants in the world. How is it possible to reduce that vast and magnificent plant world down to a mere 100? Is it not extraordinary arrogance to say there are only 100 great plants? Yes, of course, it is. But that is not what this book is saying. I am saying that you don't need every plant in the botanical encyclopedia to make a great garden. A common error many of us make when we first get into gardening is to think we have to find room for hundreds of different plants in order for our garden to be any good. Unfortunately, this kind of thinking is a major stumbling block to success. It is the reason so many of our gardens end up a jumbled, disjointed, unsatisfying mess. They are often simply packed with far too many mundane plants.

We need to reduce the number of plants and variety of plant material in our borders and flower beds to a more reliable, effective, streamlined selection. We can do this by learning to use the plant world's top performers—those specimens that not only grow best in our climate, but also look terrific most of the time.

100 best plants

This book identifies 100 of the best performance plants for creating a great garden in Ontario. It tells you why they are first-rate plants, where to plant them, how to take care of them and what other plants to grow with them. Once you have established the basic botanical bones of your garden, using all or a selection of the plants listed here in confident combinations, you can relax and take your time to add finishing touches like hanging baskets, window boxes, specialty bulbs, container plantings and garden decorations. The main goal is to provide you with a list of the most reliable plants that will allow you to construct a wonderful garden from scratch.

All the plants listed in this book have been specifically chosen for their reputation as no-nonsense, workhorse plants that will do their job without fuss or bother. They all have at least one outstanding characteristic. It could be impressive flowers, great foliage, eye-catching form or exquisite perfume, or all of these attributes. You can bring home from your local garden center any of the plants listed in this book and know that they will not disappoint and can be used to create a garden of exceptional charm and beauty.

Ontario gardens

What kills most plants is cold temperatures. This is why a plant's hardiness—the degree to which it can tolerate cold—is an important factor for gardeners to know about.

North America has been mapped into 10 climate zones, all based on average minimum winter temperatures. The lower the zone number, the colder it gets; the higher the zone number, the warmer it gets . . . and the more plants you can grow. In Zone 1, for instance, the average minimum temperature is below –50°F (–46°C). At the other end of the scale, temperatures in Zone 10 rarely dip below 30°F (–1°C).

Ontario is a huge province with vast climatic variations. Most of the province falls into one of three climatic regions: Zone 2 (–50° to –40°F/ –46° to –40°C), Zone 3 (–40° to –30°F/–40° to –34°C), and Zone 4 (–30° to –20°F/–34° to –29°C). Only the toughest plants are capable of surviving outside in the garden during the winter in these areas. But that does not tell the true story of gardening in Ontario. While most of the province lies in these zones, the majority of gardeners live in warmer areas around Toronto and the Niagara Peninsula, where temperatures push up into Zone 5 (–20° to –10°F/ –29° to –23°C) and Zone 6 (–10° to 0°F/–23° to –18°C). Around Windsor and a few protected areas close to Lake Ontario, winter temperatures even push hardiness levels into a balmy Zone 7 (0° to 10°F/–18° to –12°C).

Zone numbers are a useful guide when buying plants. If the label on a plant indicates that it is only hardy in Zone 8–9, you can safely assume the plant is too tender to survive outdoors over winter in Ontario gardens. Yet this doesn't tell the whole story. There are other climatic factors such as rainfall, winds and freeze-thaw cycles to take into account. They also play an important role in the life of plants. This is often the reason why identical plants perform differently in neighboring gardens: one is basking in the warmth of a Zone 7 microclimate, while the other plant is fighting for survival in Zone 4 temperatures in poor soil. Zone numbers are useful, but they should not stop you experimenting with plants. Many plants brought to Europe from China were initially thought to be tender and were overwintered in heated greenhouses until someone had the nerve to try growing them outside . . . and discovered that they were actually as tough as nails. So keep pushing the envelope.

What's in a name?

All the plants in this book have been given both their common name(s) and correct botanical name. This is not to impress you with clever botanical nomenclature. No, it is simply to make sure you get the right plant. For instance, if you were to wander into your local garden center and ask for a viburnum, the first thing you will be asked is, "What kind of viburnum?" The problem is there are over 200 species of viburnum. Unless you can say specifically which one you want, you are more than likely to come away with the wrong plant.

You will find the same problem if you use only common names. For instance, if you ask for a pink geranium, the person at the garden center will want to know whether you really want a geranium or if you mean a pelargonium (which is the correct name for what most people call geraniums), or whether you are looking for a hardy geranium (which is a true geranium) and if so, which kind. Now, there is no reason to be alarmed. Staff at most garden centers are very helpful in these matters, but it makes a world of difference if you can walk confidently into your garden center and ask for the plant you want by its specific botanical name. This eliminates 90 per cent of the risk of getting the wrong plant. (There is also the possibility of mislabeling, but that is happening less and less.)

Botanical names can be a pain. They are often difficult to say and even more challenging to remember. You will be surprised, however, how quickly you pick up the habit of saying them and how beautiful some of them sound as they roll off the tongue. The secret is to say the name three times in a row. By the third time, you will have it down pat and it will be safely stored in your memory.

When it comes to botanical names, there are things you need to know, and certain things that are really not worth worrying about. You need to know that each plant belongs to a particular group called a genus. This is indicated by the plant's first name. Maples, for instance, have the word *Acer* as their genus name. So you know whenever you are looking at an *Acer*, you are looking at some kind of maple. Think of it as a kind of surname. Now within that group of maples, there are many kinds, called species. Each plant has a second name which indicates its species—for instance, *Acer griseum*, *Acer davidii* and *Acer palmatum*. But if you went to the garden center and asked for an *Acer palmatum*, they would then ask you, "What cultivar?" Most plants have a third name— a cultivar name. This appears in single quotation marks—*Acer palmatum* 'Bloodgood', for example. With this information, you can ask for precisely the plant you want and get it. You need all three names to be sure.

Botanical names get more complicated after this. Sometimes a plant has an extra latinized name after the species name that indicates something about the plant's growth habit (*fastigiate*—erect; *pendulous*—weeping), or color (*alba*—white; *glauca*—blue-green), or flowers (*campanulata*—bell-shaped; *stellata*—star-shaped), or geographical origins (*japonica*—of Japan; *sinensis*—of China). This does not change things very much—all you really need for shopping is a plant's first name (genus), second name (species) and third name (cultivar).

When a plant is a hybrid between two or more species, taxonomists use a multiplication sign to let you know. *Epimedium* × *rubrum*, for example, is a hybrid produced by crossing *Epimedium alpinum* with *Epimedium grandiflorum*. Do you care? Probably not. Most home gardeners don't. If you go to your garden center and ask for *Epimedium rubrum* and neglect to include the multiplication sign, you will still come away with the right plant. For botanical accuracy, you will find plants in this book have been given their correct full botanical name and, in some cases, this includes a multiplication sign.

Plant hunting

You won't find all the plants you're looking for at your local garden center. Even the best ones have limited inventory and you will sometimes find they don't have what you want. You sometimes have to be a plant hunter. This means visiting specialty, home-based nurseries and more than one garden center.

Plant shopping is a lot like shopping for clothes—you need to look around to find what you want. Then, you may find the plant you are looking for, but it may not be healthy. Or perhaps, in the case of a tree or shrub, it may not have the shape you like. So you need to keep looking. However, you will find garden centers today are very keen to keep customers happy and many will do the plant hunting for you provided you can give them the precise name of the plant you want.

Twelve steps to a great garden

1. Have a plan. It's a mistake not to have a plan at the start. Before you rush out to buy plants, stop and consider the kind of garden you want to create. Think about the big picture. Do you need an area for children to play? Where will you put the garbage cans? What paths do you need? If your garden is on a slope or hillside, perhaps you will want to grade it into terraces.

    If you know you don't have a good eye for design, hire a professional garden designer to draw up a plan for you. Too often we simply build our gardens by following the shapes and lines left by a builder or the previous homeowner. It is easy to forget about imposing your own design and style.

Look at your garden space as a blank canvas and don't be afraid to turn rectangles into circles or wavy borders into straight lines.

2. Know your garden. Walk your garden in all seasons in all weather. Get to know the shady areas, the damp spots, the frost pockets, the fast-draining, drought-prone areas. This is valuable knowledge that will enable you to build a better garden. You may have to improve drainage in certain areas. You should do this before you try to install a lawn, shrub border or flower bed. View your garden from the inside of your home: a lot of great gardens have been designed so they can be seen at their best from a balcony, bedroom or living room window.

3. Buy plants for specific places. Don't just wander into a garden center and buy the first attractive plant to catch your eye. The key to successful gardening is to get a great plant in a good location . . . next to other right plants in right places. The most common garden error is to put shade-loving plants in sunny spots and sun-loving plants in cool damp places. You would be amazed how often it happens and it is almost always because the gardener has not taken the time to get in touch with the garden at the soil level. Promise that you won't just push a plant in the ground without first doing all the necessary soil preparation.

   Since you have spent time getting to know your garden, you can shop with confidence for plants for specific sites. Getting the right plant in the best place is the key to success. The greatest beauty in a garden is the healthiness of plants. Pests and disease descend on plants that are under stress, perhaps because they have been planted in the wrong spot. When buying trees, always ask about their height and width at maturity. You can get tall, column-shaped trees that don't get very wide, and wide-growing trees that don't get very tall.

4. Keep your soil healthy. It is such a shame to take time to pick out beautiful plants and then to stick them in miserable, infertile soil. The late great English garden guru Percy Thrower always used to say, "The answer lies in the soil." Most plants can't thrive and grow to maturity if they are trapped in lifeless, poorly drained soil. So dig deeply, enrich the soil with well-rotted compost and mushroom or steer manure and you will get your plants off to a good start. Most plants need at least 18 inches (45 cm) of decent, fertile, well-drained soil.

5. Think about the borrowed landscape. This simply means being aware of the existing scenery around your garden. Look up and around and see what kind of landscape features you get for free from your neighbors. It could be a beautiful tree that flowers in spring or a view of a distant lake, sunny hilltop or spinney. Is there a flowering shrub that gives you a wonderful show or a scrambling vine that tumbles into your yard and fills the air with an intoxicating fragrance? If you are aware of these things, you can

incorporate them into your own garden design. Many gardeners find that what visitors often admire most in their garden are trees and shrubs that are actually planted in neighboring gardens.

Thinking about "borrowed landscaping" also means being sensitive to your neighbors and thinking carefully about how or what you plant and what you take out will affect them. Gardeners with an eye for the bigger landscape picture are much more likely to create great gardens and inspire others to do likewise.

6. Send a clear invitation to linger. Too many gardens seem to say "Come and look at the plants, but leave as soon as you're done." A well-positioned bench or group of chairs can send a friendly, welcoming invitation to sit and rest. If your garden doesn't do that, think about adding a simple bench or arbor-seat in a place that will call out to your visitors when they see it.

7. Don't overlook scent. Fragrance is the most frequently overlooked element in the garden, even though it is one of the most popular. Color is important, but delicious scents add an extra dimension to the pleasure of your garden experience. Make a list of plants that provide fragrance throughout the seasons and see if you can accommodate them in areas close to porches and gateways where they will be most appreciated.

8. Don't overlook evergreens. Evergreens are important because they provide structure in the garden throughout the year. They also provide foliage contrast to other plants. Low boxwood hedges can be used to define specific areas, such as rose beds and herb gardens. You can use a spiral-shaped conifer to create a focus point or as a special accent at an intersection, or you can use two of them to flank a view.

9. Screen out eyesores. Privacy and intimacy are so important to the romantic ambience of a garden. But eyesores can spoil the fun. Block out things you don't want to see by using trellises and arbors. Fences, hedges and walls are not always the best solution. If you are trying to screen out a house, for example, think about pleaching a row of small-growing trees instead of growing a tall hedge. The pleached trees can screen the eyesore while still leaving room underneath for an interesting planting at ground level. Gazebos, arbors and pergolas are other structures you can use to create privacy.

10. Make good use of containers. Pots and troughs, planters and urns are the little touches that make the difference between a great garden and a ho-hum garden. Statuary is trickier because it makes a more personal statement, but troughs and planters are safe structures that have a universal acceptance. You don't have to overdo it. A simple boxwood topiary ball or hydrangea or rose is often all that is needed. Use containers to bring fragrance closer to your sitting areas and to create a change of pace and points of interest for visitors exploring the garden. You can also use

containers of potted plants to fill gaps left in the garden by perennials that have finished blooming.

11. Share what you grow. All expert gardeners know the best way to ensure that you have a plant forever is to give some of it away to a friend. That way, if your plant should suddenly die, you always have a friend who can give you back a replacement. Open your garden and let others see what you are doing. This is a great way to encourage and inspire others, exchange ideas and share what you know. Gardening is all about sharing—sharing plants, sharing knowledge, sharing stories of successes and failures.

12. Have fun when you garden. The saddest thing is when new gardeners get serious and forget gardening is supposed to be fun. It is playing with plants. What tends to happen is that they get pushed and prodded by fanatical gardeners to become just as fanatical and . . . unhappy. Make a decision that if ever gardening starts to feel like a tedious chore, you will stop what you are doing and find something that's fun to do. Don't let gardening become a pain in the neck. If a plant dies, you can always get another one. If you make a mistake, don't be hard on yourself—that's how most people learn what works and what doesn't. Sometimes mistakes will turn out to be surprising successes. You will always be making changes, moving plants around, even if they look fine, just to try something new. The important thing is to have fun gardening.

100

Best

Plants

*A*cer palmatum 'Bloodgood'

Common name: Japanese maple

Chief characteristics

There are many fine maples suitable for growing in small- and medium-sized gardens, but you won't go wrong if you pick a cultivar of *Acer palmatum*.

Location: Sun to part shade
Type: Deciduous tree
Size: 16 to 20 feet (5 to 6 m)
Conditions: Ordinary, well-drained soil
Zone: 5

One of the most popular feature trees for the home garden is *A. palmatum* 'Bloodgood', which has bright crimson-red foliage and attractive blackish-red bark. It is an outstanding tree because the leaves retain their striking blood-red color all summer, and then turn a spectacular fiery red in fall. With the graceful shape of its branches (a characteristic common to all palmatum maples), 'Bloodgood' also provides a delightful contrast for trees and shrubs with green leaves.

There are many outstanding cultivars of *Acer palmatum*. Few exceed 30 feet (9 m); most grow to little more than 20 feet (6 m). The coral bark maple (*A. p.* 'Sengo kaku', also known as 'Senkaki') has coral-pink bark and branches. The leaves turn a pleasant golden color in fall.

Other top cultivars to consider include 'Shojo' (similar to 'Bloodgood' but with larger leaves), 'Atropurpureum' (reddish-purple leaves that turn purple-green in summer), 'Osakazuki (large green leaves with spectacular crimson fall color) and 'Trompenburg' (deeply cut, purple-red leaves). Also keep an eye out for 'Sherwood Flame', 'Koto no ito' and 'Butterfly', all excellent trees.

Part of the beauty of these graceful upright maples is their ability to cast gentle, dappled shade that is not only pleasant to sit under, but provides the perfect light for growing a wide variety of spring-flowering bulbs and herbaceous perennials that thrive in lightly shaded areas.

Where to plant it

The beautiful foliage and graceful shape of *A. palmatum* 'Bloodgood' can provide a confident focal point and striking color contrast in the garden. The tree can stand alone as an accent by a main entrance or beside a path or gazebo, or it can be worked into a shrub border where it will happily share space with a wide variety of shrubs. It looks exceptional when planted with a taller, green-leafed tree or high cedar hedge behind it. Since the fall color of 'Bloodgood' is so outstanding, think about what else will be in bloom at that time and locate your special tree so that it can be seen without clashing or having to compete with other star performers of autumn.

How to care for it

Thriving best in Zones 6 to 9, all Japanese maples are vulnerable to cold winds in winter and scorching afternoon sun in summer, so it is wise to plant 'Bloodgood' where it will receive adequate shelter. Light shade is ideal. This can be provided by hedges, fences, trees or the house itself.

The tree will require routine maintenance. Prune away dead, damaged and diseased branches in spring. Make sure the tree is well watered in the first year; the ground should never become parched. Japanese maples thrive in rich, slightly acidic soil that stays reasonably cool and moist without being excessively wet or boggy.

Good companions

Ideal partners for 'Bloodgood' are plants that provide flower or foliage contrast to the tree's deep purple-red leaves. An underplanting of red-flowering cinquefoil (*Potentilla*) — 'Red Ace' or 'Red Robin'— would add fire to the purple tones while the golden-green foliage and burgundy-red flowers of *Spiraea bumalda* 'Goldflame' offer a cooler contrast. Other companions to consider include the light green foliage of dwarf hemlock (*Tsuga* 'Jeddeloh'), butterfly bush (*Buddleia davidii*) or a gold-leafed form of *Euonymus fortunei*.

For your collection

Here's a list of other first-rate maples.

- *Acer campestre* 'Queen Elizabeth' (hedging maple). This is an excellent tree to use for a screen of pleached trees. If you want to obscure a view that is 15 to 20 feet (4.5 to 6 m) above the ground, but are not keen on a super-high hedge and want space underneath for other plants, consider this idea. Lime and hornbeam trees have been used for screening, but *A. campestre* is a good alternative.
- *Acer griseum* (paperbark maple). When the soft light of the setting sun strikes the peeling, cinnamon-colored bark of this special tree, the sight can be quite mesmerizing. The fall foliage is also very attractive. It reaches 24 to 36 feet (7 to 11 m) at maturity.
- *Acer japonicum* 'Aconitifolium' (fullmoon maple). An excellent shade tree, this grows to about 25 feet (7.5 m). It has distinctive, deeply cut leaves with good fall color.
- *Acer platanoides* 'Crimson King'. An excellent shade tree, this is the most vigorous of the red-leafed Norway maples. It has a very

pleasant oval shape that slowly turns into a more rounded form as the tree matures. Its dark red-purple, almost deep maroon leaves provide excellent contrast to the greens of lime trees (*Tilia*) or golden yellows of honey locust (*Gleditsia*). However, a whole street full of 'Crimson King' can be overwhelming and too sober in summer.

Also consider *A. platanoides* 'Deborah', which has brilliant red-purple new foliage in spring that slowly fades to dark green and turns bronze-purple in fall.

- *Acer pseudoplatanus* 'Brilliantissimum' (sycamore maple). Not an easy tree to find, but a lovely, slow-growing specimen that is used a lot in British gardens. It has outstanding shrimp-pink new foliage in spring that easily compares to the cherry blossom for elegance and charm. It has an extremely graceful form, slowly rounding at the top as it matures into a full, lollipop shape. Once the pink leaves have unfolded, they turn a pale green. New leaves continue to appear through the summer and they decorate the tree with bright patches of pinkish-green. The effect is very subtle and attractive. Grows 15 feet (4.5 m) tall.
- *Acer rubrum* 'Red Sunset'. This has dark, glossy green leaves that turn a spectacular deep orange-red in fall. It grows 45 feet (14 m) tall, which makes it a very useful shade tree.
- *Acer saccharum* 'Legacy'. One of the best sugar maples, this beautiful big shade tree has a graceful oval shape and lush green foliage that turns orange-red in fall. It grows to 50 feet (15 m) at maturity.
- *Acer shirasawanum* 'Aureum' (golden fullmoon maple). This has beautiful, tightly clustered yellow-green leaves that can light up a corner of the garden. It grows to about 20 feet (6 m).

*A*cer palmatum dissectum 'Crimson Queen'

Common name: *Laceleaf Japanese maple*

Chief characteristics

One of the most beautiful feature trees, 'Crimson Queen' is part of a special group of maples called "dissectums." These are distinguished by their finely cut, almost feathery, reddish-purple or green foliage that cascades over twisted and contorted branches to form an extremely graceful and compact, mostly weeping, shape. Since

Location: Light shade
Type: Deciduous tree
Size: 4 to 5 feet (1.2 to 1.5 m)
Conditions: Rich, well-drained soil
Zone: 6

dissectums stay quite small, rarely growing more than 5 feet (1.5 m) tall, it is very easy to accommodate them in small- or medium-sized gardens.

'Crimson Queen' is acclaimed for its crimson-red foliage that holds its color throughout the summer. It is also extremely heat tolerant and has good fall color as the leaves turn orange-red and then bright scarlet.

Considered hardy to Zone 6, 'Crimson Queen' grows slowly to form a small, mushroom-shaped tree. It is a very useful tree for growing over low retaining walls or as a special feature in a planter box or container. You will often find it combined, in both casual and formal gardens, with its green-leaf look-alike, *Acer palmatum dissectum* 'Viridis', or 'Waterfall'. Together red- and green-leafed dissectums can be used to provide balance, harmony and visual relief. Red-leafed forms of *A. palmatum dissectum* are by far the most popular, outselling the green-leafed cultivars by at least 4 to 1.

Where to plant it

The low-growing dissectum forms of *A. palmatum* do not generally do well in open, exposed sites. They prefer a semi-shaded location where they will be well protected from the morning sun of early spring and the hot afternoon sun in summer. They thrive in rich, slightly acidic soil that stays reasonably cool and moist without being excessively wet or boggy.

How to care for it

While 'Crimson Queen' and the other dissectums mentioned here are all hardy to Zone 6, it would not be wise to leave them unprotected in winter. A simple burlap wrap will help your special tree cope a lot better with subzero temperatures. In the spring, prune away dead, damaged and diseased branches.

Make sure the tree is well watered and the ground never becomes parched in the first year of planting. Scorching of the delicate foliage can be a problem if the tree gets no protection from afternoon sun. Think carefully about the appropriate location at planting time.

Good companions

There is usually not much room to plant under the cascading foliage of dissectums. The branches tend to keep tumbling downward until they reach the ground. Some people try, without a great deal of success, to weave clematis or annual vines such as the potato vine (*Solanum*) through the lacy, deeply divided leaves. The best companions for the green and red cultivars of *A. palmatum dissectum* are each other. For a dramatic contrast, you could combine a red laceleaf with the lime-green foliage of *Spiraea japonica* 'Limemound', which also has pink flowers.

Most common partners for *A. palmatum dissectum* are well-behaved neighboring shrubs such as rhododendrons, pieris and smoke bush (*Cotinus coggygria*).

For your collection

Here are some other popular cultivars of *A. palmatum dissectum* to look for.

- 'Atropurpureum'. One of the most widely used dissectums, this is hardy to Zone 5 and is noted for the summer color of its leaves, which can range from orange-red to dark crimson.
- 'Garnet'. With exceptional crimson-red fall color, this eventually forms a beautiful mound of weeping branches. It gets its name from the rich color of its summer foliage.
- 'Inaba-shidare'. The name means "leaves of rice paper," which should signify how delicate and graceful the deep purple-red foliage is on this tree. The leaves turn crimson-red in fall and the tree has a slightly more upright habit than 'Crimson Queen' and some of the other popular dissectums.
- 'Red Dragon'. This is a relatively new introduction from New Zealand and is being touted by some nurseries as the best of the red laceleafs. It is a vigorous grower and has deep purple-red foliage and wavy branches that provide interest in winter.

ctinidia kolomikta

Common name: *Kolomikta vine, super-hardy kiwi vine*

Chief characteristics

The heart-shaped leaves of *Actinidia kolomikta* are what make it so magical. In full sun the tips turn a strawberry-pink or creamy white. Once the vine is well established, the decorative effect of the variegated color can be striking. Not everyone likes this. Critics have described the vine as "a horror of horrors" and "temperamental." I find such comments needlessly exaggerated and unfairly harsh. The vine is a popular, useful, handsome climber with a remarkable foliage color that knowledgable gardeners have described as "magnificent." It is obviously all in the eye of the beholder!

Location: Full sun
Type: Deciduous vine
Size: 10 to 14 feet (3 to 4 m)
Conditions: Ordinary soil
Zone: 4

Actinidia kolomikta is certainly a lot more graceful and easier to accommodate in the average-sized home garden than its rampant cousin, *A. chinensis* (Chinese gooseberry). That species is so vigorous it will clamber 30 feet (9 m) into a large tree or smother the wall of a house. Don't bring home the wrong plant.

As well as the interesting leaf coloring, the kolomikta vine produces mildly fragrant, cup-shaped white flowers in June. The vine gets its intriguing nickname, Arctic beauty vine, because it is capable of enduring intense cold. Although it is rarely grown on the prairies, gardeners there could consider it since it has been observed to survive even when temperatures plummet as low as $-40°F$ ($-40°C$).

Where to plant it

Actinidia kolomikta looks best against a south- or west-facing wall of a house or over a fence. It can grow more than 12 feet (3.6 m) and cover a sizable area but it must have plenty of sunshine if the leaves are going to perform their unique conjuring trick and change color at the tips.

This, however, doesn't always happen until the plant has been established for a few years. Being deciduous, it loses its leaves in winter, so it would not be the right choice if you want an area perpetually covered or screened. (Ivy would be more suitable for that task.)

When not planted in the right place — a sunny, sheltered site — *A. kolomikta* will struggle along and look rather unhappy and bedraggled. This is how many people have seen it and dismissed it. Pity. Seen at its best, it's a plant for everyone's garden.

How to care for it

While it can tolerate extreme cold, *Actinidia kolomikta* can be killed by excessively wet winters, especially if planted in poor-draining soil. It also suffers during freeze-thaw cycles when moisture in the ground around the plant turns alternately from water to ice.

Plant it in a well-drained spot in a sunny, sheltered area. Prune in late winter or early spring to encourage it to spread and increase its coverage, cutting it back to about 2 feet (60 cm) from the ground when it is still quite young. From then on it is simply a matter of pruning to size and shape.

Good companions

Climbing roses, especially pink and red ones like 'High Hopes', 'Albertine', 'Altissimo', 'Dublin Bay', 'Francois Juranville' and 'New

Dawn', and purple clematis like *Clematis* × *jackmanii* or 'Polish Spirit'
make lively companions, although *Actinidia kolomikta* is mostly seen
working alone.

For your collection

Actinidia kolomikta has been used successfully to cover garden sheds
in summer. Other shed-covering vines worth considering include
those below.

- *Polygonum aubertii* (silver lace vine). Sometimes labeled silver fleece
  vine, this produces clouds of frothy white flowers in July and August.
  It can grow to 25 feet (7.5 m) and put on at least half that growth
  in a single season. Looks especially attractive over arbors and
  entrance archways.
- *Aristolochia macrophylla* (Dutchman's pipe). Once it is established,
  Dutchman's pipe will vigorously grow to more than 25 feet (7.5 m)
  and produce large, heart-shaped leaves.
- *Parthenocissus quinquefolia* (Virginia creeper). This fast-growing, self-
  clinging vine, a cousin of Boston ivy, is famous for its vivid red fall
  color. It grows 20 to 40 feet (6 to 12 m) and can also be used as a
  groundcover. *P. quinquefolia engelmannii* (Engelmann ivy) also has
  brilliant crimson-red fall color but has smaller leaves than the
  standard Virginia creeper.
- *Polygonum baldschuanicum* (Russian vine). This immensely vigorous
  deciduous vine may cover more than the shed by the time it is
  done. It can stretch 30 feet (9 m) and produces panicles of pink-
  tinged flowers.
- *Jasminum nudiflorum* (winter jasmine). Looking for winter flowers?
  This deciduous vine, which likes sun or partial shade, will climb
  10 to 15 feet (3 to 4.5 m) and produce yellow flowers from January
  to March. It is fairly tender, hardy to Zone 6.
- *Hedera helix* (English ivy). Not the most creative choice of vines but
  certainly one of the most reliable evergreen climbers for covering
  walls, sheds or fences. The sturdy, solid green leaves will quickly
  form a lush cover. Look for 'Baltic' or 'Thorndale'. Variegated Persian
  ivy (*H. colchica* 'Dentata Variegata'), with its marbled green-gray
  leaves, may have more appeal, but it is also more tender than
  English ivy. Both will easily grow 15 to 25 feet (4.5 to 7.5 m).

$\mathcal{A}$diantum aleuticum

Common name: *Western or five-fingered maidenhair fern*

Chief characteristics

You may have thought a fern is a fern is a fern. Not so. It can come as a bit of a shock to discover just how many kinds of ferns are being commercially cultivated today. Take a deep breath and give this short list a whirl: arching wood fern, crested royal fern, ostrich fern, parsley fern, shield fern, Japanese lady fern, hard fern, fragile fern, oak fern, log fern (pause for breath), soft tree fern, scaly tree fern, Korean rock fern, licorice fern, champion's wood fern. And on and on. The list seems endless. Actually, there are no fewer than 132 kinds in commercial cultivation.

> **Location:** Shade to light shade
> **Type:** Perennial
> **Size:** 12 to 24 inches (30 to 60 cm)
> **Conditions:** Moist soil
> **Zone:** 3

Ferns are magnificent foliage plants for the shade. Along with hostas, they are the royalty of shade plants. Their main role in the garden is to provide architectural form and foliage texture and contrast. We don't expect them to have colorful flowers, although some have patterned fronds. We mainly appreciate them for their reliable, long-lasting greenness and dependable structure.

Where to begin? A great fern for any garden is *Adiantum aleuticum*, the graceful maidenhair fern, which is often sold as *Adiantum pedatum*. It has delicate fan-shaped fronds and thin black-ribbed stems. This is a supremely elegant plant, indispensable for adding a light, airy, romantic touch to the shade under trees. I have a large clump growing next to a birdbath beside a maple tree in my garden. *A. aleuticum* grows about 2 feet (60 cm) tall and will hold its form all summer, slowly giving way to frost and dying down in fall, only to return the following spring. It is truly one of the best ornamental plants available.

Where to plant it

The majority of ferns perform best in loose, fertile, well-drained soil that is regularly amended with compost or manure. Grow them under trees in dappled shade along with hostas and astilbes. You can use ferns to get a lush, jungle-like look or a soft, romantic, textured look. It is interesting to mix species to achieve even more dramatic contrast, but think carefully about their size at maturity or you may end up losing smaller plants beneath the billowy fronds of stouter giant ferns.

How to care for it

Don't let your ferns struggle in poor, arid soil in summer. Water them with the same care you show other plants in the garden. Cut away old, faded fronds in spring to allow fresh green fronds to emerge unhindered. Add organic material every year. Mulch in spring as a moisture-retaining measure. This is also an effective way of enriching the soil.

Good companions

There is no shortage of chums for ferns: hosta, hardy geranium, astilbe, cimicifuga, Solomon's seal, astrantia, pulmonaria, hydrangea, rhododendron, light shade–loving bulbs such as scilla, trillium and erythronium, and the lovely grass-like wood-rush, *Luzula*.

For your collection

Other top ferns, some bigger and more architectural than others, include those named below.

- *Polystichum acrostichoides* (Christmas fern). The dark green fronds were once used for Christmas decorations, hence the name. It is still one of the most useful evergreen ferns. It grows to 18 inches (45 cm).
- *Athyrium nipponicum* 'Pictum' (Japanese painted fern). Sometimes listed as 'Metallicum', this has attractive, deep green fronds with decorative gray-pink markings that give the plant an almost metallic sheen.
- *Osmunda regalis* (royal fern). Will ultimately reach 4 feet (1.2 m) and makes a very bold feature plant that provides structure for your garden.
- *Matteuccia struthiopteris* (ostrich fern). Grows 3 to 4 feet (90 to 120 cm) and gets its common name because the fronds look rather like the plumes of an ostrich. Also look for the deciduous cinnamon fern (*Osmunda cinnamonea*) which is somewhat similar to the ostrich fern but has cinnamon-colored fronds.
- *Dryopteris* spp. Any of the durable workhorse *Dryopteris* ferns tend to define what the word "fern" means for most people. Notable ones include the marginal wood fern (*D. marginalis*), which has bright blue-green fronds, and the lacy crested broad buckler fern (*D. dilatata* 'Lepidota cristata').
- *Dicksonia antarctica* (Tasmanian tree fern). If you have room, try growing this exotic specimen in a pot. It has huge fronds that make it look rather like a palm tree. Slow-growing, it can eventually reach

15 feet (4.5 m) with a thick tree-like trunk 3 feet (90 cm) around. It is designated Zone 8, which means it needs to be brought into a frost-free environment over winter. However, it will survive quite happily in a planter for many years.

*A*juga reptans 'Bronze Beauty'

Common name: *Common bugleweed*

Chief characteristics

One of the basic rules of gardening is that all soil should be covered, especially in summer when the sun can suck all the life-giving moisture from the ground and put your plants under stress. Most of us use grass to cover large, exposed expanses of ground. Mulch is more routinely used to protect soil around perennials in borders. If you have large areas of exposed soil under trees or shrubs, you will want to plant a suitable groundcover, preferably a low-growing, closely structured plant cover that not only holds and protects the soil, suppresses weeds and reduces moisture loss, but also has attractive flowers or foliage.

Location: Sun to part shade
Type: Perennial groundcover
Size: 6 inches (15 cm)
Conditions: Moist, well-drained soil
Flowering time: May to June
Zone: 3

Ajuga reptans is one of the best and most versatile groundcovers. A sturdy creeping plant with small, shiny, rounded leaves, this is dense enough to smother most weeds. Watch for its 4- to 6-inch (10- to 15-cm) spikes of blue flowers from May to June. There are many cultivars on the market. The best is 'Bronze Beauty', which has brilliant blue flowers in spring and reliable, ground-hugging bronze foliage the rest of the year. A few others that offer slight variations in foliage color are also worth checking out. 'Burgundy Glow' has striking variegated leaves that are a mixture of white, pink and silvery green, while 'Brockbanki' has glossy green foliage. Other popular cultivars include 'Braunherz', 'Mini Crisp Red', and 'Catlin's Giant'.

Ajuga pyramidalis 'Metallica Crispa' is a little more unusual than the common bugleweed. The crinkled leaves are compact and attractive and it's not bothered by a little sun.

Where to plant it

Ajuga is a fast-growing groundcover that forms mats of crinkly foliage in full sun to part shade in moist soil. Plant it where you will be able to see

and enjoy the bright blue flowers in spring and the lush carp
foliage the rest of the year.

Use 'Bronze Beauty' under trees and shrubs or to form a
for paths. It can be combined with other groundcovers but is fairly
competitive, gaining ground by invasive runners, and will squeeze out
all rivals but those that are equally assertive.

Hostas have sufficiently sturdy root systems to contend with it, but
daintier specimens like lamium or creeping jenny will lose out most of
the time. Most groundcovers thrive in light or full shade. The best test is
to grow a few different groundcovers in the same area and let them fight
it out. It is surprising sometimes which one wins.

How to care for it

The best rule of maintenance for ajuga is not to let it become too
invasive. It will want to creep and cover as much ground as possible. It
can, however, be easily contained by chopping it back into bounds.
Ajuga's blue flowers are wonderful, but your main reason for planting it
should be to cover ground under trees and shrubs. Regard the flowers as
a bonus. When they are finished blooming, you can shear them off or
allow them to disappear in their own time.

Ajuga is rarely troubled by pests and diseases and can be easily
transplanted. Simply separate one of the offshoots and relocate it.
Provided this is not done in the heat of summer, the offshoot will root
and should be kept well watered.

Good companions

Mix ajugas with other ajugas. Blue-leafed hostas make nice companions,
as do lungwort (*Pulmonaria*) and maidenhair ferns. Astilbe, viola,
bergenia and hardy geranium can also be planted close by to create
foliage contrasts.

For your collection

There are many other notable groundcovers. Here are some of the best.

- *Arctostaphylos uva-ursi* (bearberry, kinnikinnick). A first-rate evergreen
  groundcover that will thrive in sun or partial shade. The glossy leaves
  are decorated by pink bell-shaped flowers in spring followed by
  bright red berries. Grows 4 to 6 inches (10 to 15 cm) high.
- *Artemisia stelleriana* 'Silver Brocade'. A low-growing, compact plant
  with soft gray foliage similar to dusty miller, this is a first-rate
  rockery edging and looks good in hanging baskets.
- *Asarum* (wild ginger). Not widely used, but an excellent groundcover
  plant with dark green, glossy, evergreen heart- or kidney-shaped

leaves on thin stems. It gets its name from its gingerlike fragrance. Look for *A. canadense* or *A. europaeum*. Wild ginger performs best in moist, acidic, deep shade under rhododendrons or hydrangeas.

- *Bergenia cordifolia* (giant rockfoil or large-leafed saxifrage). This has large, leathery, bright green leaves that turn coppery red in fall. It thrives in sun or shade and sends up a striking pink, red, white or purple flowerhead in spring. Look for 'Baby Doll', 'Bressingham Ruby', 'Bressingham Salmon', 'Bressingham White'.

- *Cerastium tomentosum* (snow in summer). The soft gray leaves of this popular groundcover will quickly form a low carpet of foliage on a sunny bank. Some gardeners use it to simulate a stream running between and over rocks. The lovely white flowers that give it its common name are an added bonus. Grows 6 to 12 inches (15 to 30 cm) high.

- *Convallaria majalis* (lily-of-the-valley). This may not be the most original groundcover, but it is one of the most dependable and hardy. In spring, it puts out sweetly scented, white, bell-like flowers.

- *Cornus canadensis* (bunchberry). A member of the dogwood family, native to North America, it takes a little longer than other ground-covers to get established and is not your best pick if you want to quash weeds. It does have attractive, broad foliage and white flowers in late spring followed by red berries in late summer. Grow *C. canadensis* in light shade with lily-of-the-valley, epimedium or sweet woodruff.

- *Epimedium* (bishop's hat or barrenwort). Mainly grown for its leaves, which are heart-shaped and held up on delicate, wiry stems, *Epimedium* also flowers, producing tiny pink or white blooms in spring. In mild areas, the leaves change color and hang on all winter, needing only to be cut back just before spring. *Epimedium* gets its folk name, barrenwort, from the belief that it was supposed to be able to prevent conception.

- *Galium odoratum* (sweet woodruff). This has delightful white flowers and lacy foliage. It is the perfect choice for underscoring boxwood hedges or shrubs in the shady woodland border. It is a notorious colonizer. If planted in an unrestricted area, it will self-sow freely and spread rapidly. But this is perhaps precisely what you want. If you don't, then plant it under low hedges next to concrete driveways or paths, or next to lawns that get mown regularly.

- *Hedera helix* (English ivy). This plant provides the easy answer to many coverup problems. It will clamber into trees, over walls and fences and cover large areas under shrubs. Evergreen, it quickly forms a thick, leafy carpet, and it is indifferent to whether it is grown in sun or shade. While acknowledging its tremendous value as a woodland plant, critics tend to see ivy as a boring, monotonous choice for the home garden. But it does have its uses. Being fast-spreading, it will need to be kept in check, unless, of course, you want it to cover a large area.

* *Houttuynia cordata* 'Chameleon'. This has small, showy, heart-shaped leaves with yellow, green, bronze and pink coloring. It is a vigorous grower, especially in moist soil, and produces white flowers in summer. It grows 2 to 3 inches (5 to 8 cm) high.

* *Hypericum calycinum* (St. John's wort). A bit too common for the taste of some gardeners, it is always reliable, producing attractive leaves on low arching stems, and distinct yellow flowers for great summer color. It is not bothered about the quality of soil in which it is planted and flourishes in both sun or part shade.

* *Lamium maculatum* (spotted dead nettle). Not to be confused with stinging nettle, this has the look but not the stinging hairs of its pain-inflicting cousin. The soft, green leaves have a greenish-white mottle or stripe, and purple flowers. It will quickly form a mat of foliage in sun or light shade. 'Beacon Silver' has silvery leaves and purple flowers. Also look for 'Pink Pewter', 'White Nancy', 'Chequers' and 'Aureum'.

* *Lysimachia nummularia* (creeping jenny). One of the prettier groundcovers, this has soft yellow-green leaves and tiny, bright yellow flowers. It is ideal for brightening up a dampish, semi-shady corner in summer. The trailing stems should be snipped to make the plant thicken up. It also goes by a variety of other names including moneywort, twopenny grass, meadow runagates, string of sovereigns and wandering tailor.

* *Pachysandra terminalis* (Japanese spurge). This will do as thorough a job as ivy at covering ground with a thick carpet of handsome, evergreen foliage, only it will take longer to do it. Hardy and drought tolerant, Japanese spurge has creamy white flowers in late spring. It is especially useful in areas where nothing else will grow.

* *Vinca minor* (periwinkle). Next to grass, this is one of the most widely grown groundcovers and for a good reason—it does a steady, dependable job and requires minimal attention. Flourishing in shade or part sun, it spreads rapidly, rooting its trailing stems as it goes. The dainty, five-petal, lilac-blue flowers are not unattractive either.

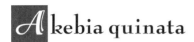

Akebia quinata

Common name: *Chocolate vine*

Chief characteristics

The chocolate vine has two endearing
qualities: it has superbly graceful five-lobed
leaves, which are a delicate shade of green,
and it has mildly vanilla-scented chocolate-
colored flowers in spring.

> **Location:** Full sun
> **Type:** Semi-evergreen vine
> **Size:** 20 to 26 feet (6 to 8 m)
> **Conditions:** Well-drained,
>   average soil
> **Flowering time:** June
> **Zone:** 4

The worst thing anyone is going to
tell you about this vine is that it can be
too vigorous. How vigorous? In ideal
conditions, it can travel 30 feet (9 m), although it may take its time to
get started on that journey. In most situations, however, it grows 15 to
20 feet (4.5 to 6 m).

The pluses far outweigh the minuses. Its ambitious ways can be
controlled and the plum-purple flowers, which some have compared to
the fragrance of expensive French soap, more than compensate for any
overenthusiasm.

Where to plant it

The chocolate vine is ideal for covering fences or growing into trees and
shrubs. Its vigor can also be harnessed to bring the garden up to isolated
decks and balconies. Pergolas and arbors provide ideal homes. Akebia
likes moist soil and plenty of sunshine. It grows by twining skinny
tendrils around whatever it can get a grip on, so provide a little support
at the beginning. Train the vine where you want it to go and, once it is
established, you can simply concentrate on pruning it to shape. The
roots don't like to be disturbed once they are settled.

How to care for it

How do you keep chocolate vine from taking over? You prune it late in
spring, the second it has finished flowering. The new growth that results
will be less vigorous.

Good companions

Chocolate vine combines well with clematis and roses. Consider
planting 'Albertine' or 'Francois Juranville' roses or a wine-red clematis
like 'Madame Julia Correvon'.

For your collection

- 🌺 *Campsis radicans* (trumpet vine, trumpet creeper or trumpet honeysuckle). This does well in a sunny, sheltered, moist, but well-drained location. The trumpet-shaped red flowers are especially popular with hummingbirds. Cultivars to look for are *C. radicans* 'Flava' or *C.* × *tagliabuana* 'Madame Galen'.
- 🌺 *Cosmos atrosanguineus* (chocolate cosmos). Chocolate-scented flowers are an interesting conversation piece in the garden. To go with your chocolate vine, you could grow a chocolate cosmos in a container. The rich maroon flowers smell of dark chocolate. This combines very nicely with *Melianthus major*, which has grey foliage that smells like peanut butter when touched. The "chocolate" and "peanut butter" combo is fun to show children. Throw in a pot full of poached egg plant (*Limnanthes douglasii*), a cherry pie plant (*Heliotropium*), some specialty mints and some scented geraniums and you can have a novelty food garden right on your patio or deck.
- 🌺 *Tropaeolum speciosum* (flame creeper). If you're interested in unusual summer climbers, how about a flame creeper, which has leaves quite similar to those of the chocolate vine? It has bright, red flowers in July and is a tender perennial climber.

𝒜lchemilla mollis

Common name: Lady's mantle

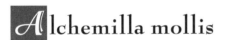

Chief characteristics

All the great cottage gardens of England have this old-fashioned favorite. It is loved for its seemingly magical ability to display raindrops like diamonds on its rough, hairy leaves. It is also valued for the light lime-green color and frothy texture of its effervescent sprays of flowers that first appear in June and last for several weeks.

Location: Full sun to light shade
Type: Perennial
Size: 12 to 14 inches (30 to 36 cm)
Conditions: Ordinary garden soil
Flowering time: June to August
Zone: 2

The name *Alchemilla* is rooted in the word alchemy. When the plant was used as a herb it was thought to possess magical healing properties. *Mollis* refers to the soft hairs of the leaves, which lock together in a way that looks rather like a lady's cloak or mantle.

While its performance is always predictable, lady's mantle can be used in a variety of ways—as a groundcover or container plant or for foliage contrast. Its most popular use is as a mounding foliage plant for filling out the front of a perennial border or as a plant for overgrowing and softening the straight edges of a path or walkway.

Originating in meadows and woodlands of eastern Europe and western Asia, *Alchemilla mollis* copes comfortably with cold winters. Hardy to −20°F (−29°C), it reaches about 14 inches (36 cm) high when in full bloom and is one of the first perennials to bounce back to life in spring. A time-bomb of a plant, lady's mantle is certainly a specimen to pass over the fence if you want your neighbor's empty yard to turn into a garden. It will quietly tick over the first year, then seed itself so rampantly that by the second year the whole yard will be covered.

Where to plant it

Lady's mantle will grow almost anywhere, but it looks best planted where it gets at least three hours of sun a day and protection from afternoon sun. Grow it in well-drained soil in light shade in a place open to the sky, but shaded on the west side. It will do well in a container provided it is not forgotten and left to wilt.

Some gardeners have used the frothy lime-green flowers of lady's mantle very artistically along the banks of a stream or creek to mimic the rush and spray of water. Others have used it to create the effect of a lush oasis in a dry gravel area or alongside a stone path.

How to care for it

Lady's mantle requires minimal maintenance. It grows happily for several years without needing to be divided and flourishes even in poor soil. When clumps do become dense, they should be lifted and divided. Do this in early April when the soil is most workable.

Lady's mantle is a prolific self-seeder. If you are not careful it will propagate itself with promiscuous abandon in a free-spirited bid to take over your entire garden. The simple solution is to remove the browning flowerheads before they have a chance to shake down their seeds. The plant can also become somewhat untidy in late summer. The solution again is to clip off the unsightly leaves; this will encourage fresh new foliage to form. Shear back old foliage at the end of fall as part of your routine garden cleanup.

Good companions

The tiny lime-green flowers and thick green leaves work well with almost any other garden plant, but lady's mantle combines exceptionally well with such shade-lovers as astilbe, bleeding heart, hosta, aquilegia, solomon's seal and sunnier performers like yellow achillea and white *Lychnis coronaria*. The flower sprays can be used in floral arrangements.

For your collection

🌿 *Alchemilla alpina* (alpine lady's mantle). This compact rockery plant grows to only 5 or 6 inches (13 or 15 cm) high and also produces tiny yellow-green flowers in summer. It is not as versatile as its cousin *A. mollis*, so show it more care and grow it in slightly moist, well-drained, fertile soil.

*A*llium aflatunense

✓**Common name:** *Ornamental onion, flowering garlic, cricketball allium*

Chief characteristics

Location: Full sun or light shade
Type: Bulb
Size: 3 feet (90 cm)
Conditions: Well-drained soil
Flowering time: May to June
Zone: 5

Close your eyes and picture this: dozens of perfectly spherical purple flowerheads reaching up beneath a canopy of yellow blooms cascading from rows of laburnum trees. Purple *Allium aflatunense* looks equally sensational popping up to complement the pink bottlebrush spikes of *Polygonum bistorta* (knotweed). Both these images are testament to the talent of gardeners who had the wit and wisdom to plant allium bulbs in the fall with a vision of what a spectacular picture they would create for spring.

Allium aflatunense is the most companionable and versatile of the flowering garlics to use in the garden landscape. It has a more stately presence than its diminutive relative, *A. schoenoprasum* (chives). But, at 3 feet (90 cm) high, *A. aflatunense* is less towering than its robust relative *A. giganteum*, which stands 4 feet (120 cm) and has flowerheads the size of a grapefruit. All add charm, character and regal color to the early summer garden. Bulbs are not expensive and they come back year after year to give a magnificent display. An extra bonus: squirrels hate the smell of them and won't disturb them unless there are tulips planted nearby.

Rosemary Verey, the grande dame of English horticulture, was one of the first to see how well they fit under laburnum trees. Others have copied her celebrated planting in her garden at Barnsley House in Gloucestershire. *Allium aflatunense* also performs very well interplanted with roses.

Where to plant it

Plant the bulbs in late September or early October, at 3 or 4 times their own depth in fertile, well-drained soil in a sunny or lightly shaded spot. They will have no trouble pushing up through hardy geraniums or daylilies or rising up through the soft leaves of *Polygonum bistorta*.

How to care for it

Once they are in the ground there is very little that can go wrong with alliums. Slugs will sometimes nibble young foliage and bulbs have been known to rot in excessively boggy ground. One of the most common mistakes is to buy the wrong bulb. It can be disappointing if you plant *Allium karataviense* instead of *A. aflatunense* and then discover in spring that the lovely flowerhead is lost in a jungle of taller foliage.

The decision to leave the faded flowerheads is purely an esthetic one: some gardeners love the look, others don't. English gardener, author and photographer Nigel Lawson once saved the dried flowerheads and re-introduced them to his garden in the winter to add architectural interest and intrigue.

Good companions

Without doubt, the best partner for *Allium aflatunense* is knotweed (*Polygonum bistorta* 'Superbum'); they bloom together for about a month starting around the middle of May. *A. aflatunense* also appears at its best when mass-planted under a row of yellow-flowering *Laburnum × watereri* 'Vossii' trees. Other excellent partners for the outstanding ornamental onion include yellow-leafed hostas, blue-flowering *Centaurea montana*, and the delicate magenta-red flowers of *Geranium macrorrhizum*.

Show off the magnificent starry flowerhead of *A. christophii* against the dark foliage of *Cimicifuga* 'Brunette' or the soft foliage of bleeding hearts. *Allium christophii* flowers around the same time as *Aubrieta, Phlox subulata,* foxgloves (*Digitalis purpurea*), perennial cornflower (*Centaurea montana*), coral bells (*Heuchera sanguinea*) and various hardy geraniums.

For your collection

Allium aflatunense is not the only star performer in the allium family. It has a few relatives that also deserve a place in the home garden. All the alliums make excellent cut flowers, especially the star of Persia (*A. christophii*), if you have the nerve to take them out of the garden when they are at their most glorious. When they finish flowering, the large globular heads slowly fade to brown and produce tiny charcoal-black seeds that add an unexpected beauty to the spheres.

- *Allium bulgaricum* grows 3 feet (90 cm) tall and produces graceful clusters of drooping pagoda-shaped flowers that have a curious blue-gray-purple color.
- *Allium caeruleum* (sometimes sold as *Allium azureum*) has lovely clusters of light blue flowers at the top of thin 18- to 24-inch (45- to 60-cm) stems. It flowers in midsummer, and looks best planted in large clumps.
- *Allium christophii* (star of Persia) resembles a space station when it is a fully formed cluster of countless five-point stars, each one a shiny, metallic purple-silver color.
- *Allium* 'Globemaster' is a true giant, producing huge 10-inch (25-cm) purple flowerheads at the top of sturdy 40-inch (100-cm) stems. It is the result of a cross between *A. christophii* from Iran and *A. macleanii* from Afghanistan.
- *Allium karataviense* produces a light purple-pink globe only 8 inches (20 cm) high.
- *Allium rosenbachianum* is very similar to *A. giganteum* but has daintier violet-purple flowerheads on a 40-inch (100-cm) stem.
- *Allium schoenoprasum* (chives). The most common of all alliums, chives can be incorporated into the perennial border, or used as a decoration in a pot on the patio close to the kitchen.
- *Allium sphaerocephalum* (drumstick allium, roundheaded leek) has a spherical, reddish-purple flowerhead at the top of a 2-foot (60-cm) stem. It makes an excellent cut flower in a sunny perennial border in late July and August.

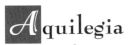

*A*quilegia

Common name: *Columbine*

Chief characteristics

Columbines are exquisite woodland plants. Their bell-shaped flowers nod expressively and look rather like a committee-made decision to cross a daylily with a daffodil and toss in the wings of a dragonfly for good measure. They are a perfect plant for any garden, flourishing in the moist, dappled shade of overhanging trees and popping up serendipitously between perennials and shrubs to form lovely pictures.

Location: Sun to light shade

Type: Perennial

Size: 2 to 3 feet (60 to 90 cm)

Conditions: Ordinary soil

Flowering time: April to May

Zone: 3

Columbine foliage is graceful and distinctive, but it is the modest, lantern-shaped flowers most gardeners fall in love with. Colors range from rich blues to muted pinks to soft pastel shades of purple and yellow. *Aquilegia vulgaris* is the old-fashioned "granny's bonnet" flower, which can be found in most English cottage gardens. It is the parent of many of the new cultivars, including blue 'Hensol Harebell', green-red 'Nora Barlow' and maroon-white 'Biedermeier'.

Other modern favorites include the McKana Hybrids, which produce big flowers in pastel and two-tone hues and grow to just over 2 feet (60 cm), and the Mrs. Scott Elliott's varieties, which are slightly more purple and darker than the others.

Although relatively short-lived, especially in heavy and wet soils, columbines are easily raised from seed, so there is no reason to lose them once you have them established in the garden. Other well-known ones to watch out for include the Dragonfly Hybrids, which have long spurs and bright colors. They are very similar to the McKana Hybrids but do not grow quite as tall.

Where to plant it

Grow columbines in well-drained leafy soil in a sunny or partly shady location. They flourish naturally under trees or in among the lush foliage of hostas and bleeding hearts. They have been known to attract hummingbirds, but their main role is to provide a romantic cottage-garden atmosphere. They make fine cut flowers.

How to care for it

Columbines are short lived but come easily from seed, which should be collected and germinated in trays or pots and then re-introduced to the garden each year.

Watch out for aphids. Red spider mites can sometimes be a problem but columbines are mostly trouble-free.

Good companions

Purple alliums and late-blooming tulips mix well with columbines, which tend to blend most naturally with other cottage garden favorites, such as bleeding heart, lady's mantle, ferns, hostas, campanulas, cornflowers, foxgloves and shade lovers such as masterwort and ligularia.

Columbines also thrive happily among shrub roses and they always find their own place in the cheerful chaos of a spring perennial border with hardy geraniums, peonies and blue salvia.

For your collection

In the rock garden, try growing any or all of these.

- *Aquilegia alpina* (Swiss columbine) grows only 12 inches (30 cm) high and has gray-green leaves.
- *Aquilegia bertolonii*, the dwarf species from Italy, grows only 6 inches (15 cm) high.
- *Aquilegia caerulea* is a pale blue and white flower from Colorado's mountains.

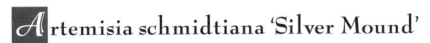

rtemisia schmidtiana 'Silver Mound'

Common name: *Wormwood*

Chief characteristics

Location: Full sun
Type: Perennial
Size: 12 to 15 inches (30 to 38 cm)
Conditions: Average, well-drained soil
Zone: 2

Gray foliage is essential for creating classy color and texture contrasts in the perennial border. There are quite a few plants that will give you the look you want, but few are as reliable as the artemisias, which not only have outstanding gray-silvery foliage but a respectable tolerance for spells of drought.

One of the best cultivars is 'Silver Mound'. Its feathery, silver foliage forms a compact, low mound. Drought tolerant and noninvasive, it blends superbly with other plants in the perennial border and makes a nice addition to the rock garden. The common name, wormwood, refers to the plant's history — herbalists used it for a medicine to kill parasitic worms.

Where to plant it

Grow 'Silver Mound' in well-drained soil in full sun. It will tolerate some shade. It can be used in the rockery, in containers or as a front-of-the-border plant. It looks good when allowed to intermingle freely with other perennials.

How to care for it

Cut back 'Silver Mound' to a few inches (8 to 10 cm) off the ground the moment it shows signs of flowering in midsummer or it will quickly become ragged and lose its wonderful dome shape. Don't worry, it may look rather brutally razored for a week or two, but fresh new growth will quickly return the plant to its former beauty.

Good companions

Black mondo grass (*Ophiopogon planiscapus* 'Nigrescens'), blue ornamental grasses, Marguerite daisies, *Scabiosa* 'Butterfly Blue' and rock rose (*Helianthemum*) are all interesting partners for 'Silver Mound'.

For a purple and silver theme, how about *Verbena* 'Homestead Purple' or *Geranium* 'Ballerina'? Combine it in a container with bronze sedge (*Carex buchananii),* blue lobelia and white bacopa for a sophisticated but zesty display for patio or balcony.

For your collection

- *Artemisia lactiflora* 'Guizhou' (white mugwort) has very different foliage—dark maroon-colored stems with purple, near-black leaves and sprays of creamy white flowers from late summer to early fall. It grows to about 4 feet (120 cm), making it a good choice for the back of the perennial border. Hardy to Zone 4.
- *Artemisia ludoviciana* 'Valerie Finnis' has soft, willow-like silvery leaves on erect stems. It grows 18 to 24 inches (45 to 60 cm) and is the perfect partner for some of David Austin's English roses, such as 'Mary Rose' or 'Heritage'. Hardy to Zone 4.
- *Artemisia* 'Powis Castle'. When it first appeared a few decades ago, this superb plant caused quite a stir in English garden circles. With its soft, feathery gray foliage, it was immediately recognized as one of the new aristocratic plants, was welcomed wholeheartedly into the garden, and has never left. It grows to 2 to 3 feet (60 to 90 cm). It is rated as hardy to Zone 6, but it is turning out to be a lot tougher than expected and has survived in colder areas.
- *Artemisia stelleriana* 'Silver Brocade' is a low-growing, compact plant with soft gray foliage similar to the popular bedding plant, dusty miller (*Cineraria maritima*). An excellent groundcover, 'Silver Brocade' is also useful for rockery edging and can even be put to work in hanging baskets to add texture and interest.

$\mathcal{A}$ster × frikartii 'Monch'

Common name: *Michaelmas daisy*

Chief characteristics

You know the end of summer is just around the corner when you start to see asters coming into bloom along with rudbeckia and Japanese anemones. Asters, better known as Michaelmas daisies, are available in a wide range of colors from red to pink, light blue to purple-blue. They also range in size from tall, gangly 5-foot (1.5-m) giants to short, compact dwarf specimens that can be grown in a rockery. Asters are valued for their long blooming period, the cheerfulness of their daisylike flowers, and their appearance when it seems as though the festive fun of summer is finished. They are a welcome late arrival to the party.

Location: Full sun
Type: Perennial
Size: 28 inches (70 cm)
Conditions: Moist, well-drained soil
Flowering time: July to October
Zone: 4

The best Michaelmas daisy for the average garden is *Aster × frikartii* 'Monch', which has bright lavender-blue flowers with yellow centers. It grows 3 feet (90 cm) tall and about 18 inches (45 cm) wide and flowers from the end of July to October. It is sturdy enough not to require staking, provides excellent cut flowers, and is a useful addition to any perennial border.

Where to plant it

Grow *Aster × frikartii* 'Monch' in full sun in rich soil that stays moist in summer but does not become water-logged in winter. Taller forms of aster often need staking, although they can be pinch-pruned to make them bushier. They are best placed at the back of the border where they can provide a wall of color.

The best place to grow 'Monch' is mixed in with other perennials and shrubs in a location where it can come into its own in August, bringing reinforcements of color to flagging flower beds, but not where it has too prominent a profile from spring to midsummer. The shorter asters can be grown at the front of the border, tucked in between summer-flowering fare, such as echinacea, daylilies, liatris and phlox.

How to care for it

The key to growing asters successfully is to make sure they get plenty of sun and are planted in fertile soil that does not dry out completely in the summer. Staking needs to be done early in July or even in late June to make sure the taller forms don't flop all over or start to twist.

Good companions

Gray-leafed plants such as *Artemisia ludoviciana* 'Valerie Finnis' and *Stachys byzantina* 'Primrose Heron' make effective partners, as do canna lilies, peanut butter plant *(Melianthus major)*, the steel-blue flowers of globe thistle *(Echinops)* and sea holly *(Eryngium)*, and the gold-yellow blooms of black-eyed susan *(Rudbeckia fulgida)*. The exquisite flowers of Japanese anemones such as 'Honorine Jobert' (white), 'Queen Charlotte' (pink) and 'September Charm' (silvery pink) are also good partners. You can select your asters so they flower when ornamental grasses such as *Miscanthus* and *Pennisetum* species are at their peak in late summer and early fall.

For your collection

- *Aster divaricatus* (white wood aster) will grow to 3 feet (90 cm) in light, dry shade. Its bright spray of white flowers adds interest to a dappled woodland area.
- *Aster dumosus* (bushy dwarf hybrids). These grow only about 12 to 15 inches (30 to 38 cm) tall and are ideal for the front of the border. Best bet: 'Lady in Blue', which has violet-blue flowers with a yellow center. This is easy to place in the border and it keeps its color long into fall. Other names to look for include 'Audrey' (mauve-blue), 'Diana' (rose-pink), 'Little Pink Beauty' (bright pink), 'Violet Carpet' (violet-blue), 'Nesthaskchen' (clear pink), 'White Opal' (white) and 'Jenny' (red).
- *Aster ericoides* (heath aster) will mound into a bush about 3 feet (90 cm) tall with clouds of lilac-blue or pale pink flowers. Look for 'Blue Cloud' or 'Pink Cloud'.
- *Aster novae-angliae* (New England aster). This is a taller species growing 5 feet (1.5 m) high. It can become gangly and benefits from being pinch-pruned at the tips in early July to make it bushier. Good names to look for include 'Andenken an Alma Potschke', 'Hella Lacy', 'Pink Winner', 'Purple Dome', 'September Ruby', 'Mrs. S. T. Wright' and 'Harrington's Pink'.
- *Aster novi-belgii* (New York aster). These grow 3 to 4 feet (90 to 120 cm) tall and are the hybrids of a species that is native to New York State. Top cultivars include 'Alert' (crimson), 'Coombe Rosemary' (violet-purple), 'Royal Ruby' (deep red), 'Coombe Margaret' (reddish-pink), 'Ada Ballard' (mauve-blue) and 'Chequers' (purple-violet).

A stilbe × arendsii 'Fanal'

Common name: *False spiraea*

Chief characteristics

It is impossible to imagine a garden without astilbes. It was once rumored that the English had given up on them completely and had banned them from their borders. If ever that were true, it would have been a most foolish choice. Astilbes are such thoroughly dependable plants. They send up lovely white, pink or red feather duster–like plumes from spring to late summer and their foliage forms great healthy mounds of leaves, which give the shade border its necessary bulk and full-bodied appearance. An old country garden plant, astilbe has had hybridizers playing with its genes for years, with the result that now we have literally dozens of cultivars with outstanding flower color and performance.

Location: Part sun to light shade
Type: Perennial
Size: 22 inches (56 cm)
Conditions: Fertile, well-drained soil
Flowering time: June to July
Zone: 3

'Fanal' is the most popular of all astilbes, partly because of its mahogany-red foliage in spring and partly because of its deep red, narrow flower spikes that appear in early spring and last well into summer. 'Fanal' grows 22 inches (56 cm) high and its small, attractive leaves slowly turn green by midsummer. What makes this plant special is its utter reliability, its cheerful blooms that allow it to blend effortlessly with other perennials, and its good timing. It produces abundant plumes from June to July, which is precisely when the garden needs to start exhibiting a sense of vitality and fullness.

Astilbe chinensis taquetii 'Superba' is another first-rate performer. It flowers later in the summer and has tall, deep purple-pink plumes reaching over 3 feet (90 cm). It is usually the last astilbe to flower. Other outstanding cultivars include 'Erika' (light pink), 'Bridal Veil' (white), 'Anita Pfeifer' (salmon), 'Rheinland' (pink), 'Glow' (deep red), 'Bressingham Beauty' (pink), 'White Gloria' (white), 'Elizabeth Bloom' (blowsy, pink), 'Diamant' (frosty white) and 'Granaat' (rose-pink).

There are so many kinds of astilbe now on the market, you might prefer to shop for them the way you do for rhododendrons—wait until they are in bloom and then pick the color you like best. Summer is a good time to make a note of plants and flowers you like. Be sure to find out not only the full botanical names but also the cultivar names so you can buy exactly what you want with confidence in spring.

Keep in mind flowering times when choosing astilbes. You will want to get a few late-blooming Chinese astilbes (*A. chinensis*) such as 'Pumila' (rose-purple), 'Superba' (lavender-pink), 'Purple Lance' (purple-red) or 'Intermezzo' (orchid pink). You might have a spot for a shorter astilbe. One that can be used almost as a low-growing groundcover in drier soil, or in the shady rock garden because of its dwarf habit, is *A. × crispa* 'Perkeo', which has reddish-pink spikes and grows to 6 to 8 inches (15 to 20 cm) tall.

Where to plant it

Astilbe is outstanding when grown in bold drifts, especially in sunny spots by small streams that keep the surrounding soil perpetually moist. It doesn't take a lot to create a drift. Put in 3 or 5 plants to start and within a few years you will have twice that number. Grow astilbe in light shade in rich soil where root competition from trees and shrubs is not too vigorous. Astilbe will flourish in a sunnier spot provided the soil does not dry out completely. It can also be grown in full shade, although it blooms more impressively when it gets a few hours of warm sunlight.

How to care for it

If clumps of astilbe are not divided every 3 or 4 years, they start to flower poorly and the whole plant begins to look unhappy. Division invigorates the plant and it will bloom enthusiastically again. The magnificent plumes can be cut and used in flower arrangements; you may find them giving off a sweet sugary scent that cannot really be described as perfume but is not unpleasant.

Good companions

Hosta, ligularia, primula, hardy geranium, lady's mantle (*Alchemilla mollis*), coral bells (*Heuchera*), Jacob's ladder (*Polemonium caeruleum*) and a whole range of other light shade–loving plants work well with astilbes. The delicate, muted white or soft pink flowers of *Astrantia major* are outstanding combined with astilbe blooms in a vase. Outstanding variegated hostas such as 'Great Expectations', 'Frances Williams' or 'Frosted Jade' can help to sustain interest and provide foliage contrast once astilbes have finished flowering.

For your collection

- *Aruncus dioicus* (goatsbeard). If you like the light airy plumes of astilbe, you will probably love the giant plumes of this plant. It grows to 5 feet (1.5 m) and looks like a giant astilbe with large attractive white plumes.

🐾 *Rodgersia pinnata* 'Superba'. It has impressive astilbe-like white or pink flower spikes held up above large, distinct leaves, rather like those of the horse chestnut. It grows 3 to 4 feet (90 to 120 cm).

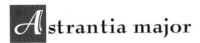strantia major

Common name: *Masterwort*

Chief characteristics

Astrantia major is loved by gardeners for the delicacy and sophistication of its flowers. They are a subtle, greenish-white with light pink centers. Very charming, very elegant. Astrantia grows happily in the shade or light shade of trees or protective shrubs. It is an old-fashioned perennial, one that has long been used in English cottage gardens. Yet it is invariably overlooked at garden centers because it has a difficult time competing with more showy annuals and perennials with vivid blooms. In the garden, however, astrantia's low-key, non-pushy presence brings a natural refinement to the shade border. The flowers are excellent for cutting. Indoors they can be appreciated close up for the true beauties they are.

Location: Part sun to part shade
Type: Perennial
Size: 30 inches (75 cm)
Conditions: Moist, but well-drained soil
Flowering time: June to August
Zone: 4

Where to plant it

Astrantia thrives in ordinary, well-drained soil in semi-shade. It will grow in deep shade, but you tend to forfeit some of its remarkable flower power. The clumps of leaves smother out weeds and associate well with the foliage of other shade plants like bleeding heart and Solomon's seal.

How to care for it

Astrantia is a most reliable, clump-forming perennial. It needs very little care. It may topple onto its neighbors, especially after a heavy rain storm, but while some see it as untidy, others recognize the relaxed look as rather charming and natural. If you want your astrantia to behave more formally, install link stakes as the new growth emerges in early spring and establish some parameters.

It should be watered well in the dog days of summer. Dry shade can kill it. Cut back the foliage after flowering to promote healthy new growth. Divide clumps every few years.

Good companions

Astrantia combines well in the shade border with astilbe, hosta, rodgersia, ligularia and ferns. It can also be worked in with shrub roses in light shade areas. One excellent combination puts *Astrantia major* 'Rubra' against the young burgundy leaves of the dwarf shrub *Berberis thunbergii* 'Atropurpurea Nana'. Also try marrying it with the blue cranesbill (*Geranium pratense*).

For your collection

- *Astrantia carniolica* 'Rubra'. This dwarf red masterwort grows less than 18 inches (45 cm) tall, has crimson-red flowers, and is slightly more compact, making it a useful plant for the front of the border.
- *Astrantia major* is the most dependable, but *A. major* 'Rubra' is very popular because of its wine-red flowers. It grows to 2 feet (60 cm).
- *Astrantia major* 'Shaggy', or 'Margery Fish', has larger, frillier white bracts and forms bold clumps of deeply cut leaves.
- *Astrantia major* 'Sunningdale Variegated'. This variegated form does not look as sickly as so many plants with green-white variegated foliage. In spring, this cultivar produces a bright mound of yellow-cream leaves.
- *Astrantia maxima* has slightly larger, more pronounced shell-pink flowers with densely clustered pincushion centers, somewhat similar to scabiosa. It grows to 2 feet (60 cm).

*B*etula utilis jacquemontii

Common name: *Himalayan birch*

Chief characteristics

In his superb poem, "Birches," Robert Frost imagines himself escaping the troubles of the world for a while by climbing a birch tree's "snow-white trunk toward heaven." Perhaps he was thinking of a grove of magnificent European weeping white birches (*Betula pendula*), one of the most widely planted deciduous trees. The white-barked birch is certainly a heavenly tree with graceful, drooping branches and attractive fall foliage. But if you are wondering which birch to plant in your garden, you will likely want either the Himalayan birch

Location: Full sun or light shade
Type: Deciduous tree
Size: 40 feet (12 m)
Conditions: Good, well-drained soil
Zone: 2

(*B. utilis jacquemontii*) with its snow-white bark or Young's weeping birch (*B. pendula* 'Youngii'), depending on how much space you have.

The Himalayan birch grows 40 feet (12 m) in 20 years. Its most attractive attribute is its brilliant white bark—the brightest white of any birch—which is exceptional in the barren winter landscape. It is available in two- or three-trunk clumps and is considered impressively resistant to birch borer.

Young's birch, on the other hand, is ideal for the courtyard or small garden because it is short and compact. It is usually sold as a weeping standard, top-grafted onto a trunk about 6 to 8 feet (2 to 2.4 m) off the ground. It soon forms an attractive umbrella shape that can look particularly handsome next to a small pond or as the centerpiece of a flower bed. The leaves often drape to the ground, hiding the silvery white trunk, which goes unnoticed until the bare days of winter.

Where to plant it

Birches are relatively short-lived trees. After 25 years they tend to lose their vigor and start to go downhill. More optimistic estimates give them 50 years, still not a long life in tree terms. Often decay starts with attacks from insects like the bronze birch borer and leafminers, but birch trees also suffer from inadequate watering after being wrongly planted in an excessively sunny, fast-draining location. All birches are happiest in rich, acidic soil where the roots can get down into moist, cool soil while the top of the tree can enjoy full sunshine. They suffer miserably if exposed to too much hot sun in summer while being denied plenty of water.

Plant your birch in early fall or mid-March. Where space permits, a clump of upright white-barked birches can be dramatic, especially if contrasted against a dark background of conifers or hedging. If you can't find a clump of birches already established by a nursery, you can make your own easily enough. Simply plant a few saplings 10 to 15 inches (25 to 38 cm) apart in the same large hole with each trunk pointing in a different direction.

How to care for it

Birches will "bleed" sap heavily if pruned at the wrong time of year. Don't prune when the sap is running in spring. Wait until fall or midwinter. Deadwood should always be taken out. In birches, it can become more of a problem because it may signal the start of fungal rot, which can quickly spread. If you plant your birch in a lawn, remember to give it an extra drink in the summer because the grass will rob it of water.

Good companions

Both Himalayan birch and Young's weeping birch can be underplanted with spring-flowering bulbs such as glory-of-the-snow, grape hyacinth, scilla, iris, scented narcissus and exotic tulips. Or consider underplanting with annuals like coleus and impatiens or low-growing perennials like heuchera, ajuga, wild ginger, lamium and bergenia. Black mondo grass provides a particularly striking contrast against the white bark in winter. You might consider making use of the hardier ornamental grasses, such as *Pennisetum alopecuroides*, and shorter hardy geraniums such as *G. macrorrhizum*.

For your collection

- *Betula albosinensis septentrionalis* (Chinese red birch). Another less common birch, this has orangy coffee-colored, flaking bark, and lovely light green leaves in summer followed by yellow foliage in fall. Hardy to Zone 5, it grows to 50 feet (15 m).
- *Betula nigra* 'Heritage' (river birch) is hardy to Zone 4, grows to 40 feet (12 m) and has pinkish-brown peeling bark.
- *Betula papyrifera* (paper birch). This is less common but also worth getting to know. It has peeling, chalky white bark, is hardy to Zone 2 and grows to 60 feet (18 m). It is also known as the canoe or white birch.
- *Betula pendula* 'Purple Rain' (purple-leafed weeping birch) is hardy to Zone 3 and grows to 33 feet (10 m).
- *Betula platyphylla japonica* 'Whitespire' (Whitespire Japanese white birch) is said to be the most disease and insect resistant. It has a pyramidal form and grows to 30 feet (9 m). It has proved itself tolerant of hot weather and impressively resistant to birch borer.
- *Cercidiphyllum japonicum pendulum* (weeping katsura). A graceful, weeping tree that covers itself with blue-green leaves and grows to about 20 feet (6 m). The foliage has been described as "giving the appearance of cascading water."
- *Salix caprea* 'Pendula' (Kilmarnock willow or weeping pussy willow). Another good choice for a small garden, it has catkins that turn yellow and thrives in moist soil.

Brugmansia × candida

Common name: *Angel's trumpet*

Chief characteristics

You can grow all kinds of plants in pots on your balcony or deck in summer, but few of them will match the dramatic impact of angel's trumpet in full flower. These extremely exotic plants, mostly from the American tropics, have spectacular, long, trumpet-shaped flowers that come in a rich range of colors from soft white to orange-red to peachy pink.

> **Location:** Full sun or light shade
> **Type:** Tender shrub
> **Size:** 5 to 6 feet (1.5 to 1.8 m)
> **Conditions:** Fertile soil
> **Flowering time:** July to September
> **Zone:** 8

At one time, they were all classified as *Datura*, but now angel's trumpets have been separated into two groups—one still called *Datura*, and another known as *Brugmansia*. If you go looking for any of the plants mentioned here you may find them listed in seed catalogues or at garden centers as either *Datura* or *Brugmansia*. It really won't matter that much to you: the botanical name game has not affected the beauty of the flowers.

There are a variety of species you can grow. There's *Brugmansia sanguinea*, an outstanding orange-red; *B. suaveolens* with white flowers; *B. versicolor*, white or peach-colored flowers; *Datura meteloides*, which has white or rose-lavender blooms; and *D. metel*, which has white or red-purple flowers.

You can wait until midsummer for your garden center to bring in a pots of angel's trumpets, or you can grow them yourself from seed. There are some exceptional *Datura* hybrids available including 'Double Blackcurrant Swirl', which has large, frilly flowers of purple-mauve; 'Cherub', which has white frilly trumpets that resemble "ballroom frocks"; and 'Double Golden Queen', which has large canary-yellow flowers. These are all short, bushy plants that grow 2 to 4 feet (60 to 120 cm) high.

For something a little more unusual, track down *Brugmansia × candida* (similar to *B. suaveolens*), which is a tree-form angel's trumpet, growing 6 feet (1.8 m) in a single season in a pot and producing gigantic, drooping, trumpet-shaped blooms with a very strong perfume. The white flowers can measure up to 15 inches (38 cm) long.

Where to plant it

Grow angel's trumpet in a pot or planter in full sun or part shade in rich soil. Locate it where it's protected from gusts of wind. Its role in the garden is as an accent or feature plant, so place it in a prime location to achieve the most dramatic visual impact. The plant's exceptionally sweet fragrance is often more noticeable in the warm evening air at twilight.

How to care for it

Grow angel's trumpet in a container that allows some room for root growth but not too much. It performs better when it is somewhat potbound. Feed with 20-20-20 every week. It is a heavy feeder and the fertilizer will encourage a profusion of blooms.

The plant should come with a label saying "handle with care" since the leaves and flowers contain toxic chemicals. Touching the leaves and rubbing your eyes can cause your pupils to dilate.

You can overwinter angel's trumpet or take cuttings, but this could be a lot more trouble than it is worth. It is perhaps easier, if you can't keep your plants in a frost-free environment over winter, to start afresh with new seed-grown plants.

Good companions

You don't need to plant anything in the pot with your angel's trumpet and there are few plants that will be able to compete with its formidable fragrance. You could surround it with smaller pots filled with different-colored ornamental grasses to create the illusion of the angel's trumpet rising out of a sea of blue or yellow or burgundy.

For a striking arrangement, fill a pot with the red-purple foxtails of *Pennisetum setaceum* 'Rubrum Dwarf' and place it next to a pot of golden yellow *Hakonechloa macra* 'Aureola' or with a couple of containers of bright blue lyme grass (*Elymus racemosus*) and blue oat grass (*Helictotrichon sempervirens*). The colors will create a sensational contrast with the super-scented angel's trumpets.

For your collection

- *Cosmos atrosanguineus* (chocolate cosmos). Another pleasantly scented container plant, this has maroon-colored flowers that smell like chocolate. It combines well with *Heliotropium arborescens* (cherry-pie plant), which smells like fresh-baked pie to some, baby powder to others.
- *Tibouchina urvilleana* (glory bush) and *Lantana camara* (shrub verbena) are two popular patio trees that can be brought out of

storage with your angel's trumpet in late spring to give your summer deck a warm, exotic look. *Tibouchina* produces exquisite purple flowers quite similar to pansies, while *Lantana camara* produces dainty clusters of orange-yellow flowers.

Buddleia davidii

Common name: *Butterfly bush, summer lilac*

Chief characteristics

Location: Full sun

Type: Deciduous shrub

Size: 8 to 13 feet (2.4 to 4 m)

Conditions: Average to poor soil

Flowering time: July to October

Zone: 5

Walk into any garden and most of the plants you see probably come from other parts of the world. There is really no such thing as a Canadian or American garden any more than there is an English garden. Most gardens are composed of a rich assortment of plants gathered from different parts of the world over centuries of patient, and at times courageous, plant-hunting followed by years of painstaking hybridizing and propagation. Part of the fun of showing people around your garden can be to point out plants that originated in China or South Africa, Greece or Turkey, New Zealand or South America.

The butterfly bush originates from the Sichuan and Hubei areas of China. It gets its name not because its flowers or foliage look anything like a butterfly, but because it has the uncanny knack of attracting butterflies. It does this by waving around long, arching stems of sweet-scented cone-shaped flowers. The nervous butterfly apparently feels some security when it lands in the long arms of the buddleia. *Buddleia davidii* comes in a rich variety of colors. Top names include the dark violet-purple 'Black Knight', rich-red 'Royal Red', bright pink 'Pink Delight', and variegated-leafed 'Harlequin.' Excellent whites include 'White Cloud', 'Peace', 'White Bouquet' and 'White Profusion'. There are two excellent dwarf forms — 'Nanho Blue' and 'Nanho Purple'. Buddleia has other fine qualities besides its flowers. Not particularly fussy about the ground it grows in, it will thrive in the poorest of soils in the least charming, most neglected corner of the garden, and still deliver an impressive show of colorful blooms. Even in its first year it will start to pump out fragrant clusters of flower cones that can measure up to 9 inches (23 cm) in length.

Where to plant it

Grow buddleia anywhere you like, but if you want to make it very happy, plant it in loose, loamy, ordinary garden soil that has good drainage in a spot that gets lots of sun. The only thing buddleia won't tolerate is too much lime.

How to care for it

Left unpruned, *Buddleia davidii* can get right out of hand. Within a couple of years, it can easily top 15 feet (4.5 m). After that it will start looking for new places to conquer. The key is to prune it back each year to about 2 feet (60 cm) off the ground. Do this in spring and dig in a little bonemeal at the same time. It also helps if you mulch really well around the shrub in early summer as a water-conserving measure. Even if you do this don't forget to water, especially during the first year when your buddleia is trying to establish itself.

Good companions

Where space is not limited, you could use the fairly tall-growing joe-pye weed (*Eupatorium maculatum*). It grows to 6 feet (1.8 m) and its pinky-purple flowerheads provide striking color in the late summer garden. There are two top varieties to consider: 'Atropurpureum' or the slightly more compact 'Gateway'.

Other useful perennials include *Sedum* 'Autumn Joy', *Echinacea purpurea*, *Verbascum bombyciferum* (giant silver mullein) with its gray leaves and yellow flowers. Also consider finding a spot for the spectacular combination of *Carex buchananii* and *Festuca* 'Elijah Blue'.

For your collection

- *Buddleia alternifolia* is a very decorative form of butterfly bush. It is known as the fountain butterfly bush because it produces a cascade of arching branches covered with tightly knotted mauve flowers. With a little effort, it can be nicely pruned to form an attractive small tree in the mixed border. You can also do this with wisteria, but *B. alternifolia* looks particularly handsome when trained in this way.
- *Buddleia* 'Dartmoor' is a fairly recent introduction with a romantic history. It was first spotted by a gardener during a romantic stroll with his fiancée in England's west country. 'Dartmoor' has soft lilac-purple spikes.
- *Buddleia fallowiana* 'Lochinch'. This is another shrub worth checking out. It has silvery leaves and lavender-blue flowers that smell like vanilla.

$\mathcal{B}$uxus microphylla koreana

Common name: *Korean boxwood*

Chief characteristics

There's nothing quite like a low, well-clipped boxwood hedge to give your garden a classical elegance. It immediately conjures up images of Elizabethan knot-gardens where flowers were dressed up like candies in a chocolate box. Boxwood is still used mostly for edging rose or herb gardens or to define the edges of a flower border more purposefully. Composed of small, glossy, dark green leaves that form an attractive, compact bush, *Buxus* can be clipped into a wondrous variety of eye-catching shapes—topiary pyramids, cones, squares and assorted creatures. You can find in some English gardens packs of hounds and flocks of birds all shaped out of box. It has been used particularly effectively to create wonderful architectural accents such as large round "box balls."

Location: Full sun
Type: Evergreen shrub
Size: 3 to 4 feet (90 to 120 cm)
Conditions: Ordinary soil
Zone: 5

In the sun, boxwood tends to give off a pungent smell that some people find mildly offensive. In most gardens, fortunately, this aroma is completely masked by the more pleasant fragrance of roses and honeysuckle.

Common boxwood, also known as English boxwood, is *Buxus sempervirens*. This species is hardy only to Zone 6 and is therefore not recommended for areas where winter temperatures dip below –10°F (–23°C). Korean boxwood, however, is perfectly hardy to –20°F (–29°C) and sometimes lower and will do just as efficient a landscaping job as the English box.

There are quite a few cultivars from which to choose. 'Winter Beauty' grows twice as wide as high, reaching 3 to 4 feet (1 to 1.2 m) at maturity. 'Green Velvet' has large, dark green leaves and the new growth is lime green. 'Green Mound' is ideal for forming low hedges in herb and rose gardens while 'Green Gem' has small, tight leaves. Other boxwood cultivars now available include 'Green Mountain' and 'Winter Gem', which is said to be the hardiest of all *Buxus microphylla* cultivars and is recommended for a low-clipped hedge.

Where to plant it

Use box to make neatly clipped, low, rectangular-shaped hedges. Plants are not inexpensive. You will undoubtedly face the temptation of using fewer plants and leaving wider spaces between them, with the idea that they will eventually grow together and the gaps will disappear. This can happen, but you can also end up with gaps in your hedge for a very long time—or at least for longer than you really want to have gaps. So, decide at the outset to bite the bullet and buy a few extra box plants so you can close ranks. You should really not plant them more than 9 inches (23 cm) apart. If you use 'Green Gem', plant 6 inches (15 cm) apart. Trimming off the top shoots will help. It will force the plants to bush out on the sides more quickly.

How to care for it

Box thrives in acidic soil in full sun to light shade. Don't neglect to water your new box hedge regularly during the first year after planting. Once established, the hedge will never give you any worries, but in the beginning the new plants are vulnerable to dry periods. Box is rarely bothered by pests and diseases.

Good companions

Underplant a box hedge with sweet woodruff (*Galium odoratum*). The foliage is a perfect complement to boxwood's tightly knotted leaves. Sweet woodruff also has fragrant white flowers in spring, which give the hedge a lovely touch of color. This groundcover can be dreadfully invasive, so don't let it seed itself too freely.

For your collection

It is unlikely you will want to collect varieties of box, but you might like to try your hand at doing a topiary or a box ball. The ball is made by putting 3 small plants together in a triangle form and then clipping as they grow to form the desired smooth, round ball shape.

🐦 Japanese holly (*Ilex crenata* 'Convexa') looks a lot more like boxwood than holly. It makes a very attractive compact shrub that produces tiny black berries in winter. It is ideal for hedging and thrives in full sun or partial shade. 'Green Thumb' is hardy to Zone 5 but *Ilex crenata* 'Hetzii' is also an excellent choice for hedging and formal landscaping.

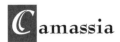amassia

Common name: *Quamash*

Chief characteristics

Daffodils. Tulips. Snowdrops. Crocuses. These are flowering bulbs we all know very well. They are all useful—crucial, some would say—for providing a burst of color to lift our spirits in spring after a long dark winter. Today, you can get some superb tulips: parrot tulips, fringed tulips, lily tulips, species tulips. They are all a lot fancier than the plain old tulip of yesteryear. Even daffodils are not what they used to be. Now you can get narcissi with multiple flowerheads that are also extremely fragrant.

Location: Sun to light shade
Type: Bulb
Size: 2 feet (60 cm)
Conditions: Moist soil
Flowering time: May to June
Zone: 5

The best bulbs for a garden are the ones that do not need to be lifted and replanted every year but can be left to naturalize under trees and shrubs, over grassy banks and at the foot of hedgerows. Some of the best for this purpose are grape hyacinth, crocus and scilla. But it is also fun to find room for a few more unusual, slightly exotic bulbs for a change of pace and to provide a conversation piece when you show visitors around.

Camassia is a perfect bulb for the job. It thrives in average, moist soil and produces very elegant blue or white flowers in late spring to early summer. Prince Charles liked this bulb so much he told his head gardener to plant 3,000 of them in the garden at Highgrove in Gloucestershire. After searching the nurseries of the world, it seems the only place the gardener could find enough camassias for the job was in Canada.

Look for *Camassia leichtlinii* or *C. cusickii*, both of which produce a profusion of blue flowers. *Camassia quamash* also has white to pale blue to purple-blue flowers.

Where to plant it

Grow *Camassia* in wet or moist fertile soil in full sun. If you don't have wet or damp ground, make sure to water the bulbs even when they are not in flower in summer. They will do very well even in ordinary soil and will tolerate light shade. Plant the bulbs, which are suprisingly large, in groups (the more the merrier) in September or early October.

If you have a stream running through your property, you can plant them on the sunny banks at the side. They are also happy in damp, open grassy areas, which is *Camassia's* natural habitat. In the small garden, they are a choice plant to mix in with the perennial border where they can rise and shine and then disappear without leaving untidy gaps.

How to care for it

After a few successful years of growing *Camassia*, you will need to lift and divide clumps, and space out the bulbs to avoid congestion.

If they are planted in well-drained soil, remember to water during dry periods. Once the flowers have faded, snip the flower stalks back to the ground.

Good companions

Iris sibirica, daylilies, catmint, gooseneck loosestrife, masterwort, hardy geraniums and astilbes can all thrive in moist soil in sunny or partially shaded locations. For color companions, however, you could try the blue of perennial cornflower (*Centaurea montana*) or the white of campanulas or the pink spikes of *Polygonum bistorta*, all of which flower about the same time as *Camassia*.

Fritillarias are another possibility. Not everyone likes them because they are a bit stinky, but there are a few worth adding to your garden. They make good supporting plants, especially when mixed in with other spring-flowering bulbs. *Fritillaria meleagris*, sometimes called snake's head fritillaria, has a colorful purple and white checkerboard flower. One of the most eye-catching fritillarias is *F. imperialis* 'Lutea', which has giant yellow flowers.

For your collection

Here's a list of other exciting bulbous plants to liven up your garden.

- *Eremurus* (foxtail lily). Not technically a bulb, this lily has a spidery, tuberous root and produces majestic 6- to 8-foot (1.8- to 2.4-m) spires of yellow or pale pink flowers that resemble long, bushy foxtails. Despite being somewhat temperamental (it requires a well-drained, sunny spot), it is a spectacular flower, especially when planted in clumps. Look for *E. stenophyllus*, *E. robustus*, *E. himalaicus*, or the two most popular hybrid strains, Ruiter or Shelford.
- *Colchicum* (autumn crocus). We've all seen crocuses in spring, but these crocus-like flowers bloom in fall. Look for *C. autumnale* (mauve), 'The Giant' (rose-lilac) and 'Princess Astrid' (deep purple-pink). The species crocus, *Crocus speciosus*, also flowers in fall, producing striking violet-blue, goblet-shaped flowers.
- *Erythronium* (dog's tooth violet). These are graceful woodland flowers with extremely attractive, nodding, lantern-like heads. They get their

rather unflattering common name from the appearance of the corms, which look like dog's fangs. You won't go wrong with *E. dens-canis* 'Purple King', 'Pink Perfection', 'Frans Hals'or 'Rose Queen'. One of the most reliable erythroniums is 'Pagoda', which has terrific yellow flowers. *E. californicum* 'White Beauty' is one of the most beautiful currently available and has delightful white flowers.

- *Galtonia candicans* (summer hyacinth). Use these pure white, drooping, bell-shaped flowers on 2-foot (60-cm) stems to add a boost of color to the perennial border in August. It can be grown in a pot—along with the white form of the tender agapanthus—and then discreetly tucked into the border to provide illuminating whites for summer evenings.

- *Eucomis bicolor* (pineapple lily). Yes, the flower really does look just like a pineapple. *Eucomis* grows 18 inches (45 cm) tall and flowers in July. Grow it in a pot and then tuck the pot into the flower bed. This allows you to bring the pot into a frost-free place over the winter.

- *Cardiocrinum giganteum* (giant Himalayan lily). A real showstopper in any garden, this grows 9 feet (2.7 m) tall and has pure white, 6-inch-long (15-cm) fragrant, trumpet-shaped flowers with red throats. The heart-shaped leaves also live up to their name, being a gigantic 18 inches (45 cm) long. Gardeners often leave the seed heads of the plant for decoration in the garden. Great conversation piece.

- *Tigridia pavonia* (tiger flower). This is a true exotic beauty with yellow or red flowers and speckled throat. It flowers from August to September and grows about 18 inches (45 cm) high. The daylily-like flowers last only a day but new ones continue to appear for a time. Since they are tender (hardy only in Zones 7 to 10), you need to treat them like dahlias and gladioli: plant in spring when the ground has completely warmed up and lift them in fall once the leaves have turned yellow.

- *Leucojum* species (snowflake). This is certainly a spring bulb worth planting. It has small, nodding white flowers somewhat similar to snowdrops but with distinctive fine green or yellow spots on the tip of each petal. Look for *Leucojum vernum*, which flowers in February or March. *L. aestivum* 'Gravetye Giant', the late-flowering summer snowflake, gets its name from the garden of 19th-century British garden guru William Robinson.

- *Canna* × *generalis* (Canna lilies). These large, bold, tropical-leaved specimens add drama and exotic color to the August garden. Start the rhizomes indoors in March and plant out in June in a hot, sunny spot. Lift and store the roots in a frost-free place over winter. They go well with dahlias.

ampanula persicifolia

Common name: *Bellflower*

Chief characteristics

There are few flowers as cheery in the summer garden as the light sky-blue blooms of *Campanula persicifolia*. They have immense charm and bring a natural, relaxed style to the perennial border. They also make a first-rate cut flower. The campanula family is large and serves reliably, year after year, in various parts of the garden.

Location: Full sun to light shade

Type: Perennial

Size: 3 to 4 feet (90 to 120 cm)

Conditions: Well-drained soil

Flowering time: June to August

Zone: 4

Campanula persicifolia is usually found in the perennial border, but you will find other campanulas tumbling over walls, filling crevices between stepping stones, adding color to the rockery or alpine garden, or just giving flower beds the charming look of an old English cottage garden.

Campanula persicifolia, also known as the peach-leafed bellflower, is one of the most popular perennials, partly because of the loveliness of its flowers and partly because it is so easy to grow. *C. persicifolia* 'Alba' has dazzling white flowers with the same delightful bell shape as the blue version and there is a smashing variety called 'Chettle Charm' now available that has pale china-blue flowers. After flowering, the long stems can be cut down, allowing the plant to act as a low-mounding groundcover.

Unfortunately, my favorite campanula is not so easy to find at local garden centers. It is the giant or great bellflower, *Campanula latifolia* 'Alba', which grows about 4 feet (1.2 m) tall and has very attractive white flowers. The flowers have a more tubular, bonnet-like shape than the blooms of *C. persicifolia*. They are a highlight in my garden in late June.

Where to plant it

Grow *Campanula persicifolia* in a sunny location in ordinary well-drained soil. It will also flourish in light shade. It looks terrific in the middle or at the back of the border—you get to see the flowers without having to look at their less attractive stems. The worst use is as a solitary clump on an exposed boulevard or alone in an empty flower bed. Bellflowers will generally stand tall and erect, but expect some flower stems to flop over. This is often preferable to having the flowers stand perfectly at attention.

How to care for it

New clumps will form without permission or invitation. Bellflowers like to self-seed and new plants are always cropping up in unexpected places. If you don't like where they are, simply shovel them out and move them to a better spot. Clumps divide easily. You'll have plenty of plants to give away to friends.

Good companions

A truly gregarious plant, *Campanula persicifolia* gets along well with roses and lilies and is at ease sharing ground with perennial cornflower (*Centaurea montana*), foxgloves, lupins, geraniums, lady's mantle, daylilies, artemisia, asters and phlox. It invariably ends up forming its own associations, creating its own good companions.

For your collection

There are dozens of campanulas, all with slightly different growth habits, making them useful in different ways in different parts of the garden.

- *Campanula carpatica* (the delicate Carpathian harebell) grows only 9 inches (23 cm) high.
- *Campanula cochleariifolia* (fairy thimbles) is a low-growing plant for the rockery, with tiny, nodding thimble-shaped flowers in either white or blue.
- *Campanula glomerata* 'Superba' (clustered bellflower) has eye-catching spherical clusters of dark violet-purple flowers from June to July.
- *Campanula lactiflora* (milky bellflower) forms compact clumps and sends up tall stems of star-shaped flowers. There is a pink-flowering cultivar called 'Loddon Anna'.
- *Campanula medium* (traditional Canterbury bells) produces deep purple-blue flowers with a bonnet shape.
- *Campanula poscharskyana* (Serbian bellflower) is a trailing rockery plant that produces masses of star-shaped blue flowers and can be used as a groundcover.
- *Campanula takesimana* (Korean bellflower) has large pale-lilac flowers with strawberry spots inside. A good plant for dry shade.

Campsis radicans

Common name: *Trumpet vine, trumpet creeper, trumpet honeysuckle*

Chief characteristics

The trumpet vine is a beautiful hot-blooded creature. The rich, deep-throated, red flowers have an extremely sensual, pouty look to them. That's why hummingbirds can't stay away. But love will not make this vine flower. Only hot sun will do it. The vine is also a vigorous climber, capable of clambering at least 15 feet (4.5 m) high and 3 or 4 feet (90 to 120 cm) wide in the right spot.

Location: Sun
Type: Deciduous vine
Size: 20 feet (6 m)
Conditions: Fertile, well-drained soil
Flowering time: July to August
Zone: 5

You can grow *Campsis radicans* into trees or use it to cover sheds or old tree trunks. All it needs is a simple trellis or post for support to get started. It climbs stealthily, without a lot of wasted effort, clinging as it goes to whatever it can use to attach its tiny aerial roots. If exposed to too much frost, it will die back to the ground, but, being a born survivor, it invariably rallies the following year. The trumpet vine is a little tougher and more free-flowering than its Asian cousin, the Chinese creeper vine (*C. grandiflora*), which has scarlet-colored blooms. Neither vine is as famous as the hybrid they produced—*C.* × *tagliabuana* 'Madame Galen', which has salmon-red flowers.

Where to plant it

Without plenty of sun (and heat), your trumpet vine will put on lots of leafy growth and will end up looking extremely lush and healthy, but may not bloom. To get it to flower freely, the vine needs a warm, sunny spot, which is why it does so well in places with hot, arid summers. Grow it in fertile, free-draining soil.

One of the best plantings I've seen was over the roof of a carport in a very sheltered west-facing courtyard garden. In my garden, I have a trumpet vine smothering an old telegraph pole. For the last three years, it has leafed out very enthusiastically, but has yet to flower. This is partly because it is lightly shaded by nearby trees at the crucial time of day when it needs more heat. This is probably easily remedied by clipping back a few branches to allow in more light. Working with your plants to help them achieve their purpose is part of the thrill of gardening.

How to care for it

Protected from cold winds and severe frosts and planted in well-drained soil, trumpet vine will sail through a winter of heavy rain and snow. It flowers on the current season's growth and should be lightly pruned in early spring just for size and to thin out the top growth.

Good companions

Stonecrop, roses, daylilies and shrubs like potentilla, weigela and viburnum can all be used to fill out around the base of a trumpet vine. For a dramatic contrast, grow it against a wall along with honeysuckle, wisteria, akebia and clematis.

For your collection

- *Campsis radicans* 'Flamenco'. Has orange-scarlet blooms.
- *Campsis radicans* 'Flava'. A yellow-flowering trumpet vine.
- *Eccremocarpus scaber* (Chilean glory vine). This vine will scramble up 10 feet (3 m) and has orange-red tubular flowers. It can be grown successfully in sheltered spots in mild areas in rich, well-drained soil.

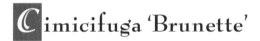

Cimicifuga 'Brunette'

Common name: *Bugbane, snakeroot*

Chief characteristics

Every now and then, gardeners get very excited about some new perennial with one or more outstanding qualities. When *Artemisia* 'Powis Castle' first came on the scene, it sparked an avalanche of interest in gray foliage. For a time, the Christmas rose (*Helleborus niger*) and the Lenten rose (*H. orientalis*) were all the rage because of the delicate beauty of their flowers and the luster of their leathery green foliage. Currently in vogue are variegated Jacob's ladder (*Polemonium* 'Brise d'Anjou') and purple-leafed coral bells (*Heuchera* 'Plum Pudding').

Location: Full sun to light shade
Type: Perennial
Size: 5 to 6 feet (1.5 to 1.8 m)
Conditions: Fertile, well-drained soil
Flowering time: September to October
Zone: 3

However, the perennial that has been enjoying the most popularity over the last few years has been *Cimicifuga* 'Brunette', which has fabulous dark black-purple foliage and arching stems bearing white bottlebrush flowers with a light purple tint. What is all the fuss about? The dark foliage is the perfect foil for the hot colors of canna lilies or for contrast against the golden yellow leaves of hostas. And cimicifuga's white flowers are a welcome arrival, waving at the top of 6- or 7-foot (1.8- to 2.1-m) stems when they appear at the end of summer, usually in September. 'Brunette' is also extremely adaptable, flourishing in a variety of situations and behaving consistently, with near indifference to soil conditions. A lot of gardeners first got to know cimicifuga through the cultivar 'Atropurpurea', which also has dark foliage. But once they meet 'Brunette', there is usually no going back. 'Hillside Black Beauty' has even darker purple foliage than 'Brunette'.

There is one other proven winner in the cimicifuga family and that is *C. simplex* 'White Pearl', which has spikes of bright white flowers and green lacy leaves in September. It grows a little shorter than 'Brunette', reaching only 3 to 4 feet (90 to 120 cm), but putting on a terrific flower display in late summer.

The name bugbane, by the way, is applied to a wide variety of plants. It simply means that the leaves have some ability to repel insects.

Where to plant it

There are a few ways to use *Cimicifuga* 'Brunette' effectively. You can plant it in the perennial border to provide foliage contrast, include it in a large container planting or mass-plant two or three of them to create a special landscape feature. 'Brunette' will thrive in full sun provided it is well watered in the hottest days of summer, but it will do better for you if grown in part sun or light shade in moist but well-drained soil. Cimicifuga is mostly considered a woodland plant and the traditional planting site is the dappled shade of a woodland garden. It is still considered by many expert gardeners to be an indispensable perennial for the light shade garden.

How to care for it

Since 'Brunette' will easily grow to 6 feet (1.8 m) it is sometimes necessary to use stakes to support the free-moving flower stems. One of the most unobtrusive ways to do this is to use a few thin, stiff branches that either fall into your garden from deciduous trees or can be judiciously pruned away without showing any serious loss. These supports look more natural than high-tech plastic stakes, almost charmingly rustic, and they certainly look more attractive than having your plant hog-tied with wire or heavy-duty string.

If you have the nerve, pinch out the bud the first year and allow your plant to put more energy into developing a deep root system. It will pay off the following year when you get twice as many flowers. Well-developed clumps can be divided in April every three years.

Good companions

The dark foliage of 'Brunette' blends very nicely with the hot summer colors of canna lilies, phlox or bee balm. In light shade, blue-leaf or yellow-leaf hostas make interesting partners, while the silver leaves of artemisia, the straplike leaves of fountain grass or the carmine-red flowers of the dahlia 'Bishop of Llandaff' can all be used to create a wonderful picture. Other good companions for 'Brunette' include *Euphorbia* 'Chameleon', *Rodgersia podophylla*, *Heuchera* 'Palace Purple' or *Penstemon* 'Husker's Red'.

For your collection

🐾 *Cimicifuga japonica*. This is different from the other cimicifugas in that it only grows to 30 inches (75 cm) and has maple-like leaves. It also has white bottlebrush-like flowers. It is often sold under the name *C. acerina*. A great plant for the woodland, it thrives in average soil in semi-shade.

Clematis × jackmanii

Common name: *Virgin's bower, old man's beard, traveler's joy*

Chief characteristics

The most sociable of climbers, clematis is deservedly called the "queen of vines." No garden should be without at least one or two. Some gardeners have planted as many as half a dozen at a time to cover a single trellis or arbor.

Choosing the right clematis is the key to success. The selection can be overwhelming. In commercial cultivation at the moment there are at least 50 blue-flowering, 34 pink, 30 purple, 16 two-tone; 34 white, 21 red, and 10 yellow-blooming varieties. Once you've chosen the color you like, the next step is to decide what time of year you want it to flower. You can get clematis that bloom in early spring or summer or fall.

The most popular of them all is *Clematis × jackmanii*, the most reliable performer of the summer-flowering cultivars. It grows 12 to

Location: Full sun to light shade

Type: Deciduous vine

Size: 12 to 20 feet (3.6 to 6 m)

Conditions: Fertile, well-drained soil

Flowering time: June to July

Zone: 3 to 7

20 feet (3.6 to 6 m) and produces masses of 4- to 6-inch (10- to 15-cm) purple flowers from June to August. 'Superba' is very similar to C. × *jackmanii* but the flowers are more substantial and bloom a little longer.

Other outstanding summer bloomers include the red 'Ville de Lyon', blue 'Polish Spirit', pale mauve with red stripe 'Nelly Moser' and pristine white 'Henryi'.

Where to plant it

Grow clematis so the roots are in the shade and the foliage and flowers are in full sun. Plant the vine deeply, in a hole at least 18 inches (45 cm) deep. This will mean burying a little more of your new plant than seems right but it will ensure that it gets well established.

To flower properly, clematis need at least five hours of full sun. The ideal location is a west-facing trellis that is shaded at its base all afternoon. This allows the vine to get maximum light and warmth at the top while the roots get the cool, moist shade they need. Plant a small shrub in front or use large stones to create shade for roots if there is no other available protection.

How to care for it

"How do you prune it?" is the most commonly asked question about clematis. There is no simple answer: it really depends on what kind of clematis it is. 'Nelly Moser', for example, requires only modest pruning in early spring while *Clematis* × *jackmanii* should be cut back to 2 feet (60 cm) off the ground every February.

The key is to know your vine. Watch it and make note of when it flowers and how it grows. As a general rule, if it flowers in spring on last year's wood, prune after flowering. If it flowers in summer on new supple shoots, prune in early spring. If it blooms twice, on old wood in spring and new wood in fall, prune lightly for appearance and size after it has finished blooming.

Good companions

Clematis are their own best friends. You can plant several side by side. The art, however, is to plant those that will give you a natural sequence of blooms from spring to fall. This is easier said than done. Your best bet is to play with the colors and forms you like and see what happens.

Clematis is a natural partner for climbing roses, especially to complement an arch arbor. The purple smoke bush (*Cotinus coggygria*) is an excellent companion for red-flowering clematis such as 'Madame Julia Correvon' or 'Ville de Lyon'. *Magnolia* × *soulangiana* is also a good partner to provide a frame for the outstanding, early flowering *Clematis alpina* 'Pamela Jackman' (deep blue) or 'Jacqueline du Pre' (rosy mauve).

For your collection

There are a few other excellent clematis that are also worth accommodating.

- *Clematis florida* 'Sieboldii'. A more unusual vine bearing creamy white blooms with distinctive deep purple centers, it can be grown in a pot on a patio as it grows only 8 feet (2.4 m) high and requires minimal pruning. It is more tender than other clematis, but can be over-wintered if protected from frost.
- *Clematis montana*. This vigorous deciduous species flowers in early spring, usually a little after the evergreen variety. Look for the names 'Tetrarose', 'Alba', 'Elizabeth', 'Pink Perfection' and *C. montana rubens*. The montana clematis originates in the Himalayas and has been used to form thick, leafy coverings over arches or arbors. It is even vigorous enough to scramble high into tall trees. This type of clematis flowers on growth produced the previous year.
- *Clematis tangutica* (golden clematis). This is an exceptionally vigorous form that produces nodding, lantern-shaped yellow flowers in July. The flowers magically transform into soft, silvery seed heads in the fall.
- Two other star performers are deep violet-purple 'Mrs. N. Thompson' and white 'Guernsey Cream'.

Coreopsis verticillata 'Moonbeam'

Common name: *Tickseed*

Chief characteristics

Location: Full sun
Type: Perennial
Size: 18 inches (45 cm)
Conditions: Ordinary, well-drained soil
Flowering time: June to August
Zone: 3

Yellow is not everybody's favorite color in the garden. It is, however, one of nature's favorites. There are some exceptional plants that produce first-rate yellow flowers and *Coreopsis verticillata* 'Moonbeam' is one. It flowers profusely from late spring into summer, growing about 18 inches (45 cm) tall and producing hundreds of small, pale yellow flowers that are not at all jarring to the eye. Called thread-leaf coreopsis because of its lacy foliage, 'Moonbeam' was named Perennial Plant of the Year in 1992 by the Perennial Plant Association of North America.

Other cultivars to look for include 'Golden Showers', which has large six-petaled open-faced flowers and 'Zagreb', a more compact dwarf form that grows only 15 inches (38 cm) high. *Coreopsis grandiflora* 'Early Sunrise' has much larger yellow flowers. It is a fuss-free award winner that forms a small bushy mound about 2 feet (60 cm) high and won't stop flowering until you force it by cutting down the stems in early fall. Other notable cultivars of coreopsis include 'Double Sunburst', 'Golden Showers, 'Sunray' and 'Baby Sun'. Coreopsis earns its common name— tickseed—from its seeds, which look like tiny bugs.

Where to plant it

Grow coreopsis in well-drained but moist soil in full sun toward the front of the border. 'Moonbeam' is perfect for growing either at the front of the border or as a supporting plant in a container scheme. 'Golden Showers' and 'Zagreb' are also excellent choices for pots or planters. The most endearing characteristic of 'Early Sunrise' is its ability to keep on blooming throughout summer. The cheerful sunny flowers add zest to floral arrangements.

How to care for it

While it will perform in fairly dry, well-drained soil, coreopsis still needs to be watered. It is a common mistake to treat coreopsis like an utterly drought-tolerant plant. It is also a mistake to allow 'Early Sunrise' and other grandiflora varieties to flower perpetually until they are killed by hard frosts in October. Much better to cut back the stems in early to mid-September and give the plant a few weeks to bulk itself up in preparation for winter.

Good companions

For striking contrast to the yellow flowers of coreopsis, look to blues and purples. There are the blue spikes of *Lavandula angustifolia* 'Munstead' and 'Hidcote Blue' or the blue flowers of agapanthus or vivid blue grasses such as *Festuca glauca* or *Helictotrichon sempervirens*. The blues of *Salvia × sylvestris* 'May Night' or the annual *Salvia farinacea* are also very useful. The woody shrub *Caryopteris × clandonensis* 'Dark Knight' (sometimes called blue spiraea) flowers late in August and offers an exciting contrast to the yellows of rudbeckia as well as coreopsis.

There's also the purple of blazing star (*Liatris spicata*) or *Verbena canadensis* 'Homestead Purple' or plain old chives (*Allium schoenoprasum*). For lively pastel combinations, you could try using some of the new yarrow (*Achillea*) hybrids, such as 'Summer Pastels', 'Heidi', 'Apple-blossom' or 'Christel'. For a little more punch, how about the cherry red of 'Paprika' or 'Red Beauty'? Three other achilleas that can be incorporated into the composition are 'Cerise Queen' (deep pink), 'Coronation' (golden yellow) and 'Moonshine' (bright yellow). *Coreopsis verticillata* 'Moonbeam' partners well with the silvery gray foliage of artemisias, daylilies such as the almost perpetual-blooming 'Stella de Oro' or the richer reds of 'Bess Ross', ' Buzz Bomb', 'Summer Wine' or 'Russian Rhapsody'. Consider mixing it up with the pink-purple foxtails of *Pennisetum setaceum* 'Rubrum', the maroon flowers of *Cosmos atrosanguineus* or the orange-red flowers of *Crocosmia* 'Vulcan', a shorter, more compact montbretia.

For your collection

There are several other superb yellow-flowering perennials that deserve a spot in your garden. Here's a pick of the best.

- *Kirengeshoma palmata* (yellow waxbells). This is an excellent plant for cool woodland gardens and considered a choice specimen by plant connoisseurs. It has waxy, yellow, bell-shaped flowers from July to October that hang down from purplish stems of 4 or 5 feet (1.2 to 1.5 m). It thrives in rich, leafy, moist, but well-drained soil.
- *Ligularia stenocephala* 'The Rocket'. A bold background plant with large, decorative leaves, this has long rocket-tail spikes of yellow flowers. It looks wonderful in June and July and not so terrible even when the flowers have faded. Even so, you should still cut down the spikes once they are done.
- *Oenothera tetragona* (evening primrose). This grows 2 feet (60 cm) tall and produces striking lemon-yellow flowers from June to August. It is drought resistant and can spread to fill a sizable area. It is best displayed with another low-growing plant to cover the gawkiness of its stems at the front.
- *Rudbeckia* (black-eyed susan). The large yellow daisy flowers with dark purplish-brown centers are a mainstay of the fall border, flowering from late summer into October. *R. fulgida* 'Goldsturm' is very reliable and grows to 2 feet (60 cm), but there are also excellent taller cultivars such as 'Double Gold' and 'Irish Eyes'.
- *Heliopsis* (false sunflower). These tall daisies make a bright backdrop, growing up to 4 feet (1.2 m) high. They are also long lasting, flowering from early summer to fall. *H. helianthoides* 'Summer Sun' is the best and can be combined with blue veronica or salvia for a striking mix of colors.
- *Verbascum bombyciferum*. Not only does this plant have striking yellow flowers, it also has attractive, soft, silvery gray leaves. It needs plenty of room to achieve its potential. Grows 5 to 6 feet (1.5 to 1.8 m) in full sun.

🍂 *Argyranthemum frutescens* 'Jamaica Primrose'(formerly *Chrysanthemum*). This perennial grows to 3 feet (90 cm) and has lovely soft yellow flowers that blend well with the midsummer border. Combines well with trailing petunias and bacopa.

Cornus alba 'Elegantissima'

Common name: *Silverleaf dogwood*

Chief characteristics

Location: Full sun to light shade

Type: Deciduous shrub

Size: 10 feet (3 m)

Conditions: Good, well-drained soil

Zone: 2

There is no question that every garden should have at least one dogwood. The key issue is what characteristic you're looking for—lovely flowers or winter interest or feature foliage. If you want beautiful white blooms, you can't go wrong with Chinese dogwood (*Cornus kousa*), which has creamy flowers, or the Cloud Nine dogwood (*Cornus florida* 'Cloud Nine'), which has snowy white flowers. Both bloom in June. For winter interest, there are the beautiful red- or yellow-twig dogwoods, *Cornus sanguinea* 'Winter Beauty' (blood-red stems) or *Cornus stolonifera* 'Flaviramea' (bright yellow twigs).

But for feature foliage that can brighten shady corners and provide long-lasting color and contrast, you can't beat silverleaf dogwood (*Cornus alba* 'Elegantissima'). This has been a popular and reliable performer for years and has established itself as one of the mainstays of a mixed border and an integral part of the botanical bones of many outstanding home gardens.

The pink-flowering dogwood (*Cornus florida rubra*) looks sensational in full bloom in May and pagoda dogwood (*Cornus alternifolia*) has graceful, horizontally tiered branches and blue-black berries in fall, but the silverleaf dogwood's green-and-white variegated foliage and burgundy-red branches in winter make it my pick as a "best plant" among the dogwoods. This is primarily because of the simple elegance of the attractive two-tone foliage (it isn't named 'Elegantissima' for nothing) and the shrub's general usefulness and reliability in the garden. It produces tiny clusters of pale white flowers but these are insignificant and often come and go unnoticed.

An offspring of the common Tatarian dogwood (*Cornus alba*), 'Elegantissima' has a couple of very attractive cousins worth knowing — 'Gouchaultii' (also known as the mottled Tatarian because of its green-

and-cream streaked foliage) and 'Sibirica' (Siberian dogwood, which has striking red stems in winter). 'Elegantissima' and 'Sibirica' grow 8 to 10 feet (2.4 to 3 m) but 'Gouchaultii' is not quite as vigorous, growing to 6 or 8 feet (1.5 to 2.4 m).

Where to plant it

All dogwoods grow best in full sun or light shade in rich, slightly acidic, well-drained soil. They need some protection from cold winds. 'Elegantissima' can be planted to brighten a shady corner or mixed in the shrub border to add foliage color and contrast. It is also useful for screening out eyesores or creating privacy in the summer. In the winter, the bare structure of the branches, which have a dull red tinge, can be quite attractive. It is worth locating 'Elegantissima' where it can be seen in winter so these characteristics can be enjoyed.

How to care for it

All the cultivars of Tatarian dogwood, including 'Elegantissma', are disease resistant and easy to maintain. They can be pruned for size and shape as required, usually in early spring, mainly to remove any dead or damaged branches. The varieties that are specifically grown for their vivid red or yellow twigs ('Sibirica' or 'Flaviramea') should be cut down to a few inches (8 to 10 cm) from the ground every March to promote new, vigorous, colorful growth.

Good companions

When you buy a silverleaf dogwood, don't be surprised if you are asked, "Do you want a purple leaf sand cherry to go with that?" The two shrubs do work well together—the dark plum-colored leaves of the sand cherry (*Prunus* × *cistena*) contrasting very nicely with the white-and-cream leaves of the dogwood. A smoke bush (*Cotinus coggygria*) would also make a good partner, with its striking purple leaves. Other companionable shrubs for your dogwood include rhododendrons, magnolias, witch hazels and deciduous azaleas.

Dogwoods can be underscored with spring-flowering bulbs such as dog's tooth violets, flowering perennials like Lenten rose (*Helleborus orientalis*) and groundcovers like ajuga and hardy geraniums.

For your collection

Here are some other outstanding members of the dogwood family.

- *Cornus alternifolia* (pagoda dogwood). Hardy to Zone 4, this small tree grows to 20 feet (6 m), and gets its names from the pagoda-like structure of its horizontally tiered branches. It has fragrant, yellowish-white flowers from May to June. It thrives in moist, acidic soil in light shade.

- *Cornus controversa* 'Variegata' is a much coveted tree because of its rarity, its green-white variegated foliage and its graceful growth habit—horizontally tiered branches that maintain a pyramidal shape. It also produces masses of white blooms. It is best seen with setting sunlight behind it, which brings out the magic of the two-toned foliage. A relatively fast grower, it reaches about 30 feet (9 m) at maturity.

- *Cornus florida rubra* (red-flowering dogwood) is a very popular small tree that produces light pink flowers. *C. florida* 'Cherokee Chief' has the deepest red flowers, bright red foliage in May and burgundy foliage in fall. It grows to 20 feet (6 m).

- *Cornus kousa* (Chinese dogwood) is actually a native of Japan, not China. It flowers in June, about a month after most other dogwoods, and is much loved for its creamy white flowers that are larger than those of other dogwoods. It grows as wide as it does tall, reaching 15 feet (4.5 m) after about 10 years. A beautiful red-flowering variety called 'Satomi' has crimson-purple foliage in fall and grows to 30 feet (9 m) at maturity.

- *Cornus mas* (Cornelian cherry) is a small tree or multi-stemmed bush with yellow flowers on bare branches in April and bright "cherry" red fruits in fall. It grows to about 10 feet (3 m).

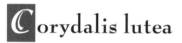orydalis lutea

Common name: *Yellow corydalis*

Chief characteristics

This is a magnificent, perpetually flowering perennial for semi-shade areas of the garden. It bears clusters of tiny yellow, tubular flowers above lush mounds of frothy foliage. The first flowers appear in mid-spring and continue to the end of summer. Corydalis can be mass-planted in long rows to provide an effective edging for a stone or brick path in light shade or as a groundcover under trees or shrubs. The worst thing anyone is going to tell you about *Corydalis lutea* is that it likes to seed itself everywhere. Of course, this may be exactly what you

Location: Sun to partial shade

Type: Perennial

Size: 12 to 18 inches (30 to 45 cm)

Conditions: Average, well-drained soil

Flowering time: April to September

Zone: 5

want it to do. If not, you can either resign yourself to pulling out the seedlings, which can be given away to friends, or grow the plant only where its free-seeding habit is not going to be a problem. The benefits of growing corydalis far outweigh the disadvantages.

There are now three other immensely popular cultivars of corydalis, all of them blue-flowering—'Blue Panda', 'China Blue' and 'Purple Leaf'. With its sky-blue, fragrant flowers, *Corydalis flexuosa* 'Blue Panda' has proven itself to be the best performer of the three. None of the blues, however, flowers quite as profusely as the yellow form.

Where to plant it

Corydalis will grow in average, even inferior soil. Grow it under shrubs or combined with other perennials for its foliage contrast. Even if it falls on stony ground, corydalis seed never fails to germinate.

How to care for it

Sometimes called the "yellow bleeding heart," *Corydalis lutea* has loose, lacy foliage that's similar to *Dicentra*—in fact, it's a close relative. Clumps can be divided every few years. The foliage tends to look a little disheveled by the end of summer and can be cut back. It will soldier on for awhile, eventually dying down with the first frost. In spring, it will bounce back, good as new.

Good companions

Blue always makes yellow more striking, so combine *Corydalis lutea* with one of the great blue varieties of Jacob's ladder, either *Polemonium caeruleum* or *P. reptans* 'Blue Pearl'. The blue flowers of *Geranium* 'Johnson's Blue' would also work. Other good partners include bleeding hearts like *Dicentra spectabilis* or *D. formosa* 'Luxuriant'. The frothy lime-green sprays of lady's mantle also fit well with yellow corydalis. Experiment with growing spring-flowering bulbs—bluebells, grape hyacinths, tulips—to achieve some eye-catching contrasts.

For your collection

Yellow flowers are not everyone's favorite but others love their cheerfulness. Here are some other great yellow-flowering perennials to check out.

- *Heliopsis helianthoides* 'Loraine Sunshine', which has variegated foliage and large golden-yellow daisy-like flowers from June to October. It grows 30 inches (75 cm) high. Other varieties to consider include 'Midwest Dreams' and 'Summer Sun'.

- *Phlomis fruticosa* (Jerusalem sage) has soft gray foliage.
- *Lysimachia punctata* (loosestrife) has buttercup-like flowers on 18- to 36-inch (45- to 90-cm) stems.
- *Meconopsis cambrica* (Welsh poppy) has soft yellow flowers in late spring.
- *Ligularia stenocephala* 'The Rocket' produces 4- to 6-foot (120- to 180-cm) tall spires of golden yellow foxtail–lily-like flowers.
- *Oenothera fruticosa* (evening primrose) flowers from spring through to the end of summer and has bright yellow flowers at the top of 3-foot (90-cm) stems. Look for the German hybrid 'Sonnenwende'.
- *Rudbeckia fulgida* (black-eyed susan) is the flower that signals the end of summer and the coming of the cool days of September.

Cotinus coggygria 'Royal Purple'

Common name: *Smoke tree, smoke bush*

Chief characteristics

Location: Full or part sun
Type: Deciduous shrub
Size: 10 feet (3 m) or more
Conditions: Well-drained, ordinary soil
Flowering time: July to August
Zone: 5

This is a most attractive and useful foliage shrub for gardens of any size. The distinctive plum-purple, oval-shaped leaves are exceptional when contrasted against the dark green background of a cedar or yew hedge.

Native to southern Europe and eastward to China, smoke bush gets its common name from the delicate feathery panicles of pinkish-purple flowers that form in summer and give the impression of puffs of smoke. At one time, it was called *Rhus cotinus*. In Europe, it is known as the Venetian sumach and it is sometimes called wig tree. Left to grow without interference, *Cotinus coggygria* 'Royal Purple' will quickly soar to more than 15 feet (4.5 m) and can achieve almost that in width. It will, however, tolerate regular pruning and can be kept down to a manageable size. In gardens where space is limited, it is often pruned back to form a small, single-stemmed tree.

Where to plant it

Cotinus coggygria 'Royal Purple' will grow in any ordinary, well-drained soil, but prefers fertile, humus-rich, moist ground. To get the best "smoke" effect, it needs full sun. In large, spacious gardens it can be used as a giant, showy specimen shrub, which will look like a great cloud of frothy purple at the height of summer. In most gardens, however, 'Royal Purple' is more realistically grown in the mixed border to contrast with other medium-sized shrubs.

It can also be grown as a patio tree. In a container, its roots will be restricted, which will keep it from getting out of hand, but you will need to top-dress the soil every year and add slow-release fertilizer.

How to care for it

It is a trouble-free shrub with few pest or disease problems. Powdery mildew can sometimes be a problem and verticillium wilt has been known to slowly kill the shrub in some locations, but these are not common occurrences. Prune for size and shape and to eliminate shoots that pop up from the roots.

Good companions

Clematis 'Ville de Lyon' or 'Madame Julia Correvon' can be grown into a smoke bush. Both have red flowers that are striking with the shrub's plum foliage. The pink or red flowers of potentilla, the dainty purple flowers of *Geranium* 'Ballerina', and the bright leaves of mock orange (*Philadelphus coronarius* 'Aureus') are also worth considering. You can create room under a smoke bush for silver-foliage plants such as lamb's ears and artemisia or golden yellow hostas. Other excellent summer underplantings are the fiery red forms of coleus or small white marguerite daisies.

For your collection

Other purple-leafed plants you might like include the following.

- *Euphorbia amygdaloides* 'Rubra' has wine-colored foliage that plays nicely against the small yellow flowers that appear in spring. It is hardy to Zone 6, so needs winter protection in colder zones.
- *Salvia officinalis* 'Purpurascens' (purple-leafed sage) is an excellent foliage contrast plant with soft purple, slightly aromatic leaves. Hardy to Zone 6.
- *Sedum telephium maximum* 'Atropurpureum' is one of the more unusual varieties of stonecrop. It has fleshy, dark burgundy leaves, pinkish-white flowers in August and September, and grows about 2 feet (60 cm). Also look for such names as 'Matrona', 'Morchen', 'Vera Jameson' or 'Bertram Anderson', which all have darkish burgundy-purple or mahogany-red foliage.
- *Heuchera* 'Palace Purple' has striking, crinkled, dark purple foliage and 'Plum Pudding' has bright plum-colored foliage. They make good groundcovers, or feature plants in the border.

Crocosmia 'Lucifer'

Common name: *Montbretia*

Chief characteristics

The soft, semi-spherical mound is one of the most ubiquitous shapes in the garden. Weeping or cascading forms, or bold, upwardly thrusting, sword-like leaves make a wonderful contrast. Such trees as mulberry (*Morus alba* 'Pendula'), Young's birch (*Betula pendula* 'Youngii') and Camperdown elm (*Ulmus glabra* 'Horizontalis') will give you first-rate

Location: Full sun
Type: Perennial
Size: 4 feet (1.2 m)
Conditions: Fertile, well-drained soil
Flowering time: July to September
Zone: 5

weeping foliage, while ornamental grasses like *Miscanthus sinensis* 'Gracillimus' will provide superb, tallish, cascading structure.

For bold, sword-shaped foliage, you can't beat *Crocosmia* 'Lucifer'. As well as superbly architectural, stiff, gladiola-like leaves, this exceptional perennial also produces antler-like stalks of flame-red from July to September. A member of the iris family (*Iridaceae*), this native South African plant grows from a corm and can often be found listed as a bulb. Its botanical name was once *Montbretia* and some people still call it that. For the longest time, the best form of *Crocosmia* was the species, *C. masonorum*, which has bright orange flowers. Then in the 1970s, British nurseryman Alan Bloom, of Bressingham Gardens in Norfolk, produced some new, exciting hybrids, one of which was 'Lucifer'. Other Bloom creations were 'Vulcan', orange, 2 feet (60 cm); 'Bressingham Beacon', orange and yellow, 40 inches (100 cm); 'Emberglow', orange-red, 30 inches (75 cm); 'Firebird', orange, 32 inches (80 cm); and 'Jenny Bloom', yellow, 40 inches (100 cm).

Where to plant it

Grow *Crocosmia* 'Lucifer' in average, well-drained soil in full sun or light shade. It will also thrive in sandy soil provided it is watered well in summer and the soil is enriched with a mulch over winter.

This taller variety of *Crocosmia* looks terrific as an accent piece in the center of an island perennial bed. It is especially useful for adding height, an exotic look and a sense of drama to the perennial border. Shorter varieties such as 'Vulcan' and 'Emberglow' are often used in mass plantings to create a lush bank of daylily-like foliage.

How to care for it

Disease and pest resistant, *Crocosmia* 'Lucifer' is remarkably trouble free. It will stand perfectly erect but sometimes needs the support of a stake once the flowers form in July and the stalks become a little top-heavy. The seeds can be gathered and propagated over winter in a cool greenhouse. They will germinate fairly easily but don't expect to see flowers for at least two years. 'Lucifer' will double in size within a few seasons but clumps can easily be lifted and divided to create new colonies.

Although it is hardy to Zone 4, it is still wise to mulch crocosmia well at the end of fall. In extremely cold areas, clumps should be treated like dahlias or gladioli and lifted and stored in a frost-free environment until spring.

Good companions

There is no shortage of good companions, but you need to be a little careful about eye-jarring clashes of color. Without a lot of effort, it is easy to find the red antlers of *Crocosmia* 'Lucifer' in battle with yellow rudbeckia and pink *Phlox paniculata*. If you use phlox, think carefully about the color. Safe companions include bee balm, artemisia, shasta daisies, globe thistle (*Echinops*), sea hollies (*Eryngium*) and late irises.

For your collection

Here are a few other attractive plants with sword-like foliage.

- *Yucca filamentosa* (Adam's needle). A first-rate plant for contrast purposes, this grows 5 feet (1.5 m) high and produces creamy white flowers in July. Grows best in well-drained soil in full sun.
- *Iris pseudacorus* 'Variegata'. This thrives in damp sites, grows about 4 feet (1.2 m) tall and has green leaves with bold white or creamy yellow streaks.
- *Phormium tenax* (New Zealand flax). An excellent plant for growing in a large pot at the side of a pool. This is tender, so you will need to protect it in a frost-free environment over winter. As an added bonus, it has dark red flowers if it gets enough heat.

Delphinium Pacific Hybrids

Common name: *Larkspur*

Chief characteristics

Location: Full sun

Type: Perennial

Size: 4 to 6 feet (1.2 to 1.8 m)

Conditions: Moist, rich soil

Flowering time: June to August

Zone: 3

The tall, soaring spires of blue or white delphiniums can be an awesome spectacle in the summer garden. Delphiniums have been described as "glamorous" and "romantic" and "compulsory for the perennial border." The white forms can look especially lovely at twilight when all the reds and blues have faded into the dusk. Delphiniums certainly have a long and glorious association with the cutflower garden. They were one of the mainstays of the classic Victorian-Edwardian perennial border and their popularity has never subsided. When planted with care, they rarely disappoint.

The secret to success is picking the right type. The best and most dramatic performers are the Pacific Hybrids, which grow 4 to 6 feet (1.2 to 1.8 m) tall in perfect conditions. Many of them are named after characters in the legend of King Arthur and the Knights of the Round Table. Names to look for: 'Black Knight' (dark blue), 'Galahad' (white), 'King Arthur' (purple), 'Guinevere' (lavender-pink), 'Summer Skies' (light blue), 'Camelliard' (lavender-blue), 'Blue Bird' (blue) and 'Blue Jay' (light blue).

The other popular delphiniums are the belladonna types, which are shorter than Pacific Hybrids, growing only 3 to 4 feet (90 to 120 cm). They display their flowers in loose, open clusters rather than dense spires. Chinese delphinium (*D. grandiflorum* 'Blue Butterfly') has intense blue flowers in June and August and grows only 10 inches (25 cm) high.

Where to plant it

Grow delphiniums in rich, well-drained soil in sun or light shade at the back or middle of the perennial border. They should be positioned so their magnificent flowers can easily be seen above medium-sized perennials. Delphiniums are also effectively combined with ornamental grasses to provide the height needed at the center of an island bed.

How to care for it

Cut off the flowerheads when they are faded. This will promote a second flush in late summer. Delphiniums are heavy feeders so make sure you enrich the soil at planting time with well-rotted compost or manure. An application of slow-release 14-14-14 fertilizer in late spring will ensure the plants do not starve. Staking is almost always necessary with the super-tall Pacific Hybrids, especially where the towering plants are exposed to sudden gusts of wind.

Staking is also useful in preventing them from tumbling over in the event of a heavy rainstorm. Give your delphiniums the support they need, but don't tie them so tightly they're throttled to death. Unfortunately, delphiniums don't go on forever. They become less and less vigorous in subsequent seasons and end up having to be replaced. But by that time they will have given many, many hours of pleasure for very little expense.

Good companions

The red flowers of *Crocosmia* 'Lucifer' or the single or multi-colored blooms of *Phlox paniculata* give bold and dramatic support to the simple blues and whites of delphiniums. Taller ornamental grasses such as *Miscanthus sinensis* 'Gracillimus' or *Pennisetum alopecuroides* can join forces with the rose-pink flowers of Mexican evening primrose (*Oenothera berlandieri* 'Siskiyou') to surround delphiniums with interesting and unusual colors and textures. For more standard companions, look to pink and red *Monarda* 'Gardenview Scarlet', silvery *Artemisia* 'Powis Castle' and the lacy foliage and buttery yellow flowers of *Coreopsis* 'Moonbeam'. Delphiniums also look first-rate rising up among roses.

For your collection

- *Delphinium cashmerianum* has especially graceful and delicate blue flowers and is one of the best delphiniums for connoisseurs. Blue and white are not the only colors of delphinium. You can get yellow (*D. semibarbatum*), red (*D. cardinale*) and pink (*D.* × *ruysii*).
- If you are looking for other tall, attractive plants to add strength to the back of the border, consider the giant plume poppy (*Macleaya cordata*) or goatsbeard (*Aruncus dioicus*) or the foxtail lily (*Eremurus himalaicus*).

*D*icentra spectabilis 'Alba'

Common name: *Old-fashioned bleeding heart*

Chief characteristics

Location: Shade to semi-shade

Type: Perennial

Size: 3 feet (90 cm)

Conditions: Moist, well-drained soil

Flowering time: May to July

Zone: 2

What is the loveliest flower in the spring garden? Tulip? Daffodil? Lenten rose? All are quite wonderful but few can compare with the transcendent, classical beauty of old-fashioned bleeding heart. It has such a simple, elegant, graceful appearance and exquisite white or red blooms. It is easy to understand why it has been a favorite of gardeners worldwide for generations.

You will find dicentra listed in many people's top 10 perennials. The heart-shaped flowers are suspended individually like precious lockets along gently arching stems that reach out romantically from a lush clump of soft green leaves. If the outer petals of a single flower are carefully removed, a perfectly formed, miniature Valentine's Day heart can be found in the center. The plant derives its common name from the appearance of the red form of *Dicentra spectabilis*, which has tiny heart-shaped inner petals enclosed by blood-red outer petals.

Dicentra spectabilis 'Alba' and plain old *D. spectabilis* are outstanding, but they do have a drawback. The bushy clumps of leaves, so vigorous and full in late May and June, start to fade by the end of June. The flowers disappear and the plant slowly dies back and usually needs to be cut down to keep the rest of the border looking neat and tidy. This can leave an unsightly gap. One of the simplest solutions is to have a mature hosta—perhaps 'Krossa Regal' or 'Francee' or 'Frances Williams'—in a pot, standing by to move into the vacated spot. The pot can be easily disguised and the hosta will fit very naturally into the scheme of the border. Or you could take the opportunity to add some color to the border and bring in a semi-shade flowering perennial such as blue- or yellow-flowering corydalis, taller forms of impatiens or begonias to fill the space.

There are, however, other cultivars of bleeding heart (none quite as attractive in my opinion as the ones just mentioned) that do not go dormant in the heat of summer. The best is *Dicentra eximia* 'Alba', one of the fringed bleeding hearts, all of which have lacy, fernlike foliage. 'Alba' grows about 12 to 15 inches (30 to 38 cm) high and produces white pouch-shaped flowers all summer, making it a good selection for the front of the border. A good red variety is *D. formosa* 'Luxuriant', which has cherry-red flowers.

Where to plant it

A native woodland plant, bleeding heart is best grown in cool shade under trees as a companion to other perennials in the herbaceous border. In my garden, both red and white forms of *Dicentra spectabilis* have a place in a semi-shaded mixed border. The red variety is tucked beneath a slow-growing sycamore maple. The dwarf varieties of bleeding heart can be mass-planted to create drifts of frothy bluish-green foliage and white flowers in summer.

How to care for it

Dicentra spectabilis can be spotted emerging from the ground in April. It will also be immediately noticed by any passing slugs. Keep an eye on the new growth to make sure it gets off to a good start. The plant does not need staking but in ideal conditions the stems can grow 3, even 4 feet (90 to 120 cm) high and tend to cover other plants. The arching stems of flowers are not long-lasting when cut, but they still make a handsome, if temporary, addition to floral arrangements.

Bleeding heart should be cut down and tidied up at the end of June. Clumps are best left undisturbed, but if necessary they can be divided and moved in fall or before flowering in spring.

Good companions

Dicentra spectabilis combines naturally with columbines, hostas, ferns, astilbes, alliums and hardy geraniums, especially the dark-flowered cranesbill, *Geranium phaeum* (mourning widow), or *G. pratense* and, in sunnier spots, *Geranium* 'Johnson's Blue' and pink-flowered *G. sanguineum*. Early spring-flowering bulbs such as scillas and grape hyacinth can be planted around the clump to add color while the bleeding heart is getting underway and in late spring, tulips can inject interesting color contrasts.

For your collection

- *Dicentra* 'Goldheart' has golden yellow foliage. It is still very much a novelty plant and the jury is out on whether there is much of a demand for it.
- *Dicentra* 'Langtrees' (also known as 'Pearl Drops') has white flowers with pink tips.
- *Dicentra* 'Snowflakes' is a new introduction from England that has white flowers and is noted for its vigorous growth habit and rich green foliage.
- *Dicentra* 'Stuart Boothman' has bright pink flowers and pale green foliage and grows about 15 inches (38 cm) high.

Digitalis purpurea

Common name: *Foxglove*

Chief characteristics

Location: Sun to semi-shade
Type: Perennial
Size: 5 feet (1.5 m)
Conditions: Moist, well-drained soil
Flowering time: May to July
Zone: 4

Foxgloves are majestic, romantic plants. The story goes that a fox used the silky tube-shaped flowers as gloves so he could sneak into the hen house without awakening the farmer. Foxgloves can be grown in just about any medium-sized garden with a semi-shady woodland-type corner. They are superb in large groups, gently swaying in the breeze. They also have character and charm as solitary specimens, rising up like sentries here and there around the garden. They spend the first year establishing themselves and then flower the following year. You will always be nursing a few foxglove plants, allowing them to occupy space in the garden even though they produce no flowers and the small clumps of coarse leaves are not at all attractive.

The most common foxglove, *Digitalis purpurea*, produces lovely pink-purple tube-shaped flowers with a speckled throat. These flowers are tightly arranged in drooping layers up the sturdy stem. The flowers open first at the bottom, giving the impression that the spires of blooms come to a sharp point. The Excelsior Hybrids are the most impressive foxgloves. They produce white, purple and pink flowers and grow to 5 feet (1.5 m) tall from May to July. One of the best cultivars is 'Apricot Beauty' which has soft apricot-pink flowers in May and grows 4 feet (120 cm). The Merton foxglove (*Digitalis* × *mertonensis*) is a true perennial. It grows less than 3 feet (90 cm) and has deep copper-pink flowers. Foxy Hybrids are available in a range of colors and are more compact than Excelsior Hybrids. They grow to about 3 feet (90 cm).

Where to plant it

Plant foxgloves in semi-shade in ordinary garden soil that stays reasonably moist all the time. Grow them in colonies or small groups in the middle or at the back of the perennial border, where they are particularly useful for creating height and architectural interest. Once they have finished flowering, they will leave a gap that will need to be filled or covered by other perennials. Some people like only white foxgloves, so they pull out any with purplish leaf stalks, supposedly a sign that the flowers will not be pure white.

How to care for it

After they have finished flowering, foxgloves produce thousands of tiny coal-black seeds that spill everywhere from fragile brown pods. You can collect the seed and sprinkle it where you would like foxgloves in the future or sow it in pots and raise plants for transplanting into specific locations later on.

Plants that have established themselves through the summer can be lifted in the fall and moved to wherever you want them to flower the following year. You don't need to leave all your foxgloves until they have gone to seed. One or two produce enough seed to ensure survival. The rest can be tugged very easily from the ground and disposed of once they have finished blooming.

Good companions

Foxgloves are great minglers. They get along very well with virtually every plant in the garden, especially daylilies, campanula, hardy geraniums, bleeding hearts, ferns and columbines. The beauty of foxgloves is that they are always forming their own spontaneous partnerships. They will pop up quite unexpectedly behind rhododendrons and assorted shrubs. They even find a place next to roses.

If you don't mind a little rustic, old-world charm in your garden, you won't be too hard on foxgloves and you will give them their day. If they are quite out of place at bloom time, simply snip the flower stalk and use it in an indoor bouquet.

For your collection

- *Digitalis ferruginea* (rusty foxglove) has yellowish flowers with rust-red speckles.
- *Digitalis grandiflora* (yellow foxglove) has pale yellow flowers and smooth green leaves and grows less than 3 feet (90 cm) tall. It blooms from June to August. It can be used to form a striking contrast with red shrub roses.
- *Digitalis viridiflora* has white flowers with a yellow-gold throat and green markings.

*E*chinacea purpurea

Common name: *Purple coneflower*

Chief characteristics

This native North American flower is closely
related to another very popular cottage
garden perennial, black-eyed susan
(*Rudbeckia fulgida*). It has a similar daisy-
like flower, but rudbeckia is yellow with
a black center and echinacea has bright,
pink-purple petals around a large, orange-
brown cone.

Location: Full sun
Size: 3 feet (90 cm)
Type: Perennial
Conditions: Ordinary, well-
    drained soil
Flowering time: July to
    August
Zone: 3

Echinacea purpurea 'Magnus' is a dependable cultivar with cheerful
rose-pink petals. There is also an attractive white cultivar, *E. purpurea*
'White Swan', which has flowers with a rather regal gold and black cone
at the center. Everyone falls in love with echinacea when they first see
a mature clump of it with dozens of the purple flowerheads. It can take
a few years of patient nurturing to get a plant to that level of lushness,
but the effort is worthwhile. In addition to producing spectacular,
colorful, honey-scented blooms, which make excellent cut flowers,
echinacea attracts butterflies to the garden. You may also come across
E. angustifolia, which is similar to *E. purpurea* but a little taller, with
slender, drooping petals.

The name *Echinacea* is derived from the Greek word for "hedgehog,"
referring to the prickly cone at the center of the flower. Echinacea is said
to have healing properties and is still used by herbalists to stimulate and
strengthen the immune system and cleanse the body of toxins.

Where to plant it

Echinacea can be grown in the perennial border and makes a good cut
flower. It thrives in average soil in a warm, sunny location.

It is best planted slightly back from the front of the border, where
the beautiful flowerheads can be easily seen and reached for cutting and
the less attractive stems are concealed by shorter flowering perennials.

How to care for it

To get the best results from echinacea, remember that it has an appetite.
Work in plenty of well-rotted compost and manure at the time of
planting and mulch around the plant in spring. A sprinkling of slow-
release fertilizer or rose food in spring doesn't hurt either.

Staking is often needed. Don't be too aggressive or you'll end up with straggly foliage and choked flowerheads—not a pretty picture. Deadhead faded flowers regularly. The whole plant can be cut down close to the ground at the end of the season. Clumps take a few years to build up, but once they have, you probably won't feel like dividing them. If you do get around to it, do it in late September.

Good companions

Ornamental grasses and lavender offer credible companionship for *Echinacea purpurea*. You can use fountain grass (*Pennisetum alopecuroides* 'Hameln') or the very attractive tender summer variety *Pennisetum* 'Rubrum' as a light and breezy neighbor. For a lavender, try 'Munstead'.

Shasta daisies, asters, crocosmia, rudbeckia and other late summer-flowering perennials can create appealing combinations. One of the best ways to focus echinacea's purple blooms is to provide a backdrop of color. The orange in the flower cone will be heightened by a backdrop of blue monkshood (*Aconitum napellus*) or stand out against the dark burgundy foliage of *Cimicifuga* 'Brunette'. Or you could try a silver blend, using *Artemisia ludoviciana* 'Silver King' or Artemisia 'Powis Castle'.

For your collection

- *Echinacea tennesseensis*. For something more exotic, track down this native of Tennessee. It is a rarer form of the purple coneflower, growing to about 3 feet (90 cm). If you manage to get one you have something quite special. Growing naturally on rocky hillsides, it has thin, linear leaves and smaller petals than *E. purpurea*.
- *Gaillardia grandiflora* (blanket flower). If you like echinacea, you will probably like this plant, which also has large, colorful, daisy-shaped flowers with a central cone. It grows in full sun, can reach 3 feet (90 cm) high, makes an excellent cut flower, and comes in a range of colors including red with yellow tips, burgundy and yellow.

*E*laeagnus angustifolia

Common name: *Russian olive, oleaster*

Chief characteristics

The beauty of the Russian olive is that you can grow it either as a tree or a shrub without forfeiting any of the attractiveness of its graceful, silver-gray, willow-like foliage. Native to Europe and the Himalayas, it thrives in climates with hot summers and cold winters, which makes it a good choice for Ontario gardens. In June, it has fragrant yellow flowers, followed by small, silvery yellow, berry-like fruit in late summer.

Location: Full sun to light shade
Type: Deciduous tree
Size: 15 feet (4.5 m)
Conditions: Ordinary, well-drained soil
Zone: 2

It is, however, the lovely gray foliage that we all love the most about Russian olive. The leaves look splendid moving in a breeze and they contrast beautifully with the dark foliage of other trees and shrubs. In the winter, the bark and bare brown branches can be picturesque. It grows to 15 feet (4.5 m), which means *Elaeagnus angustifolia* is easy to accommodate even in a small garden or boulevard.

Russian olive is often confused with another outstanding feature tree—the weeping willow-leafed pear (*Pyrus salicifolia*). This tree is slowly becoming more appreciated as more gardeners discover its virtues and versatility. It doesn't look like much in the nursery as an infant, but as it matures it has a special presence. With minimal care, it will grow to form a shimmering, round-headed mass of silver leaves. Look for 'Silver Cascade' or 'Silver Frost'. Hardy to Zone 5, this tree is a great centerpiece for an all-white garden.

Where to grow it

Grow Russian olive in full sun or light shade in well-drained soil. Use it either as a stand-alone specimen tree or plant it in the mixed shrub border for foliage contrast.

You can grow it as a multi-stemmed shrub or train it as a standard tree-form with a clear stem 4 to 6 feet (1.2 to 1.8 m) high. It adapts to most soil conditions and since it is also very salt-tolerant, Russian olive is an excellent tree for a front garden where it will be exposed to the salted street in winter. It is also a first-rate shrub for creating a privacy screen.

How to care for it

It is said that *Elaeagnus angustifolia* can take any amount of punishment . . . except being planted in a garden where the winters are mild and the summers lukewarm. It needs a good, cold winter and the heat of a glorious summer to flourish and look its best. It requires little pruning, but it is indifferent to whatever pruning you do, bouncing back with renewed vigor.

Good companions

If you are using Russian olive as a feature tree, it should stand alone in the lawn or boulevard, but if you use it in the mixed border or as an accent plant within a flower bed, think about colors that will contrast with the silvery leaves. The purple foliage of such shrubs as smoke bush or sand cherry offer exciting contrast. You could attempt a white theme and use *Hydrangea* 'Annabelle', *Pieris japonica*, white potentilla, white roses, white campanula and white lavatera. Plants with blue foliage or flowers would also make excellent partners; consider blue junipers, hibiscus, lavender and assorted blue-flowered spring bulbs.

For your collection

There are two cousins of Russian olive that you may come across.

- *Elaeagnus commutata* (silverberry). This commonplace native North American has shiny silvery leaves and grows 10 feet (3 m) tall. It is useful for screening or as a windbreak.
- *Elaeagnus umbellata* (autumn olive shrub). This has silver-green leaves, fragrant yellow flowers and red fruit. It grows to 10 feet (3 m).

uonymus fortunei 'Emerald Gaiety'

Common name: *Emerald Gaiety euonymus*

Chief characteristics

It is so important for a garden to have good "botanical bones"—plants that provide structure year round. Perennials will rise and fall, annuals add their slash of vibrant color, but there is a special place in the heart of most gardeners for those no-fuss plants that give a garden consistent and reliable color and form.

Location: Sun or shade
Type: Evergreen shrub
Size: 3 to 5 feet (1 to 1.5 m)
Conditions: Ordinary, well-drained soil
Zone: 3

The most useful and versatile in this category is *Euonymus fortunei*. Not only does it provide excellent foliage contrast, this popular and dependable evergreen shrub can be grown a variety of ways in a variety of locations. There are several cultivars from which to choose, but 'Emerald Gaiety' is the most elegant, having a crisp, gray-green and creamy white variegated foliage that can settle very unobtrusively into most garden landscapes. A compact bush, 3 to 5 feet (90 to 150 cm), it can easily be pruned for size and shape. In winter the leaves turn a little pink, adding some seasonal interest. You can also get this variety in a patio-tree form. The foliage is usually tightly pruned into a handsome globe shape to add a little formality and structure to a mixed border. Another popular cultivar of *Euonymus fortunei* is 'Emerald 'n' Gold', which has what some consider "startling" bright yellow and green variegated leaves. It grows 2 to 3 feet tall (60 to 90 cm), making it suitable as a groundcover or dwarf hedge, and its foliage also gets a pinkish tinge in winter.

Other top varieties to check out include 'Canadale Gold' (green with gold edges), 'Country Gold' (green with gold edges), 'Gold Tip' (green with gold markings) and 'Surespot' (green with yellow center).

Where to plant it

'Emerald Gaiety' thrives in full sun or shade in ordinary, well-drained soil. The leaves are small and dense and the overall form is more compact and slow-growing than some of the other kinds of euonymus.

Use it to bring textural relief to the front of a wall or dark hedge. The variegated leaves make it an outstanding feature plant, or it can be planted in small groups as a groundcover or low, informal hedge. If planted close to the side of the house, it can be encouraged to slowly climb and form an attractive espalier.

The secret to using variegated euonymus to the best effect is to surround it with plenty of plain green plants. Too much variegated foliage can make a garden look gaudy and unkempt, but one or two well-placed plants can have the opposite result, producing a balanced, elegant, well-structured landscape.

How to care for it

Euonymus fortunei is extremely disease and pest resistant. You can encourage bushiness by pinch-pruning the growth tips of branches when the shrub is still young.

Euonymus can be grown in a container on a patio or balcony, but the roots would need extra protection in winter. Aphids and powdery mildew can sometimes be a problem, but this is invariably caused by stress from inadequate watering, planting in impoverished soil, inferior air circulation or all three.

Good companions

Don't plant 'Emerald Gaiety' close to other brightly variegated plants such as silverleaf dogwood (*Cornus alba* 'Elegantissima'). *Pieris japonica*, boxwood, dwarf blue juniper, potentilla and plain green ivy and hostas all make good partners. Perhaps the best partner is a plain brick wall against which the variegated leaves can be seen without competition.

For your collection

- *Euonymus alatus* (burning bush). This is valued mostly for the spectacular scarlet-orange leaf color in fall. It grows to 10 feet (3 m) in full sun. Look for 'Chicago Fire', which is famous for its fire engine–red leaves in October and orange-red fruit in November. A compact variety, *E. alatus* 'Compactus', can be used to create an informal low hedge and is also available in a tree form.
- *Euonymus japonicus* 'Silver Queen'. One of the most popular taller varieties, this is more tender than 'Emerald Gaiety'. It's only hardy to Zone 6 and requires protection in colder areas. 'Silver Queen' grows 3 feet (90 cm) tall and has striking green and white variegation, making it an excellent accent plant.
- *Euonymus* 'Sarcoxie' and 'Colaratus' are two cultivars that are capable of climbing if they are planted close to a sheltered wall. 'Sarcoxie' (dark green foliage) will reach 5 to 6 feet (1.5 to 1.8 m); 'Colaratus' (green leaves that turn red-purple in winter) will climb to 10 feet (3 m) and can also be used as a groundcover.

Euphorbia griffithii 'Fireglow'

Common name: Spurge

Chief characteristics

Everyone knows poinsettia, the popular Christmas plant. But a lot of people don't know that the familiar poinsettia is actually part of a grand group of plants called *Euphorbia*. These are first-rate garden plants, extremely useful for providing unusual foliage, form, texture and color contrast.

Every garden should have at least two or three different kinds of euphorbia.

Location: Sun or light shade
Type: Perennnial
Size: 3 to 4 feet (90 to 120 cm)
Conditions: Well-drained, acid soil
Flowering time: April to May
Zone: 2

'Fireglow' is a good one to start with. It bounces back to life early in spring, pushing up sturdy stems with coppery orange tones. These quickly open into thin, attractive green leaves that within a few short weeks develop to form a small bush of lush, red-tinted foliage 3 or 4 feet (90 to 120 cm) high. We're not finished. 'Fireglow' then goes on to reveal how it got its name . . . by producing a subtle splattering of muted orange-red flowers all over the plant. These flowers last for several weeks and continue intermittently all summer.

In my garden, I grow 'Fireglow' with *Sedum* 'Autumn Joy' close to a small rectangular water feature in a retaining wall. By the middle of summer, the soft leaves of 'Fireglow' are reflected in the water and they help soften the brickwork.

Like most other euphorbias, 'Fireglow' will emit a mildy toxic milky sap if pruned or if the leaves are pulled off. This sap can irritate the skin, so it is good to be aware of this when trimming it back or simply gardening around it. I have never found the sap to be a problem. In fact, it can be an interesting conversation piece when showing visitors around. I often introduce my 'Fireglow' as "the plant that fights back."

Where to plant it

Grow 'Fireglow' in full sun or light shade in fertile, well-drained soil. Give it plenty of space because it will want to expand with creeping underground roots that produce new stems. It makes a very handsome, structural plant for the herbaceous border or you can work it quite easily into a mixed shrub border as it does look rather like a low-mounding bushy shrub.

Being herbaceous, it dies down after the first hard frost and can be cut down to keep the garden looking neat and tidy. It helps to insert green support stakes as the new stems are emerging. These will ensure 'Fireglow' stays compact and maintains its attractive rounded form.

How to care for it

If you don't want *Euphorbia griffithii* to take over, keep it within bounds by removing the new stems its creeping roots produce every spring. These can be potted up and given away to friends or planted in other parts of the garden to create a new clump.

'Fireglow' is drought tolerant, but it still needs to be watered in the summer to keep it looking its best. The flowers fade and fall away without leaving a mess, so there is no need to deadhead. If the plant does get a little ragged, prune it back, and once the sap has ceased running, new leaves will appear to cover the wounds.

Good companions

Euphorbia contrasts well in the perennial border with red-hot poker, lavatera or lavender. It can be underplanted with lamb's ears, if you don't mind clipping off the flower stalks, or *Artemisia schmidtiana* 'Silver Mound', which can be used to soften spurge's stiffer, more formal profile.

For your collection

Other euphorbias worth checking out include those below.

- *Euphorbia amygdaloides* 'Rubra' (purple wood spurge). Mounding purple foliage and clusters of lime-green flowers make it a very useful groundcover in lightly shaded locations.
- *Euphorbia characias wulfenii*: This majestic plant sends up long sturdy flower stems with large, lime-green, multi-eyed flowerheads in spring. It has graceful, spear-shaped, blue-green leaves and grows 4 feet high by 4 feet wide (1.2 by 1.2 m) within a couple of years. It is, however, extremely well behaved. Its sturdy stems can be trimmed easily, making it far more manageable than its appearance suggests.
- *Euphorbia dulcis* 'Chameleon'. One of the newer hybrids, it has the remarkable characteristic of changing color three times during the year. The new leaves start out bronze-purple and then fade to green and turn a muted red-yellow in fall. It also produces tiny yellow-green flowers. It grows to about 2 feet (60 cm) and produces offspring from seed after a year or two.
- *Euphorbia myrsinites* (donkey-tail spurge). A succulent, evergreen species with distinctive blue-green tail-like leaf curls and yellow flowers in spring. It's a good plant for growing in a sunny spot over a wall or rockery, as it is highly drought tolerant.
- *Euphorbia polychroma* (cushion spurge). This drought-tolerant, clumping plant produces a cushion or dome of light yellow-green flowers in spring. A very desirable, mounding spurge that grows 1 to 2 feet (30 to 60 cm) and looks good under trees or around the base of shrubs.

ℱoeniculum vulgare 'Purpureum'

Common name: *Bronze fennel*

Chief characteristics

You might not find bronze fennel terribly attractive if you saw it for the first time on its own in a pot at the garden center. Nor would you be the first person to dismiss it as a gangly, weedy-looking thing. It is one of those plants that doesn't always make a good first impression. However, it will do a first-rate job of providing light, airy color contrast and textural interest to your garden.

Location: Full sun
Type: Perennial
Size: 6 feet (1.8 m)
Conditions: Good, well-drained soil
Flowering time: July to September
Zone: 3

Growing 5 or 6 feet (1.5 to 1.8 m) high, *Foeniculum vulgare* 'Purpureum' has feathery, bronze-green foliage with a very pleasant anise-like scent. All parts of the plant are edible. Cooks and herbalists have used it for years to give food flavor and help the digestive system work more efficiently. It can also be fun to pinch off a few sprays of the finely textured foliage and invite visitors to your garden to taste it. If they have no idea what the plant is, they tend to hover a little apprehensively. This hesitancy soon passes once they recognize the distinctive licorice flavor of the soft foliage.

In July and August, bronze fennel develops flat, dill-like umbels of tiny, dull-yellow flowers which make the plant even more decorative and interesting. The seeds that follow will fall and germinate with no assistance.

Where to plant it

Grow bronze fennel in a sunny spot at the back of the perennial border in average, well-drained soil. Once established, it will come back every year, eventually forming a dense clump you will need to split up.

Since you are mainly interested in growing this plant for foliage texture. Place it so it can mingle with its neighbors without becoming a nuisance. You don't want it to block them out completely.

Don't be afraid to take your pruners and thin out fennel clumps, even in the heart of the season, in order to maintain the look you want. It should be relaxed, breezy and elegant, not weedy, sprawling or overpowering.

How to care for it

Bronze fennel is drought tolerant and needs very little encouragement to revive in spring. The sturdy, bamboo-like stems can hold themselves up. Stakes are usually only needed to pull back thickets that are leaning to reach more light.

Fennel is very generous about seeding itself. You'll find seedlings popping up here and there. They are easily pulled and can be transplanted to other sites or given away to friends. Divide clumps to thin them or make more plants in mid-September or early March.

Good companions

The white-pink hollyhock flowers of *Lavatera thuringiaca* 'Barnsley' and soft gray leaves of *Stachys byzantina* or *Stachys* 'Countess Helen von Stein' combine well with the smoky purple of bronze fennel. Shrub roses such as 'Ballerina' and 'Mary Rose' make excellent partners. For more outstanding contrast, combine either the yellow flowers of evening primrose or verbascum, and the red of *Lobelia cardinalis* or *Lychnis viscaria*. The pure white annual mallow (*Lavatera trimestris* 'Mont Blanc') can be worked in for a little theatrical lighting.

For your collection

Herbs fulfil a very useful role as decorative plants in the ornamental flower border as well as culinary and medicinal specimens for the physick garden. Here are some others to consider.

- *Foeniculum vulgare* (common fennel). Also known as sweet or wild fennel, it has green leaves that taste like sweet licorice.
- *Foeniculum vulgare azoricum* (Florence fennel). Also known as finocchio, it has large celery-like stems and green feather-like leaves.
- *Angelica archangelica* (angelica). One of the most dramatic herbs for the perennial border, it can rise 8 feet (2.4 m) with wrist-thick hollow stems and magnificent umbels of green-white flowers. The bold flowerheads can be cut and used to great effect in floral arrangements.
- *Eupatorium purpureum* (joe-pye weed). With its pink flowers and lush foliage, it's a dynamic partner for angelica. It is put to best use at the back of the border or in an open area where it can fill ground without restriction. But think twice before getting carried away with angelica or joe-pye weed. Neither plant is really suitable for the small garden.
- *Salvia officinalis* 'Purpurascens' (purple-leafed sage). This and the gold-yellow form (*S. officinalis* 'Kew Gold') are useful for creating exciting foliage contrast and interest.

- *Allium schoenoprasum* (chives) are marvelous in sauces and salads and have fine, pale purple flowerheads.
- *Borago officinalis* (borage). Coarse, hairy foliage and bright blue flowers.

*G*eranium cinereum 'Ballerina'

Common name: *Cranesbill, hardy geranium*

Chief characteristics

Cranesbills are true geraniums. The plants many people call geraniums are not geraniums at all—they are pelargoniums. True geraniums are tough, winter-resistant plants with tiny, exquisite flowers that come in a delicious range of colors from sky blue to candy pink, royal purple to milk white. No garden should be without at least a couple of these versatile plants. They are called cranesbills because the seed heads look something like the beak of the crane. There are several exceptional hardy geraniums to choose from. Two of the best—both great favorites of mine—are *Geranium macrorrhizum* and *G. cinereum* 'Ballerina'.

Location: Full sun

Type: Perennial

Size: 6 inches (15 cm)

Conditions: Ordinary, well-drained soil

Flowering time: May to September

Zone: 4

Geranium macrorrhizum has lovely pink flowers in early spring and doubles as an extremely good mounding groundcover. Look for the baby pink 'Ingwersen's Variety', white 'Album' or the magenta-pink 'Bevan's Variety'. *G. cinereum* 'Ballerina' has exquisite purple-veined pink flowers that keep on coming all summer long. ('Lawrence Flatman' is almost identical to 'Ballerina'.)

Both *Geranium macrorrhizum* and *G. cinereum* 'Ballerina' are star performers, but 'Ballerina' is the superior garden plant overall because of its compact form, noninvasive habit, decorative foliage, and relentless flower power. It is a treasure for the sunny rockery.

But do give *G. macrorrhizum* a try, too. Its evergreen foliage has a pleasant pungent aroma when touched. Not everyone likes it, of course, but the scent does not detract from the intrinsic beauty and general usefulness of the plant.

Where to plant it

Geraniums are so adaptable they can be grown in sun or shade and will perform beautifully. *Geranium cinereum* 'Ballerina' needs to be planted in well-drained soil. Four clumps have survived two dreadful winters in my garden, quite happy in raised terraces on the sunny but protected south-facing side of the house. In summer, they never stop generating their magnificent purple-veined flowers.

The danger in growing geraniums is that you end up with too many. *Geranium macrorrhizum*, for instance, is so easy to propagate. All you have to do is pull off a few of the leggy rhizomatous stems from a mature clump, make a shallow trough and lay them in it, end to end, to create an entirely new colony. New gardeners who don't have money to buy all the plants they need in one fell swoop can certainly rely on *G. macrorrhizum* to cover the ground and hold the site until they are ready to replace them with more exotic fare.

How to care for it

Hardy geraniums are problem-free plants. The only attention they need is to be clipped back when they get too enthusiastic and tidied up once the flowers have come and gone and the plants start to look a little messy.

They can be grown in sun or shade. Most perform best if provided with shade in the afternoon.

Good companions

Cranesbills are the most gregarious of plants. Try them at the feet of lavatera, under climbing hydrangea, skirting shrubs in the mixed border or for foliage contrast with lady's mantle, variegated or yellow hostas, dicentras and fancy ferns. Columbines make excellent lanky pals to tower over hardy geraniums in the late spring.

Geranium macrorrhizum looks best grown in clumps, next to lady's mantle, or in crowded drifts, sweeping around rhododendrons or fruit trees in an orchard.

For your collection

When you go to buy hardy geraniums, you will find dozens of superb names besides those just mentioned. Where to begin? None of the following will disappoint.

🐾 *Geranium clarkei* 'Kashmir Purple' and 'Kashmir White' are other first-rate members of the geranium family, especially the white, which makes a dazzling appearance in late spring. They all grow to 2 feet (60 cm). Other superb whites are *G. sanguineum* 'Album', which forms a mound 20 inches (50 cm) high; *G. sylvaticum* 'Album', which grows to 30 inches (75 cm); and *G. phaeum* 'Album', which grows to about 2 feet (60 cm).

- *Geranium endressii* 'Wargrave Pink'. This is a must. It has rich pink flowers from June to September, mounds up to 3 feet (90 cm), and is a good-natured mixer in the perennial border.
- 'Johnson's Blue' has lovely sky-blue flowers in spring. It can get a bit leggy but you can easily scissor it back.
- 'Phoebe Noble' is requisite for all Canadian gardeners as it bears the name of the beloved Victoria, B.C., gardener and former math professor who surely ranks as the world's biggest geranium fan. Phoebe has grown dozens of cultivars for years in her 2-acre (.8-hectare) garden. So it was perhaps predictable that one day a new form of geranium would pop up there. It did, Phoebe spotted it as something quite unique, and it is now named after her and is one of the best new perennials on the market. Its official name is *Geranium × oxonianum* 'Noble'. It grows to 4 feet (1.2 m).
- *Geranium phaeum* (mourning widow) has dark purple flowers, so dark and brooding they almost look black. A good conversation piece to grow in the cool, moist shade of a woodland setting.
- *Geranium pratense* (meadow cranesbill) is far more cheerful, producing delightful deep blue flowers. It forms a terrific little plant. Growing to 4 feet (1.2 m), it needs to be staked to get it to stand upright and look its best.
- *Geranium psilostemon* (Armenian cranesbill). One of the tallest hardy geraniums, this grows 3 to 4 feet (90 to 120 cm) high and produces striking magenta flowers with black centers in early summer. It is one of the best geraniums to use as an accent plant for the middle of a perennial border.

*G*leditsia triacanthos 'Sunburst'

Common name: *Thornless gold honey locust*

Chief characteristics

If you need a large deciduous tree that will bathe your house in cool, dappled shade in summer and add a little cheerful color and charm to your neighborhood, *Gleditsia triacanthos* 'Sunburst' will do the trick. There are other wonderful shade trees available— ash, linden, maple, birch, oak—but for something a little different, the thornless gold honey locust is an excellent pick.

Location: Full sun to light shade

Type: Deciduous tree

Size: 40 to 50 feet (12 to 15 m)

Conditions: Fertile, well-drained soil

Zone: 4

Make sure you don't accidentally pick up the common honey locust. This has thorns and messy seed pods. 'Sunburst' is one of a special group of cultivars that are all thornless and virtually seedless, which makes them ideal street trees.

But the special appeal of 'Sunburst' is its golden yellow new leaves, which look exceptional against a darker background of deep green or purple-leafed trees. The golden leaves turn medium green by midsummer. The tree eventually grows into a large specimen with a loose canopy that moves with great elegance in a breeze.

The name "honey locust" refers to the sweet gummy substance found in the seed pods of the common *Gleditsia triacanthos*.

Where to plant it

Gleditsia triacanthos 'Sunburst' thrives in full sun in almost any type of soil provided it drains freely. It is very tolerant of city pollution, which makes it suitable for planting on a boulevard or sidewalk or in a front garden as a shade tree. Reasonably fast growing, it is a good choice for people who want a large tree as soon as possible. If possible, plant 'Sunburst' against dark conifers or the maroon leaves of a 'King Crimson' maple. Or place it in direct contrast with shrubs like purple smoke bush (*Cotinus coggygria*) or burning bush (*Euonymus alata*).

Try to plant this tree in well-drained soil where the roots can go deep without becoming a problem. Some people have used it very successfully to give their garden a focal point, anchor a curve in a mixed border or create a prominent feature in the center of a lawn. It is regarded by many landscape designers as an impact tree. With sunshine streaming through its leaves, it is an awesome spectacle.

How to care for it

Forget about heavy pruning. 'Sunburst' rarely needs it. The only pruning you will have to do is the basic: snip out whatever is dead, diseased, damaged or dangerous in spring. This tree is unlikely to display any of those problems if planted properly in the first place. If your garden is prone to winds, try not to plant 'Sunburst' in a site that is too exposed: its branches can be brittle and they can snap in high winds.

The golden-yellow foliage will turn green in summer but light pruning will produce new color. Avoid overwatering.

Good companions

Part of the beauty and appeal of 'Sunburst' is its ability to share ground with a rich variety of plants and tolerate the root presence of sizable shrubs. The airy foliage allows light to reach the ground rather than casting a deep shadow and that means many other plants can flourish.

Underplant with your choice of hostas or hardy geraniums. The silver foliage of *Artemisia ludoviciana* 'Valerie Finnis' and the blue flowers of *Salvia* × *sylvestris* 'East Friesland' can be combined with the green-silvery foliage of *Ruta graveolens* 'Curly Girl' to create an attractive mix of color and textures. For a dramatic display, underplant the tree with a mixture of late-blooming yellow 'Sweet Harmony' or white 'Maureen' tulips, with one or two black 'Queen of the Night' tulips in the center.

For your collection

There are three other excellent cultivars of *Gleditsia*.

- 🌿 'Shademaster'. This has a vase shape and is an excellent pick if you want light shade. It grows to 40 feet (12 m).
- 🌿 'Skyline'. A slightly taller tree, more pyramidal and symmetrical than 'Shademaster', this will reach almost 50 feet (15 m).
- 🌿 'Rubylace'. A round-headed graceful tree, this has ruby-red foliage in spring that turns bronze-green with a red tinge in fall. It grows to 40 feet (12 m).

Here are a few other excellent shade trees with golden or interest foliage.

- 🌿 *Robinia pseudoacacia* 'Frisia'. An exceptionally beautiful and graceful medium-sized deciduous tree, this is suitable for small- and medium-sized gardens. Its yellow-green leaves look sensational when seen against the backdrop of dark brooding conifers. This is a tree to lust after if you don't have one. 'Frisia' takes at least 10 years to reach 25 feet (7.5 m), and another 20 years to attain its full height, usually not more than 40 feet (12 m).
- 🌿 *Acer negundo* 'Flamingo' is another outstanding tree for the small- or medium-sized garden. Its new leaves have a flamingo-pink edge to them. The color is even more pronounced in cooler areas where the tree's Zone 5 hardiness rating gets pushed to the limit. It grows about 15 to 20 feet (4.5 to 6 m).
- 🌿 *Ginkgo biloba* (maidenhair tree). One of the plant world's great survivors, it is estimated this tree has been around for at least 160 million years! Imagine that it once shared the Earth with dinosaurs and you realize why it is so respected by horticulturists. I include it here because of the sensational golden yellow fall color of its butterfly-shaped leaves. Completely pest and disease resistant, it is a wonderful character tree with an elegant pyramidal shape. Hardy to Zone 4, it grows 35 to 40 feet (10 to 12 m). Make sure you plant the male tree, as the female produces messy, stinky fruit.

*H*amamelis × intermedia 'Diane'

Common name: *Witch hazel*

Chief characteristics

Color in the garden in the dark days of winter can lift the spirit. It reminds us that spring is only weeks away. Witch hazel, an insignificant plant most of the year, comes into its own in midwinter when it produces spidery yellow or copper-red flowers on its leafless branches. The flowers are sweetly scented with a fragrance that has been compared to that of hyacinths or lilies. For some people, witch hazel brings back childhood memories of astringents used to heal scrapes on knees and elbows. Witch hazel gets its name from its fork-shaped twigs, used as divining rods in "water witching"—a way of searching for underground water sources.

> **Location:** Sun or light shade
> **Type:** Deciduous shrub
> **Size:** 10 feet (3 m)
> **Conditions:** Well-drained, acid soil
> **Flowering time:** February to March
> **Zone:** 5

The two most popular plants for the average-sized garden are *Hamamelis × intermedia* 'Diane', which has deep crimson-red flowers, and *H. × intermedia* 'Jelena', which has coppery orange flowers. Both are hardy to Zone 5, although 'Diane' is generally less troubled by subzero temperatures. It is also regarded by some nurseries as the best red-flowering witch hazel. Both produce small, fragrant clusters of flowers in January and February. These appear on bare branches like neatly twisted tufts of shredded paper in January and February. Chinese witch hazel, *Hamamelis mollis*, one of the parents of 'Jelena' and 'Diane', has bright golden yellow flowers. *H. mollis* is slow-growing, eventually growing to 8 to 14 feet (2.5 to 4 m). The top cultivars of *H. mollis* are 'Pallida', which has fragrant, pale sulphur-yellow flowers, and 'Brevipetala', which has large, dark yellow flowers.

Where to plant it

Witch hazel fits naturally into a lightly shaded part of a woodland garden. It is best planted where the scent and color of the flowers can be appreciated in winter. Just keep in mind that the shrub offers very little interest the rest of the year. It has a valuable supporting role to play in the border, filling in gaps between other shrubs, and it is right at home in an out-of-the-way corner by a gate, driveway or path, tucked next to a hedge or under a tall tree. For best effect, 'Diane' should be planted where sunlight floods through the bush from behind.

How to care for it

Witch hazel likes rich, moist, acidic soils and it is not bothered by polluted air. The shrub can be pruned to size, but it will be happier if it is allowed to expand and fill a sizable corner. Basic pruning involves removing dead or damaged or unwanted branches after flowering but before leaves unfurl in spring. Prune judiciously to keep the shrub within its prescribed boundaries but don't resist the opportunity to take off branches for forcing indoors in early spring.

Good companions

Since witch hazels don't flower in summer and their oval leaves are not especially attractive, they should be underplanted with spring-flowering bulbs, such as dog's tooth violet, *Iris reticulata*, dwarf narcissus, scilla and chionodoxa, and groundcovers, like sweet woodruff, Japanese spurge and hardy geraniums. Witch hazel can offer support to shrubs like rhododendrons, pieris, magnolia, viburnum and mock orange.

For your collection

- *Hamamelis* × *intermedia* 'Arnold Promise' is a vase-shaped shrub with fragrant yellow flowers tinged with red. It grows to 5 to 7 feet (1.5 to 2 m) and is hardy to Zone 4.
- *Hamamelis* × *intermedia* 'Carmine Red' is a vigorous grower with bright carmine-red flowers and contorted petals. It grows 5 to 8 feet (1.5 to 2.4 m) tall and is hardy to Zone 6.
- *Hamamelis* × *intermedia* 'Fire Cracker' is a taller variety. It grows to 8 to 14 feet (2.4 to 4 m) and has crumpled, copper-red flowers. It is hardy to Zone 6.

Helictotrichon sempervirens

Common name: Blue oat grass

Chief characteristics

What makes ornamental grasses so special is not just their color and shape but the way they can catch the barest breeze and bring sound and movement to the garden. The gentle swaying of the rose-red plumes of purple fountain grass (*Pennisetum setaceum* 'Rubrum') or the rustle of the distinctive blades of zebra grass (*Miscanthus sinensis* 'Zebrinus') brings a whole new

Location: Full sun

Type: Ornamental grass

Size: 18 to 20 inches (45 to 50 cm)

Conditions: Ordinary, well-drained soil

Flowering time: July to August

Zone: 3

dimension to the beauty of a summer garden. Ornamental grasses contribute to the color and design of a garden. Grasses also remind us of open meadows and country footpaths and carefree childhood days when we would pull up a stem of grass and amble along a lane with pals, without a care in the world.

Many grasses deserve a place in the garden but few are as versatile or as easy to grow as blue oat grass. It has a fabulous mounding form, outstanding intense silvery blue blades, and long arching stalks that slowly turn to straw by the end of summer. In mild areas it stays evergreen, which brings much-valued color to the garden in winter.

Where to plant it

Blue oat grass is not a small grass. It needs room to be seen at its best. It will grow 2 feet (60 cm) high, send pale blue flower stalks up another 2 feet (60 cm), and form a round, compact mound at least 2 feet (60 cm) wide. Blue oat grass may be used as an accent plant or planted in groups for greater drama. Perfect for the sunny perennial border, its color contrasts well with silver-leafed plants such as artemisia or dark-leafed plants like *Heuchera micrantha* 'Bressingham Bronze' or *Cimicifuga* 'Brunette'.

Plant blue oat grass in fertile, well-drained, average soil in a sunny location. Make sure it gets good air circulation. If the drainage is poor, especially if the soil is wet clay, it will die from root rot. In my garden, blue oat grass flourishes beautifully next to a path on the west side of the house where it is sheltered from the hot afternoon sun by a cedar hedge, yet still gets plenty of morning sun and daylight. In a simple unadorned pot on a balcony, it can be very attractive.

How to care for it

Too much shade will lead to fungal problems. Too much sun will make blue oat grass go into early dormancy and quit performing. Cut down the spent flower stems in fall. Divide and replace every three years.

Good companions

The succulent foliage and heavy broccoli-like flowerheads of *Sedum* 'Autumn Joy' and the silver leaves of *Stachys byzantina* 'Silver Carpet' or *Artemisia* 'Silver Mound' add to the beauty of blue oat grass. The rose-red flowers of *Lychnis coronaria* and late-summer purple flowerheads of cosmos also offer a striking combination. Annuals like the purple-flowering cherry-pie plant and the spidery pink or lavender flowers of *Cleome spinosa* add excitement. Shrub roses, particularly any of David Austin's top English roses, like 'Mary Rose' or 'Gertrude Jekyll', make fine bedfellows for blue oat grass.

For your collection

If you fall in love with blue grasses, there are plenty more for your garden. Here are two of the best.

- *Festuca cinerea* 'Elijah Blue'. This has powdery blue evergreen leaves and grows only 18 inches (45 cm) high. It is rated by nursery experts as one of the brightest and best of the blue grasses. It also goes under the name *F. ovina glauca* 'Elijah Blue'.
- *Elymus racemosus* (lyme grass). This favorite blue grass of the illustrious 19th-century English garden designer Gertrude Jekyll can be used as an accent plant or as a groundcover.

Heliotropium arborescens

Common name: Heliotrope, cherry-pie plant

Chief characteristics

Location: Full sun
Type: Annual
Size: 8 to 24 inches (20 to 60 cm)
Conditions: Fertile, well-drained soil
Flowering time: June to September

An old-fashioned summer annual, heliotrope has it all: great color, memorable fragrance and a lyrical common name, cherry-pie plant. It is called that because for some people the remarkable scent of the purple flowers is reminiscent of a cherry pie, fresh out of the oven. Others think the fragrance is more like baby powder or licorice. It is a strong, but not offensive aroma. You may catch a whiff of it as you breeze by but most of the time you need to put your nose quite close to the large purple flowerheads to catch the fragrance's full strength.

Native to South America, where Europeans first encountered it in Peru toward the end of the 18th century, heliotrope is now a firm favorite of container gardeners, who like to use it in pots and hanging baskets. (It is also listed as *Heliotropium peruvianum*). An easy plant to care for, it flowers non-stop from June to September. In addition to its dense flowerheads, composed of tight clusters of tiny, individual mauve-purple flowers, it also has very attractive, dark green, corrugated leaves.

Where to plant it

Heliotrope performs superbly in patio pots, window boxes, hanging baskets and planter boxes. Or it can be grown in a sunny, well-drained site in the open garden. It is rarely troubled by pests or disease.

How to care for it

There are two golden rules for growing heliotrope. 1) Don't overwater. It hates having its roots waterlogged and perpetually damp soil will cause the leaves to turn brown and fall off. 2) Remember to feed it, especially if it is planted in a pot, with a half-strength solution of 20-20-20 at least twice a week.

Good companions

Heliotrope contrasts well with silver foliage plants such as dusty miller, white petunias, the two-tone yellow-maroon heads of French marigolds, and yellow marguerites.

For your collection

🐌 *Heliotropium arborescens* 'Alba' is a white cultivar with a slightly more powerful vanilla scent. Other scented plants that can be grown in pots on the patio include scented geraniums, mints and chocolate cosmos.

elleborus orientalis

Common name: *Lenten rose*

Chief characteristics

Location: Semi-shade
Type: Perennial
Size: 18 to 24 inches (45 to 60 cm)
Conditions: Good, well-drained soil
Flowering time: March to April
Zone: 3

There are fads and trends in gardening just as there are in fashion and the arts. For a time, hellebores were the "must-have" plants of the moment. Avid gardeners still talk of how remarkable hellebores are and how it is a major oversight not to have at least two or three types in the garden.

In reality, while they are robust, reliable plants with charming, open cup-shaped flowers, they are actually rather modest performers, not at all showy or attention-grabbing in the way roses or daylilies are. This makes hellebores something of an acquired taste. But once you like them, you will probably grow to love them. If, on the other hand, you don't see what all the fuss is about, that is also perfectly understandable.

Two of the most popular kinds are *Helleborus orientalis*, the Lenten rose, which comes in a range of flower colors from red to pink, maroon to white; and *H. niger*, the Christmas rose, which has flowers ranging from pure white to blush green. I think it's worth finding a place for both, but if I had to choose between them I would pick the Lenten rose because of its exquisite plum-colored flowers. Look for 'Red Mountain Lenten', which has pure red flowers and grows 12 inches (30 cm) high. Hellebores form low mounding clumps of firm, leathery, evergreen leaves. The Christmas rose (rarely ever in bloom at Christmas) usually flowers in March.

Where to plant it

Both Lenten and Christmas roses flourish in rich soil that is moist but well drained, in light to full shade. A dappled woodland-type setting is the perfect location for hellebores. In too much sun, the leaves tend to scorch and look tatty.

The flowers rise 10 to 12 inches (25 to 30 cm) above the foliage and nod downward. You may have to lift the shy flowers face-up to see them, something that only adds to their charm. Both these hellebores make good underplanting for rhododendrons, deciduous trees and shrubs.

How to care for it

When the Lenten rose and Christmas rose are in full bloom you will probably want to cut a few and bring them indoors. They look very good in a small glass vase but they don't last very long unless they are cut and put in water immediately. Some gardeners say adding a nip of vodka or gin to the water seems to make these flowers last longer. Grow hellebores toward the front of the shade border, where the flowers won't be hidden and can be easily reached. When flowers have faded, allow them to go to seed. Cut old, dead and decaying leaves back to the base clump of healthy green foliage.

Clumps can be divided in spring or fall, but hellebores prefer not to be disturbed and have a tendency to recover slowly and refuse to flower for a couple of seasons after being messed with. If you cut away the foliage of *Helleborus niger* as the buds expand, the flowers tend to be more showy.

Good companions

Surrounded by spring-flowering bulbs like grape hyacinths and dog's tooth violet, Lenten and Christmas roses fit well under trees and shrubs. They won't object to sharing ground with hostas, hardy geraniums, barrenwort, lungwort, jack-in-the-pulpit, lily-of-the-valley, maidenhair fern, rhododendrons and deciduous shrubs like hydrangea.

For your collection

There are other important hellebores you should consider.

- 🌿 *Helleborus argutifolius* (Corsican hellebore). This grows about 3 feet (90 cm) tall and has tough, glossy leaves with serrated edges. It has dense bunches of lime-green flowers in early spring. It may require staking to hold up the weighty flowerheads. Prune out the old flower stalks after it has bloomed and it will produce healthy new foliage. 'Bulmer's Blush', a new pink-flowered version of the standard Corsican hellebore, caused quite a stir when it was showcased for the first time at the Chelsea Flower Show. Hardy to Zone 6.
- 🌿 *Helleborus foetidus* (stinking hellebore). This is not really stinky at all unless you put your nose very close to the flowers, which are pale yellow-green and have a vaguely skunky aroma. The foliage is deeply cut and is useful in the shade border for creating textural contrasts. Hardy to Zone 4.

    Corsican and stinking hellebores are both first-rate plants but they are generally valued more by plant connoisseurs than average weekend gardeners, partly because the flowers and foliage are not especially showy and partly because you mostly find these plants at specialty nurseries that cater to knowledgeable plant-lovers.
- 🌿 *Helleborus vesicarius*, native to the oak scrub and rocky limestone outcrops of Turkey, has lovely deep-cut oak-like leaves and nodding maroon flowers. Tests have found that it is a lot hardier than was originally thought. Hardy to Zone 6.

*ℋ*emerocallis 'Stella de Oro'

Common name: *Daylily*

Chief characteristics

The daylily has two major assets: superb trumpet-shaped flowers that now come in a grand range of colors, and handsome strap-like leaves that rise and fall in cascading mounds. Both flowers and foliage play an invaluable decorative role in the summer garden.

One of the easiest and most reliable perennials to grow, the daylily gets its

Location: Full sun to light shade
Type: Perennial
Size: 18 inches (45 cm)
Conditions: Good, moist, well-drained soil
Flowering time: June to September
Zone: 3

botanical name, *Hemerocallis*, from two Greek words—*hemero* for day and *kallos* for beauty. The delicate flowers—more water than substance—last for only a day, two at most, depending how much sun and shade they receive. A major compensation for the shockingly brief lifespan of such a beautiful flower is that a mature clump of daylilies is perfectly capable of producing dozens of exquisite blooms in a single season. A three-year-old plant can produce in excess of 600 blooms in just 8 weeks. Over the last few decades, hybridizers have been astonishingly busy, with the result that today there are at least 38,000 registered hybrids, covering a vast range of colors in virtually every shade of pink, orange, yellow and red imaginable.

Like roses, daylilies all have marvelous names. 'Cherry Cheeks', 'Pandora's Box', 'Pardon Me', 'Painted Lady', 'Pineapple Frost', 'Velveteen', 'Gold Spider', and on and on. Most gardeners, however, have not the foggiest idea what they actually have growing in their garden. The fight to rectify the daylily's identity crisis is a cause célèbre for many daylily breeders. They campaign with almost evangelical zeal to persuade nurseries and garden centers to call daylilies by their full botanical name instead of dumping them into non-specific, generic color categories.

There are a few classic top performers that over the years have earned a special place of honor. Top of the class is 'Stella de Oro', a long-time favorite, loved for its short 12- to 18-inch (30- to 45-cm) form and its lightly ruffled orange-gold flowers that bloom continuously from spring to fall. 'Catherine Woodbury' is another classic, producing lovely, fragrant, pale orchid-pink blooms with a lime-green throat. 'Happy Returns' is similar to 'Stella de Oro', with canary-yellow flowers. It blooms from early summer into autumn.

'Frans Hals' is a plain golden yellow and dark orange bicolor with an elegant simplicity to it—like the work of the Dutch artist for whom it is named. 'Hyperion' is an established star performer with international appeal. It produces highly scented lemon-yellow flowers. Other top performers to look out for include 'Scarlock' (red), 'Pink Lass' (pink), 'Buzz Bomb' (scarlet), 'Gentle Shepherd' (cream) and 'Springsyde' (clear yellow).

A lot of gardeners don't know that the modern daylily is the product of some clever and complicated genetic wizardry. The tetraploid breed of daylilies has twice as many chromosomes as the old-fashioned two-chromosome (diploid) cultivars. Tetraploids have bigger, bolder flowers with brighter colors in striking patterns. These "super" daylilies also have sturdier flower stems (scapes) and more robust foliage and they have proven to be more disease and drought tolerant than many of their predecessors. However, the argument over which kind of daylily is better—tetraploid or diploid—is still a subject of much debate among professional daylily growers.

Where to plant it

Daylilies thrive in full sun or light shade. They flower best if, like roses, they get at least 6 hours of sun a day. They are marvelous mass-planted in deep drifts by the side of a path or edging the front of a raised bed. They can also perform very successfully in large single clumps in the perennial border or even in containers, provided they are well watered. Moisture is essential: they need at least an inch (2.5 cm) a week in order to produce high-quality flowers that won't shrivel the first moment the sun touches them. For this reason, make sure you plant daylilies in rich, moisture-retentive soil. Although they are sun-lovers, they benefit from being located where they get light, dappled shade in the afternoon.

When buying daylilies, look not only at the quality of the flower, but also for healthy, vigorous foliage. Daylily connoisseurs also look closely at the area where the flowers are formed. The wider the flower junctions, the less likelihood there is of blooms becoming congested and failing to appear at their best.

How to care for it

There is no need to spray daylilies. They will thrive in fertile soil that has been well amended with fully aged compost or manure. Slugs and snails can be a nuisance, especially when young daylily foliage is developing. This is a time to be extra vigilant, although most daylilies seem quite capable of compensating for any damage inflicted by slugs by producing even more flowering stems. A healthy daylily will grow at an astonishing rate, almost doubling itself in a year.

You can deadhead your daylilies—pulling off the spent blooms each day—but do it only for the sake of tidiness. It makes no difference to the plant.

Division is very easy. Large clumps can be pulled apart to make many new colonies. This is what often drives gardeners to be very selective in the first place. They know one day they will end up with hundreds of plants of whatever form they have chosen.

Good companions

Daylilies combine effortlessly with many summer-flowering perennials. Phlox and bee balm, crocosmia and lavatera are all good candidates. Ornamental grasses, artemisia and bronze fennel can provide interesting foliage contrast while yarrow, liatris and daisies offer stimulating color combinations in sunny locations. In light shade, late-flowering astilbe and ligularia offer pleasant companionship along with hostas and astrantia and the blue flowers of *Geranium pratense*. Deciduous small trees or shrubs like variegated dogwood or purple-leafed smoke bush can also provide creative backdrops to the graceful foliage and elegant flowers of daylilies.

For your collection

You can spend a fortune if you really get bitten by the daylily bug. Some plants sell for more than $200 each. You could concentrate on making collections. For example, there is the Siloam series, dozens of hybrids produced by Pauline Henry in Arkansas and each named after her hometown, Siloam. There's 'Siloam Rose Queen', 'Siloam Red Toy', 'Siloam Little Fairy', 'Siloam Ethel Smith' and many more.

*H*euchera micrantha 'Bressingham Bronze'

Common name: *Coral bells*

Chief characteristics

Heuchera can be used as a groundcover, an edging plant beside a path or a texture plant in the flower border. It looks good grown in a pot on its own or combined with colorful summer annuals. The delicate sprays of white, red or pink flowers look particularly attractive in flower arrangements and heuchera's foliage is most useful as a counterpoint to the bright blooms of lavender, salvia, achillea, coreopsis, corydalis and blue and gold ornamental grasses.

Location: Full sun to part shade
Type: Perennial
Size: 9 inches (23 cm)
Conditions: Good, moist, well-drained soil
Flowering time: June to July
Zone: 4

Heuchera wasn't always so popular. But over the last few decades, hybridizers have been very busy with the result that today there are many new, outstanding cultivars. They are available in a wide range of foliage and flower colors.

Some of the most impressive heucheras are the Bressingham hybrids, raised by the Blooms Nursery of Bressingham in Norfolk, England. One of the best of the new hybrids is 'Bressingham Bronze', which gets its name from its distinctive crinkly, bronzy-red foliage. It has tiny white flowers on thin stems in summer, but the main reason for getting this plant is to create exciting color contrasts by combining it with blue grasses and plants with silver leaves. 'Bressingham Bronze' is an improved version of another very popular heuchera called 'Palace Purple', which was so impressive when it came on the market it was voted Perennial Plant of the Year in 1991 by the Perennial Plant Association of North America. 'Palace Purple' has white flowers and dark purple-brown, maple-shaped leaves that have an almost metallic look to them. However, 'Bressingham Bronze' now routinely outperforms 'Palace Purple' in European and North American gardens, partly because its creators insist that it be propagated vegetatively (by division or from cuttings) rather than from seed, which tends to produce inferior plants that lack the all-important foliage characteristic for which the plant is famous. "Once you've seen 'Bressingham Bronze'," says Adrian Bloom, of Blooms Nursery, "you won't want 'Palace Purple'."

Where to plant it

Grow heuchera in full sun or semi-shade in well-drained soil. Don't let the ground become too dry, especially in blazing afternoon sun.

Create a tapestry of contrasting foliage by planting different heucheras together. The light sprays of flowers also command attention, frothing up in mass plantings. Or you can employ heuchera to edge a path, or try out exciting new color associations in the perennial border. The semi-shaded rockery is another place heuchera will thrive provided it is well watered.

How to care for it

Once settled in the right place, heucheras are easy plants to care for. Simply improve the soil by mulching around them with an enriching well-rotted manure or compost mulch in spring. Cut off the faded flower stalks in summer to keep the plants looking tidy. Divide clumps every few years.

You may think you have selected precisely the right spot for your heuchera, but it will sulk if given too much sun and too little water. Watch it for the first season; if it performs well and the leaves look crisp and healthy and attractive, you know you have it in the right spot.

Good companions

Some of the best companions for heucheras are other heucheras. The foliage of 'Palace Purple' can be contrasted with 'Snow Storm' or 'Chocolate Ruffles'—not hugely creative, but it does work.

The pale lemon-tinted leaves of *Stachys byzantina* 'Primrose Heron' and the white flowers of *Geranium clarkei* 'Kashmir White' would give

Heuchera micrantha 'Bressingham Bronze' two great neighbors. The small clumping grass, *Festuca glauca*, could also be tossed into the mix to add a blue note. Other possible associates are *Allium christophii*, with its silver-purple starlike blooms; black mondo grass; *Euphorbia polychroma*; and *Scabiosa columbaria* 'Pink Mist'.

For your collection

The list of heuchera hybrids now in commercial production is staggering. Other top names to look out for include the following.

- 'Brandon Pink'. One of the biggest heucheras, growing 18 to 24 inches (45 to 60 cm), it produces coral-pink flowers. It is also exceptionally hardy.
- 'Chocolate Ruffles'. You can't miss the large, dark chocolate-brown leaves with ruffled edges. It produces white flowers.
- 'Northern Fire'. This is another admirably hardy cultivar. It has variegated white-green foliage and scarlet-red flowers.
- 'Persian Carpet'. It has dark green and silver-blue foliage.
- 'Pewter Moon'. This has cool pink flowers on tall maroon stems but it is loved mostly for its oustanding silver-gray foliage with pewter-gray veins.
- 'Plum Pudding'. Very aptly named, this has rich plum-colored foliage.
- *Heuchera sanguinea* hybrids. These well-established favorites are still pretty hard to beat and they're the first coral bells to flower. They send up pink or bright red flowers from May to July. Look for 'Splish Splash', which has variegated green-white foliage with veins that turn red at the first chill of fall; 'Splendens', a compact plant with scarlet-red flowers; and 'Snow Storm', which has pink flowers and ruffled white leaves edged with green.
- *Salvia officinalis* 'Purpurascens' (purple sage) and *Euphorbia amygdaloides* 'Rubra' are two other plants with bronzy foliage that are worth having.

ℋibiscus syriacus 'Blue Bird'

Common name: *Rose of Sharon*

Chief characteristics

Rose of Sharon is a fabulous, late summer–flowering shrub with an intriguing name. It is not a rose at all but a shrub form of hibiscus. It gets its name from a vague biblical reference in the Song of Solomon to "a rose of Sharon," which in Hebrew refers to a crocus, not a rose, and certainly not hibiscus. All this, I think, is fun to tell visitors to your garden when they stand admiring the magnificent blooms of your Rose of Sharon.

Location: Full sun to light shade

Type: Deciduous shrub

Size: 5 to 6 feet (1.5 to 1.8 m)

Conditions: Fertile, well-drained soil

Flowering time: August to October

Zone: 5

What we know for sure about this shrub is that it grows into a substantial bush, 5 to 6 feet (1.5 to 1.8 m) high, and produces lovely hollyhock-like blooms in a wide variety of colors from August to September. Native to Syria (from which it gets its species name, *syriacus*), Rose of Sharon is perhaps most popular of all in France and Italy where it is used extensively in parks and gardens.

'Blue Bird' is one of the best cultivars. It has light blue flowers with a dark center and it has proven itself a reliable performer in many gardens over the years. Other top cultivars include 'Woodbridge' (rose-pink with carmine centre), 'Aphrodite' (pink with red centre), 'Ardens' (purple), 'Coelestis' (sky blue), 'Lucy' (bright red), 'Blushing Bride' (pink), 'Morningstar' (white), 'Paeoniflorus' (pink), 'Rubis' (red), 'Single White' (white) and 'Tricolor' (red, white and blue).

Where to plant it

To flower perfectly, *Hibiscus syriacus* needs plenty of sun and a long, hot summer. Plant it in ordinary but well-drained soil in the warmest, most protected site in your garden.

'Blue Bird' can be used as an accent plant in the shrub border or trained into a tree form and used to create privacy or block out eyesores. You can also grow hibiscus in containers, but regardless of where you grow it, it will need to be protected from cool breezes and chilly night temperatures. Be patient. This shrub is slow to get established and takes a couple of years before it gets into full swing and starts blooming profusely.

How to care for it

A lot of gardeners think their hibiscus is dead because it is so slow to leaf out in spring. Relax. It is not dead, just sleeping. Hardy to Zone 5, it needs winter protection in colder areas. Prune back the bush for size and shape and to encourage bushy growth. Cut back to two buds on the previous season's growth. Most important with hibiscus—keep the soil moist, but not soaking wet, especially in hot, dry summers. Also keep an eye out for aphids and mealy bugs.

Good companions

Potentilla, hydrangea, English roses, buddleia, euonymus, and spiraea are all excellent partners for Rose of Sharon. If you include it in a border with bush forms of magnolia, French lilac and burning bush (*Euonymus alata*) you get a complete sequence of color from May to October. Throw in some red- or yellow-twig dogwoods and you'll extend the colorful picture into the winter months.

For your collection

    Hibiscus moscheutos (rose mallow). This perennial produces large flowers in July to September. Top cultivars are 'Disco Belle' (pink), which grows 2 to 3 feet (60 to 90 cm), and 'Southern Belle' (white, pink and red), which is slightly taller, growing 3 to 5 feet (90 cm to 1.5 m). They both thrive in full sun in well-drained soil.

osta 'Frances Williams'

Common name: *Frances Williams hosta*

Chief characteristics

Hostas are so dependable, versatile and long lasting, it is no surprise so many gardeners regard them as the perfect perennial. They are certainly one of the structural workhorse plants of the shade garden. Once settled, they can have a formidable presence either in a large group planting or alone as a solitary feature. Hostas can be large and lush or diminutive and delicate. They come in an astonishing diversity of color and form.

Location: Light shade
Type: Perennial
Size: 2 to 3 feet (60 to 90 cm)
Conditions: Moist, well-drained soil
Flowering time: July
Zone: 2

For all-round beauty and reliability, however, one of the best hostas is 'Frances Williams', an old favorite with pale lavender flowers and variegated, heart-shaped, blue-green leaves trimmed with gold. The foliage variegation is consistent and never sick- or anemic-looking. This hosta has a reputation for being slug resistant and can also tolerate more sun than other hostas.

Other fine variegated hostas include 'Aureo Marginata', 'Francee', 'Wide Brim', 'Great Expectations', 'Frosted Jade', and 'Albo Marginata'. Another top performer is the urn-shaped 'Krossa Regal', which has frosty blue leaves, pale lavender flowers and an ability to handle more sun than a lot of other hostas. 'Krossa Regal' also forms an attractive vase-shaped clump.

There are marvelous blue hostas such as 'Hadspen Blue', 'Blue Wedgewood', 'Bressingham Blue', 'Halcyon' and 'Big Daddy'; delicious yellow cultivars like 'Sun Power', 'Midas Touch' and 'August Moon'; classy, large-leafed cultivars like 'Sum and Substance' and 'Elegans'; and rich green ones like 'Devon Green', 'Canadian Shield', 'Green Acres' and 'Royal Standard'.

Where to plant it

Hostas thrive in light or full shade in moist, well-drained soil. They need at least four hours of sunshine to flower properly, so it is best to place them in light shade rather than total shade.

Some gardeners want only the broad handsome leaves and cut off the long stiff stalks of lilac or white flowers the moment they appear. However, the flowers of some—'Honeybells' and 'Royal Standard', for example—have a delightful fragrance and it would be a pity to lose them.

Grow hostas in a mass planting as a groundcover or contrast their fabulous leaf texture against the leaves of other plants. All hostas are good candidates for containers, especially 'Wide Brim', 'Gold Standard', 'Francee', 'Krossa Regal', 'Halcyon' and 'Snowden'. Decorate decks, balconies and patios or hold them in the wings to plug gaps in the shade border in summer.

Try growing larger-leafed hostas as a dramatic focal point in the herbaceous border or beside a stream or pond. Golden yellow cultivars can be used to brighten dark corners, and the blue cultivars are almost a novelty to show off to visitors.

How to care for it

All hostas are prone to slugs. Some, like 'Frances Williams', 'Krossa Regal' and 'Sum and Substance', seem to be more resistant than others. There are numerous strategies for dealing with them. Sprinkle diatomaceous earth around the new leaves as they emerge from the ground in spring. This material has sharp edges that makes it unpleasant for slugs to slither over. Beer in a plastic container sunk into the ground is supposed to lure the slimy mollusks to a boozy last night. The chemical slug killer, metaldehyde, works, but its use is frowned upon because of the risk of poisoning birds and household pets. You could get your own pet toad—toads eat slugs and snails. Pity we don't have hedgehogs in this part of the world: they also eat slugs. The best way to deal with slugs is to regularly patrol your hosta patch. Look for them, especially after rain. You may find them sitting munching on the top of leaves or lurking in folds of as-yet-uncurled leaves or hiding under pieces of wood or close to the ground in the cool crevices of large stones.

What to do with them once you have found them? Snip them with a pair of scissors, toss them into a plastic bag bound for the garbage, drop them into a bucket of hot water or sprinkle them with salt. I have heard there are people who collect slugs and walk them a mile or two down the road to release them into a friendly wood. This sounds so fantastic, I think these people should go directly to heaven or get a sainthood. How do they bring themselves to cut flowers?

Hostas like to be left to settle down and form large clumps, but they are easily divided when clumps become too large or when you want more hostas.

Good companions

Combine hostas with shade-loving shrubs and perennials like ligularia, hydrangea, Solomon's seal, hellebore, astilbe, dicentra, lady's mantle, epimedium and rhododendron.

Don't be a slave to the shade rule, however. Hostas, especially the variegated kinds, often appreciate more sun. It is all trial and error, but it is worth combining hostas with daylilies and astilbes in more exposed, sunny locations where the soil is moist. Where the ground is perpetually boggy, you can mix hostas with the water-loving *Iris laevigata*.

For your collection

🐌 There are several novel hostas worth having just for the fun of their names. 'Hosta La Vista' is one. 'Wrinkles and Crinkles' is another. 'Raspberry Sorbet' has red flower stems, while 'Canadian Shield' has very strong, firm, metallic leaves that look like they could be used to do some steel-plating. 'Gold Standard' is 'Frances Williams' in reverse—it has gold-yellow leaves with green edges and grows 2 feet (60 cm) high.

$\mathcal{H}$ydrangea arborescens 'Annabelle'

Common name: *Annabelle hydrangea*

Chief characteristics

Hydrangeas have been called the "queen of flowering shrubs." Some garden snobs consider them coarse and boring. But even a snob can't deny the glory of a hydrangea in full bloom. To my mind, they are magnificent plants, an indispensable part of the botanical backbone of a garden.

Hydrangea arborescens 'Annabelle' is one of the most reliable. It is hardy and produces very large white flowerheads from July into October. Hills-of-snow hydrangea (*H. arborescens* 'Grandiflora') is very similar, but it grows slightly taller, reaching 5 to 10 feet (1.5 to 3 m) and producing large white trusses of flowers from July to September.

Location: Full sun to part shade
Type: Deciduous shrub
Size: 4 to 5 feet (1.2 to 1.5 m)
Conditions: Moist, but well-drained soil
Flowering time: July to October.
Zone: 3

The peegee hydrangea (*H. paniculata* 'Grandiflora') grows 8 feet (2.4 m) high and produces masses of large, cascading, creamy white or light pink, cone-shaped flowers from August until frost. It can be trained into a small tree.

The popular mopheads (*Hydrangea macrophylla*), also known as hortensias, have large, globular flowerheads. Top cultivars include 'Nikko Blue', a prolific bloomer that produces turquoise-blue globe-shaped flowers in acid soil and shell-pink blooms in neutral soil; 'Forever Pink', a dwarf variety growing only 3 feet (90 cm) high and producing pink flowers in May; and 'Merritt's Beauty', noted for its robust growth habit. You will also find 'Hamburg', 'King George' and 'Kluis Superba', all of which grow about 4 feet (1.2 m).

Lacecap hydrangeas have slightly more decorative flowerheads with dense centers skirted by a light garland of single, flat flowers. Look for 'Mariesii Perfecta' and 'Mariesii Variegata'. In Zone 6 microclimates, you could try growing one of the most outstanding of all lacecaps, *Hydrangea serrata* 'Bluebird'. This has lovely blue flowers that fade to a delicate pink if the soil is allowed to become more alkaline.

Where to plant it

Hydrangeas are versatile shrubs that fit into almost any kind of garden scheme. They look most natural in woodland settings where they enjoy the protection of high trees that allow in plenty of dappled sunshine. Hydrangeas thrive in light shade, but they are frequently grown in full sun. They won't object provided they are well watered. They also need to be well fed. Keep the soil amended by adding compost or nutrient-rich mulches in spring. Also, consider growing hydrangeas in half-barrels; they don't seem to mind having limited space for root development and they flower just as profusely.

How to care for it

Hydrangeas require good soil and plenty of water, especially during hot, dry spells. Grow them in a location protected from heavy frosts. The more acidic the soil, the more blue the flowers; the more limey or alkaline the soil, the more pink the flowers will be. For blue hydrangea flowers, add aluminum sulfate to the soil; for pink, add lime.

Faded flowerheads can be cut after flowering or you can leave them on throughout winter if you like the look of them. Snip them off in early spring when you do your routine cleanup and prune back the stems without damaging the newly developed plump flower bud. There is no evidence that leaving the faded flowers on over winter has any benefit other than providing decorative textural interest.

Good companions

Good partners for hydrangeas include buddleia, rhododendron, evergreen azalea, *Enkianthus campanulatus, Cornus alba* 'Elegantissima' and *Viburnum* 'Summer Snowflake'.

For your collection

Here are a few other kinds of hydrangea you should know about.

- *Hydrangea aspera* is a larger, shrubby hydrangea with a more natural, uncultivated, jungle-bush look to it. *H. sargentiana* is another species with an exotic jungle look. Both of these are tender and hardy only to Zone 7.
- *Hydrangea macrophylla* 'Winning Edge' is a dwarf mophead with deep pink flowers. It grows to only about 2 feet (60 cm). 'Tovelit' and 'Elf' are two other compact mophead-type hydrangeas that are ideal for container growing in semi-shade on a deck, balcony or patio. Hardy to Zone 5.
- *Hydrangea quercifolia* (oakleaf hydrangea) is an unusual plant that has white flowers and large leaves resembling those of an oak tree. It grows to 6 feet (1.8 m) and is a Zone 5.

ℋydrangea petiolaris

Common name: *Climbing hydrangea*

Chief characteristics

Location: Semi-shade
Type: Deciduous vine
Size: 30 feet (9 m)
Conditions: Fertile, well-drained soil
Flowering time: June
Zone: 4

If you have only a small wall, fence or garden shed you want covered, a climbing hydrangea is probably not the right choice. It is a slow starter but is a vigorous climber capable of reaching 30 feet (9 m) once it gets going. In the ideal spot, and left unpruned, it has been known to soar to 50 feet (15 m) or more. This is also one of its great strengths. Its energetic growth habit makes it a magnificent plant for covering large walls or long fences or growing into sturdy big trees. It leafs out quickly in early spring with handsome green foliage and goes on to produce large white lacecap flowers. These can measure as much as 9 inches (23 cm) across.

The vine is self-supporting, climbing by means of tiny aerial roots that attach themselves firmly to any available surface. It likes to grow outward as well as upward, but it does not object to being firmly pruned or clipped and trained in the way you want it to go. It can be clipped neatly into shape once it has lost its leaves in fall and will resume its normal growth pattern in spring. As years go by, it will thicken out, become woodier and eventually form a massive, majestic spectacle.

Some of the older gardens in England have made extremely good use of the climbing hydrangea to cover walls that separate different areas of a garden. In one case, the vine was allowed to swarm and completely overwhelm a long, tall brick wall. But it was also carefully pruned to leave a narrow doorway in the thick barrier of leaves. The bright opening, leading from the shade into a sunny flower garden, looked exceptionally elegant and inviting.

Where to plant it

Climbing hydrangea grows best in rich, moist, but well-drained soil in semi-shade. In too much sun, the leaves scorch and the vine becomes tatty and unattractive. It reaches the peak of performance in late spring when its leaves form glorious layered patterns and the handsome white lacecap flowers open up against the solid backdrop of lustrous green foliage.

If you grow it against the house you should realize that it is a tenacious clinger and won't let go without a fight. This is exactly what you want if you are looking for a long-lasting vine that will form a solid, structured framework. It can be made to clamber up brick chimneys or into trees or against garages or over sheds and fences in the shade of west- or east- or north-facing locations. It is also an excellent vine for screening.

In my garden, it covers a high, wide wall on the little-used west side of the house in a shady space that faces a neighbor's deck. In summer, when the vine is fully leafed out, my neighbors have a much more pleasant view from their deck than looking at an unadorned flat wall.

How to care for it

Prune climbing hydrangea in late fall or winter to keep it within bounds and to form a nicely structured shape. Branches that grow outward can be pruned back to maintain the vine's symmetry and prevent lower branches from being too shaded.

Don't be fooled if your newly planted vine doesn't grow at rocket speed. It is very deceptive at the beginning, taking its time to put in a good root system before it launches off. Have your secateurs on hand once it gets going.

Good companions

You can underplant a climbing hydrangea with *Geranium macrorrhizum* (white and pink) or *Corydalis* (yellow or white).

For your collection

- Three other powerful climbers that are useful in the right location are Virginia creeper (*Parthenocissus quinquefolia*), with brilliant red leaves turning to orange in fall; Boston ivy (*Parthenocissus tricuspidata*), with leaves that turn a striking red in fall; and silver lace vine (*Polygonum aubertii*), which puts out a white cloud of flowers from August to September.
- English ivy (*Hedera helix* 'Baltic') or Dutchman's pipe (*Aristolochia durior*) are two possible choices for decorating a large wall or covering an unsightly garage or shed. Also consider 'Hall's honeysuckle (*Lonicera japonica* 'Halliana') or *Lonicera brownii* 'Dropmore Scarlet'.

*I*ris sibirica

Common name: *Siberian iris, water iris, Siberian flag*

Chief characteristics

You can easily get lost in the jungle of irises. There are more than 200 species and thousands of cultivars. Some classifications have been so broken down into subcategories, it can be quite overwhelming to sort it all out. Of course, you don't have to. Most are us are content to grow a clump or two of Siberian iris, a few bearded iris, and some of the little early spring–flowering iris.

Location: Full sun to light shade
Type: Perennial
Size: 3 feet (90 cm)
Conditions: Moist soil
Flowering time: June to July
Zone: 3

Siberian iris is a marvelous clumping plant with thin, upright leaves and superb purple or blue flowers in June to July. Sadly, the flowers don't bloom for very long, 2 or 3 weeks at most, but the foliage stays green and attractive all summer. Like old garden roses, the beauty of the Siberian iris is in the exquisite delicacy of the blooms. Top named cultivars include 'Caesar's Brother' (deep purple), 'Butter and Sugar' (white-yellow), 'Orville Fay' (medium blue), 'Dance Ballerina' (white-purple), 'Tycoon' (violet), 'Papillon' (light blue) and 'White Swirl' (white).

Longer flowering, and generally a more familiar sight in many gardens, are the bearded irises. They bloom in June and are a lot more showy. They have a very distinctive flower, formed by 3 upright petals and 3 drooping petals, which have hairy tufts on their ridges—hence the "beard" name. Bearded irises have solid, sword-shaped leaves and the flowers come in a remarkable range of colors from blue to peach, pink to yellow, purple to black. There are many bicolor variations. It really all comes down to picking the size and color you like.

It helps to know irises come in six basic sizes—dwarf, less than 10 inches (25 cm); standard dwarf, 10 to 15 inches (25 to 38 cm); intermediate, 15 to 28 inches (38 to 70 cm); miniature tall, 18 to 26 inches (45 to 65 cm); border, up to 28 inches (70 cm); and standard tall, more than 28 inches (70 cm). The border and tall bearded irises are the most popular.

You will find dozens of bearded irises from which to choose. Top names include 'Babbling Brook' (clear blue), 'Valimar (pink), 'Butterscotch' (copper), 'Cosmic Dance' (blue), 'Frost and Flame' (white), 'Beverly Sills' (coral pink), 'Swazi Princess' (violet), 'Blue

Staccato' (bright blue with white edges), 'Cherub's Smile' (pink) and 'Dusky Challenger' (black-purple). The ones not in flower at garden centers usually come with an attached color photo, designed to eliminate guesswork.

Top dwarf irises include 'Alaska Blue' (blue), 'Banbury Ruffles' (blue), 'Bee's Wings' (purple) and 'Fleming Gold' (yellow).

Where to plant it

Grow Siberian irises in ordinary, moist soil in full sun or light shade. Make sure the rhizome is not planted too deep or too shallow. It likes to bake in the sun while its roots stay cool and moist.

Grow tall bearded irises in fertile, moist but well-drained soil in full sun. The rhizomes need to be positioned so that they get full sun on their tops while their rooted undersides are able to draw water from the soil. Bearded irises will thrive in large groups or alone, scattered in the perennial border.

How to care for it

Irises need to be well fed and watered to bloom properly. They can be fertilized in spring just before they bloom and again when they have finished flowering in July, which will encourage them to produce a second flush in late summer. Moist, well-drained soil is a must for bearded irises, so they need to be watered well, especially during their flowering stint.

Clumps can be lifted and divided using a sharp knife. Each new rhizome must have at least one fan (thick leaf-blade) in order to establish itself and flower. A sign that Siberian irises need to be divided is a bald spot in the center of a clump.

Good companions

Mix irises among your daylilies, shrub roses, peonies and hardy geraniums. The color of the flowers packs a powerful punch in early summer. Other good companions include the blue flowers of *Centaurea dealbata* and *Campanula glomerata* 'Superba'. Foliage plants, such as Penstemon 'Husker Red' with its dark maroon-red leaves or *Cimicifuga* 'Brunette' with its deep purple leaves, can offer excellent color contrasts. Yellow bearded irises look outstanding placed in front of the white flowers of a *Viburnum plicatum* 'Summer Snowflake'.

For your collection.

    ❧ *Iris pallida* (sweet iris) 'Aureo Variegata' and 'Variegata'. These cultivars have interesting variegated foliage and are good for edging or creating a bright focal point of foliage interest. They both have lavender-blue flowers.

 *Iris reticulata* and *Iris danfordiae*. These two tiny spring-flowering irises are worth getting. *I. reticulata* comes in various blues and *I. danfordiae* is yellow. They both grow 4 to 6 inches (10 to 15 cm) high and make a cheerful showing in April.

 If you have a pond, stream or lake, you could plant Japanese iris (*Iris ensata*, also known as *I. kaempferi*) or the yellow flag iris (*I. pseudoacorus*), which has canary-yellow flowers, on the banks.

*J*uniperus scopulorum 'Wichita Blue'

Common name: *Wichita Blue juniper, blue column juniper*

Chief characteristics

Structure and definition are two key elements of a well-designed garden. Herbaceous perennials are fascinating. Annuals are great fun to play with. Clematis is divine. Roses are ravishing. But evergreen shrubs and trees are what give a garden its botanical bones. Junipers are especially useful, tough, disease-resistant evergreens.

Location: Full sun to light shade
Type: Evergreen shrub
Size: 10 to 14 feet (3 to 4 m)
Conditions: Ordinary, well-drained soil
Zone: 4

Yet they are all too often dismissed as the most boring and overplanted shrubs in the urban landscape. This is partly the fault of lackluster landscapers who immediately think of junipers when asked to install a "low-maintenance" garden. The real problem, however, is that gardeners tend to go overboard and plant too many junipers in one area. While one or two well-placed junipers can add character, shape and structure to a garden, too many planted in close proximity can overwhelm a site and turn it into a tedious jungle of coarse foliage.

There are junipers for all kinds of uses: screening, hedging, groundcover, accent planting, color contrast. The key is to know the best juniper for the job. There are dozens of species. Most of the popular junipers at garden centers are cultivars of Chinese juniper (*Juniperus chinensis*), Rocky Mountain juniper (*J. scopulorum*), eastern red cedar (*J. virginiana*), scaly-leafed Nepal juniper (*J. squamata*), creeping, prostrate juniper (*J. horizontalis*) or shrubby European juniper (*J. sabina*). But all you really need to know is that they fall into one of three main types: upright column-shaped junipers; dwarf, slow-growing junipers, mostly under 4 feet (1.2 m); and ground-hugging junipers.

Best of the uprights—and an especially handsome shrub for accent or feature plantings—is the Wichita Blue juniper, which has dense, bright blue foliage all year and grows about 13 to 20 feet (4 to 6 m) high. Other excellent upright junipers to consider include *J. virginiana* 'Skyrocket', which has a slender narrow form with silvery blue foliage and grows to 15 feet (4.5 m); *J. chinensis* 'Mountbatten', which has silver-green foliage and grows 20 feet (6 m); and *J. scopulorum* 'Moffetii', which grows wider than the others, has silver-blue foliage and will reach 13 feet (4 m). Other names you will come across include 'Fairview', 'Iowa', 'Medora', 'Blue Alps' and 'Blaauw'.

Best of the dwarf junipers is *Juniperus squamata* 'Blue Star', with its steel-blue foliage. The perfect shrub for small spaces and rock gardens, it grows only 3 feet (90 cm) high and looks good year-round. Also consider *J. chinensis* 'Mint Julep', which has bright mint-green foliage, or *J. chinensis* 'Old Gold', which has bright golden foliage and is slow-growing to 3 feet (90 cm). You will also find these named varieties at your garden center—'Hertz Blue', 'Gold Star', 'Compact Pfitzer', 'Blue Danube' and 'Savin'. They all do a similar job to 'Blue Star'.

Best of the low-spreading, creeping junipers is *J. horizontalis* 'Blue Chip' with its exceptional steel-blue foliage. It spreads to 3 feet (90 cm). *J. horizontalis* 'Wiltonii' is another popular variety and forms a dense carpet of blue foliage. It can be used to cascade over walls. Other top names include 'Ice Blue', 'Blue Rug', 'Prince of Wales', 'Calgary Carpet', 'New Blue Tamarix' and 'Bar Harbor'.

Where to plant it

Junipers thrive in full sun or light shade in average, well-drained soil. This means they can be planted in virtually any location and they will perform satisfactorily. 'Witchita Blue' is best used to provide foliage and color accent as a stand-alone feature specimen. It can also be worked in to the mixed shrub border, where it tends to look most natural when supported by other conifers, such as pine and spruce.

The dwarf junipers are useful in gardens where space is limited or where a compact shape and structure are required in a more formal, low-maintenance planting scheme. They look at home under windows or beside entranceways. The groundcover junipers are reliable for carpeting banks or providing a durable, easy-maintenance landscape next to driveways, gravel paths or roads.

How to care for it

You will often hear people say they want a "low-maintenance" garden. What they really mean is they want a "no-maintenance" garden. That is, of course, not possible. Even if you cover your yard with easy-care junipers, there is still some work required to keep everything healthy and trim. Junipers respond well to pruning and this should be done not only to keep shrubs in shape but also to promote bushiness and healthy new growth. In spring, prune away any foliage that has suffered cold damage over winter and enrich the soil, especially under groundcover junipers, with well-rotted compost or manure every couple of years. Even junipers need well-nourished soil to stay healthy.

Good companions

You can create a rich tapestry of year-round texture and color using only dwarf conifers—juniper, pine, spruce, yew, cedar and cypress. You would be surprised at how attractive a patchwork of blue, green and golden-yellow evergreens can look together in an artistic arrangement. For inspiration, look at the work done in this area by Adrian Bloom, of the famous Blooms Nursery of Bressingham, England.

Support your 'Wichita Blue' with silver foliage perennials such as the hardy groundcover *Artemisia* 'Silver Brocade', hardy fountain grass (*Pennisetum alopecuroides*) or the variegated *Euonymus* 'Emerald Gaiety'. The blue foliage also looks wonderful near red-twig dogwoods or white-barked birch in winter. Other combinations to consider are the feathery foliage of a red laceleaf maple, the white or red flowers of potentilla and the crinkly leaves of heuchera or ajuga.

For your collection

Here are some first-rate dwarf conifers.

- *Thuja occidentalis* 'Danica' (white cedar). Dark green foliage turns blue-green in winter; grows to 30 inches (75 cm). Also look for 'Little Gem', which has a pyramidal shape and emerald-green foliage and grows 12 inches (30 cm) high, making it an excellent plant for a planter on a patio; 'Little Champion', which has soft bright green foliage; and 'Little Giant', a stocky shrub that keeps its bright green look in winter and grows to 42 inches (105 cm).
- *Picea glauca* 'Conica' (dwarf Albert spruce). This slow-growing, cone-shaped spruce has bright green new growth that turns gray-green with age. It can be kept under 7 feet (2 m) high.
- *Picea pungens* 'Globosa' (globe blue spruce). This has striking silver-blue needles and forms a compact mound about 3 feet (90 cm) high. It is available in a short tree form.
- *Picea mariana* 'Nana' ('Blue Nest' spruce). Grows to 2 feet (60 cm) and forms a "nest" of blue-green needles. Also consider 'Nest' (*Picea abies* 'Nidiformis'), which has dark green needles.

   🐾 *Pinus mugo* (mugho pine). One of the most common evergreens used in low-maintenance schemes, this offers excellent texture contrast. It is slow-growing to 4 feet (1.2 m) but it can be kept lower. Also consider the dwarf Scots pine (*Pinus sylvestris* 'Glauca Nana') or the dwarf mugho pine (*Pinus mugo* 'Pumilo'), which is fairly shade tolerant.

   🐾 *Taxus cuspidata* (dwarf spreading Japanese yew). This has dense, dark green foliage. It grows only 4 feet (1.2 m) high but can be kept shorter and more compact.

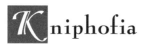niphofia

Common name: *Red-hot poker, torch lily*

Chief characteristics

Red-hot pokers are exotic, architectural plants. Kniphofia 'Royal Castle Hybrids' is one of the best. It has attractive mounds of evergreen, daylily-like foliage and in June sends up tall, two-tone flower stalks of yellow tipped with orange-red. The tops of the stiff, 3-foot-long (90-cm), "poker" stems are composed of dozens of tiny tubular flowers. The plant gets its common name from the look of the thick stems, which appear like hot pokers just drawn from the fire of a forge. Sensational for about a month, the flowers slowly lose their color, at which time the pokers need to be cut out.

> **Location:** Full sun
> **Type:** Perennial
> **Size:** 3 feet (90 cm)
> **Conditions:** Moist, well-drained soil
> **Flowering time:** June to August
> **Zone:** 5

Native to South Africa, kniphofia is a moderately drought-tolerant plant. It will flourish in a hot, sunny border in average soil that is reasonably moisture retentive. There are many good cultivars available. Some bloom in early summer, some in the middle of summer, others at the end of summer and into fall. When buying kniphofia, you need to decide what time of the year you want to see the torch-like flowers. Colors range from lemon-yellow to orange to rose-red to the popular two-tones.

For spring or early summer flowering, look for 'Alcazar' (orange), 'Bressingham Torch' (orange-yellow), 'Earliest of All' (coral-red) and 'Royal Castle Hybrids' (yellow-orange). For midsummer flowering, look for 'Jenny Bloom' (yellow-orange), 'Firefly' (orange-red), 'Shining Sceptre' (golden orange), 'Primrose Beauty' (yellow), 'Royal Standard' (brilliant red and yellow), 'Bressingham Comet' (yellow and orange) and 'Little Maid' (ivory and light yellow). For late summer/early fall, look for 'Bee's Lemon', 'Ice Queen', 'Cobra', 'Wayside Flame', 'Underway' and 'Fiery Fred'.

Where to plant it

The perfect plant for the sunny perennial border, kniphofia needs to be supported at the front and rear by plants that can take over when the poker flowers have gone. The mound of green leaves that is left is not particularly unattractive but neither does it add much to the garden once the flowers are over. So it is best placed a little back from the front of the border to allow for suitable companion planting.

How to care for it

The secret is to plant in well-drained soil in a spot where it also is protected from severe frosts. The leaves can be tied up over winter to reduce the amount of water and cold getting into the central crown. Just untie and clean them up in early spring. Clumps can be divided in March every few years.

Good companions

Liatris will send up spikes of purple or white flowers after kniphofia has finished flowering. Daylilies combine nicely, compensating for the kniphofia's loss of flowers with their own tall flower stems. Daylily leaves also blend perfectly with kniphofia's foliage. Other possible companions include the sulphur-yellow flowers of *Achillea* 'Moonshine', the red and orange blooms of *Crocosmia* 'Lucifer', 'Bressingham Beacon' and 'Firebird' and the blues of globe thistle (*Echinops ritro*) or sea holly (*Eryngium alpinum*). Late summer–flowering grasses like purple-leafed fountain grass (*Pennisetum setaceum* 'Rubrum') and late summer–flowering perennials like black-eyed susan and *Aster* × *frikartii* would also make good companions.

For your collection

Orange is not the easiest color to place in the garden, but if you wanted to create an orange monocolor garden, there are lots of suitable kniphofia cultivars. One of the best is 'Orange Torch', which was cultivated by the famous English plantswoman Beth Chatto, a lover of kniphofia, especially the yellow-green 'Little Maid', one of her own selections.

ℒavandula angustifolia

Common name: English lavender

Chief characteristics

You don't have to grow heaps of lavender in your garden, but you probably should grow a clump or two. Lavender has been a mainstay in gardens for as long as gardens have existed. Over the centuries, it has transcended mere popularity and entrenched itself as much more than an aromatic herb. It has risen to a place of honor accorded few plants in horticulture. Today, it has almost a defining presence, giving a garden, large or small, the stamp of authenticity and credibility. A favorite in the organized floral chaos of English cottage gardens for generations, lavender has a long history of supplying its powerful fragrance for use in sachets to freshen fusty closets and wardrobes and as a key ingredient in potpourris for sweetening the air in stuffy rooms. It is now used in aromatherapy, where its old nickname, the "herb of devotion," is taking on a whole new meaning.

Location: Full sun
Type: Evergreen shrub
Size: 18 to 24 inches (45 to 60 cm)
Conditions: Well-drained soil
Flowering time: June to August
Zone: 4

Lavender's primary scent is located in the dense clusters of tiny light blue or purple flowers. These are tightly bound together at the top of slender grasslike stalks that rise up above thick clumps of grayish-green foliage. One of the most intense and familiar of all garden aromas, the fragrance is released by brushing the flower stalks or foliage with your hand.

There are more than 25 different types of lavender. The best are two cultivars of *Lavandula angustifolia*—'Hidcote', which has bluish-purple flowers on long, tumbling stalks; and 'Munstead', which has violet-blue flowers. 'Sarah' is very similar to 'Munstead' but grows a little taller and has larger flowers that bloom longer. There are also pink forms, 'Loddon Pink' and 'Jean Davies'. One of the very best new lavender cultivars is *L. angustifolia* 'Lady', an All-American Selections winner in 1994. 'Lady' can be grown from seed and will produce beautiful lavender spikes the first year.

Where to plant it

Drainage is crucial. Nothing kills lavender faster than boggy, waterlogged soil. Native to the Mediterranean region, it thrives in full sun in well-drained soil. Its love for dry places makes it very useful for covering drought-prone slopes and exposed sunny sides of paths. You can plant it as a special feature or grow it as a low hedge or driveway edging. It will also grow very happily in a pot.

How to care for it

Plant lavender properly and prune it routinely and forget about it. The secret to keeping lavender healthy and bushy is to clip the flower stalks back once the blooms have faded in summer. Plants can also be pruned to tidy them up at the end of summer, and given a slightly harder pruning in spring after the buds have begun to break. Whatever you do, however, lavender will eventually become woody and ragged. Pruning back into the old wood rarely works, as buds have a difficult time breaking from old wood. You usually end up having to replace plants with new ones.

You may find "cuckoo spit" on the flower spikes in damp springs. The "spit" is home to a little green insect called a froghopper. You can wash it away or squish it between your fingers or ignore it because it doesn't do too much harm anyway.

Good companions

Lavender fits in beautifully around roses and looks good sharing ground with blue ornamental grasses like *Festuca glauca* 'Elijah Blue' or the blue flower spikes of *Salvia* 'May Night' or 'East Friesland'. *Sedum spectabile, Coreopsis grandiflora* 'Early Sunrise' and *Scabiosa columbaria* 'Butterfly Blue' or 'Pink Mint' all offer worthwhile partnerships. The soft purple heads of chives (*Allium schoenoprasum*) will combine very attractively with the deeper violet-blue of 'Hidcote' lavender.

For your collection

- *Lavandula stoechas* (Spanish lavender) is very beautiful. It has attractive, violet butterfly-like petals at the top of deeper purple, pineapple-shaped flowers. The blooms have a pleasant scent reminiscent of varnish. It is a lovely plant to grow in a pot, but needs to be brought into a frost-free place in winter, not being hardy enough to survive outside.
- *Lavandula dentata* (French lavender) is also a good container plant with fragrant flowers. It needs to be brought indoors in winter.

*L*avatera trimestris 'Mont Blanc'

Common name: *Annual mallow*

Chief characteristics

The summer garden needs one or two special annuals to add splashes of color or simply a sense of fun and frivolity, drama and romance. I always manage to find room for a few snapdragons (ones with a dragon jaw for snapping), a pillar of sweetpeas (for their intoxicating fragrance) and a window box of petunias (for hummingbirds). There are, however, a few bedding plants that always strike me as doing more than is asked of them. They go the extra mile and seem to raise the value of the plants around them with their dynamic color and form.

Location: Full sun to light shade

Type: Annual

Size: 2 to 3 feet (60 to 90 cm)

Conditions: Ordinary, well-drained soil

Flowering time: June to September

One of the most eye-catching is *Lavatera trimestris* (annual mallow). Top cultivars to look for include 'Mont Blanc', which has pure white, trumpet-shaped flowers; 'Silver Cup', which has rose-pink flowers; and 'Pink Beauty', which has pastel-pink blooms with wine-red veining. All three grow to about 2 or 3 feet (60 to 90 cm) and are easily propagated from seed indoors and transplanted in spring. The special beauty of 'Mont Blanc' is that, like all brilliant white flowers, the flowers stand out like a soft light in the garden at twilight. White flowers are always popular for this reason. They add such a lovely sense of romance and calm to the evening garden and make it so enchanting to walk in, especially if you have a few candles burning here and there.

If you want to try a shrub form, *Lavatera thuringiaca* 'Barnsley' (tree mallow) is a shrub lavatera. It is an exceptionally lovely plant, but tender in all but the warmest areas of Zone 6. Nevertheless, it is worth pushing the botanical envelope and 'Barnsley' can always be grown in a container and overwintered that way. What makes it so desirable is its lovely white-pink hollyhock-like flowers. Grow it in a sunny spot in your garden and it will quickly swell up to become a substantial bush, reaching 6 or even 8 feet (1.8 to 2.4 m). 'Barnsley' gets its name from Barnsley House, the home and garden in Gloucester, England, of one of Britain's most respected garden experts, Rosemary Verey. The plant first surfaced in 1985 and has since become an international favorite. There are a few other notable cultivars of *Lavatera thuringiaca*: 'Kew Rose' has deep pink flowers; 'Burgundy Wine' has purplish-red flowers; 'Ice Cool', which also goes under the name 'Peppermint Ice', has pure white flowers with attractive green centers; 'Bredon Springs' has rose-pink blooms with shallow-notched petals that give the flowers an unusual hexagonal shape; and 'Candy Floss' has bright pink flowers.

Where to plant it

Plant *Lavatera trimestris* 'Mont Blanc' in full sun or light shade in ordinary, well-drained soil. Since it grows only 2 feet (60 cm) high, you can risk bringing it very close to the front of your perennial border or use it to add light beneath shrubs such as *Viburnum* 'Summer Snowflake' or French lilacs that have finished flowering.

It is best to plant at least three to five plants to give the white hibiscus-like flowers greater impact. Or use 'Mont Blanc' as one of the ingredients in a half-barrel planting. Mix in some blue salvia (*Salvia farinacea*) and you have a lovely tub of color for your sunny patio or deck. If your garden center can't supply plants, start 'Mont Blanc' from seed indoors in March and transplant the seedlings in early May.

How to care for it

Space 'Mont Blanc' about 18 inches (45 cm) apart and deadhead (pinch away) the flowers regularly as they fade. This will encourage the plant to keep producing flowers all summer. Don't forget to water it, especially if you are growing it in a container. Water all your annuals with a half-strength solution of 20-20-20 fertilizer once or twice a week to keep them in tip-top shape.

Good companions

The white flowers of 'Mont Blanc' mix very nicely with ornamental grasses and summer-flowering perennials such as yellow coreopsis, red bee balm, echinacea and silver artemisia. Use 'Mont Blanc' to lend support to angel's trumpets or *Lantana camara* or to provide a backdrop to a soft gray carpet of lamb's ears.

For your collection

Here are two other white-flowering annuals you may want to find a spot for.

- *Cosmos bipinnatus* 'Sonata' is another special bedding plant with stunning white flowers that will do a similar job to 'Mont Blanc'. 'Sonata' grows 18 inches (45 cm) high and has feathery foliage, an added bonus.

- *Bacopa* 'Snowflake' is a beautiful white-flowering plant for use in hanging baskets or window boxes. One of the new generation of bedding plants introduced in the early 1990s, bacopa produces tiny white flowers against a lush backdrop of dense green foliage all summer long, from June to September.

- Coleus, once a firm favorite with Victorian gardeners, is another tender plant worth having fun with in your summer garden. It is making a big comeback as a plant for creating an exuberant, frivolous splash of color in the summer garden. The vibrant, multi-colored leaves may, at first glance, strike you as terribly garish, but you will be surprised how effective they can look when mass planted and carefully contrasted with varieties with simpler green-and-white or green-and-burgundy variegation. Look for 'Volcano' (bright red) or 'Black Dragon' (deep maroon with pink center). These look wonderful mixed in with other annuals that enjoy light sun or partial shade and they are very easy to propagate from cutting. Simply finger-pinch off a tip, pop it in water, and pot it up once the white roots have formed.

- *Amaranthus caudatus* (love-lies-bleeding) makes a dynamic centerpiece. It looks sensational, weeping its long blood-red tassels over low boxwood hedging or contrasted against a mass planting of blue annual salvia.

- *Zinnia* 'Profusion Orange' and *Zinnia* 'Profusion Cherry'. These two new varieties of zinnia have caused quite a stir, being awarded a gold medal by the All-American Selections judges for being a "breeding breakthrough." In AAS trial gardens all over North America, these trouble-free zinnias proved more resistant to mildew and leaf spot and they also produced striking cherry-red and tangerine-orange flowers all summer. They both perform very well in containers, offering wonderful, exotic colors for any balcony or deck. Grow them from seed or pester your garden center to get them in for you.

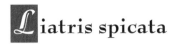iatris spicata

✓ **Common name:** *Gayfeather, blazing star*

Chief characteristics

Many new gardeners are astonished to discover they can actually grow liatris in their own garden. They are so used to seeing the slender, pokerlike, pinkish-purple flower spikes in florist shops and exotic flower arrangements, it comes as a surprise to learn the plant will thrive very nicely in sunny, well-drained sites in the open garden. Native to North America, liatris grows naturally in moist meadows and on the edges of marshes in sunny, open areas.

> **Location:** Full sun to light shade
> **Type:** Perennial
> **Size:** 2 to 3 feet (60 to 90 cm)
> **Conditions:** Ordinary, moist, well-drained soil
> **Flowering time:** July to September
> **Zone:** 2

Liatris is a welcome sight in the late summer garden. It brings a fresh burst of color and provides exciting vertical architecture in the flagging perennial border or cutflower garden. The most popular form is *Liatris spicata*, which has 2- to 3-foot (60- to 90-cm) spiky-leafed stems with pinkish-purple, bottlebrush flowers. 'Kobold' is a more compact form, growing only 18 to 24 inches (45 to 60 cm), which makes it a good candidate for the front of the border. You can also find a white liatris—'Floristan Violet'—which serves very well in an all-white scheme.

Where to plant it

Everyone talks about how liatris is so drought tolerant, yet it really grows best in free-draining soil that is able to retain moisture while allowing the plant to enjoy a full-sun exposure. This can pose a challenge when it comes to choosing an appropriate site. Liatris can easily be overwhelmed by more aggressive neighbors like shasta daisies, asters, daylilies and bee balm. So it is also important to plant it where it can be seen and enjoyed when it finally blooms in mid-July. It is an exceptional cut flower, if you can bear to leave the garden empty of its royal spikes.

How to care for it

Cold winters are no threat to *Liatris spicata*. It is hardy to Zone 2, but it won't tolerate waterlogged soil. Good drainage is essential.

Once the flowers appear, you want them to be seen, so you may have to clear away the foliage of other perennials to give liatris its day. When flowers fade, cut the stems down for neatness.

The plant will disappear completely in winter and it's not a fast plant out of the ground in spring, which can be a problem. It is easy to forget it was ever there and dig it up accidentally in the spring while finding slots for new perennials. It is best to mark its place in the garden at the end of summer. Clumps can be divided every few years.

Good companions

The spectacular blue spheres of globe thistle and steel-blue flowers of sea holly both come into flower around the same time as liatris in July and are even more drought tolerant. Other good partners for liatris include *Phlox paniculata*, yarrow, *Crocosmia* 'Lucifer', black-eyed susans, *Anaphalis* (pearly everlasting) and *Aster dumosus* 'Lady in Blue' or *A.* × *frikartii* 'Monch'.

For your collection

There are a few excellent plants with purple flowers worth collecting.

- *Astilbe chinensis* 'Purple Lance' has large, bright purple flower plumes in August. Also look for 'Superba' which has softer, lavender-red plumes.
- *Echinacea* 'Magnus' has striking purple flowers in late summer that stand very solidly atop 30-inch (75-cm) stems.
- *Penstemon fruticosus* 'Purple Haze'. It has masses of tube-shaped purple flowers in June and is a very useful plant for cascading over walls and banks. It grows 8 inches (20 cm) tall.

*L*igularia stenocephala 'The Rocket'

Common name: *Ligularia*

Chief characteristics

Ligularia is a magnificent plant with spectacular flowers. The challenge is to get it to maturity without having it chewed to pieces by slugs.

There are two first-rate species you should get: *Ligularia stenocephala* ('The Rocket') and *L. dentata* ('Desdemona' or 'Othello'). Your garden will be all the richer for them. 'The Rocket' has soaring yellow-gold flower spikes similar in shape to

Location: Shade to semi-shade

Type: Perennial

Size: 4 to 6 feet (1.2 to 1.8 m)

Conditions: Good, moist soil

Flowering time: June to August

Zone: 3

foxgloves or foxtail lilies while 'Othello' and 'Desdemona' have spreading heads of golden yellow, star-shaped flowers. All three have great foliage, but 'Desdemona' and 'Othello' are noted for their exceptional, big, purple-black leaves. Both species are summer flowering. 'The Rocket' blooms slightly earlier than 'Desdemona' or 'Othello', which flower at the end of July and continue into September.

Yellow can be a difficult color to place, but the warm golden yellow flowers of 'The Rocket' are easy on the eye. They also bring architectural strength and height to the summer garden.

Where to plant it

Grow 'The Rocket' in the bog garden or at the back of the shade border in a spot where it has plenty of room to spread sideways. It also needs open space above so nothing interferes with its soaring yellow flower spires. It flourishes nicely in dappled shade beside a stream in a woodland setting. In bright shade it will look healthy and happy until the warm late-morning sun touches its large leaves. Then it will slump and look wilty and miserable even if the ground is watered copiously. However, once the sun has slipped by and 'The Rocket' is again in the shade, it will perk up and resume its previous splendid form.

The lesson in all of this is to locate 'The Rocket' in a shady spot where it gets light but not a lot of heat, and in soil that never dries out.

How to care for it

Slugs are the biggest problem with growing ligularia. They simply cannot resist its leaves, which have been described as "cheesecake for slugs." The young leaves of both kinds of ligularia need to be diligently inspected and protected from the moment they appear. Slugs are so intent on eating the tasty leaves, they will find a way over the sharpest and most threatening of obstacles. The only real defence is to patrol at night with a flashlight and a pair of sharp scissors.

Heavy rain can knock over the flower spikes of 'The Rocket', leaving it looking rather disheveled. Staking is not always necessary but it's not a bad idea if it can be done unobtrusively. A lot of the time the flowers get adequate support from the plant's own muscular, rough-cut leaves.

Good companions

Rodgersia, hosta, astilbe and ferns are all robust companions for 'The Rocket'. Primroses, lysimachia, astrantia and polygonum also make good partners.

For your collection

- ❧ *Rheum palmatum* 'Atrosanguineum' (ornamental rhubarb). If you are interested in collecting big, bold plants, check this plant out. In addition to having gigantic leaves, it also has bright crimson flower plumes in June.
- ❧ *Macleaya cordata* (plume poppy). You will also want this plant, which has gray-green leaves and can jump up to a mature height of 7 feet (2.1 m). It produces white flowers from July to August.
- ❧ *Gunnera manicata*. This is the grand-daddy of all bog plants. It can drink a lake by itself. It is the perfect plant for setting on the edge of a sizable pond or the edge of a stream.

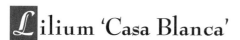 **ilium 'Casa Blanca'**

Common name: *Casa Blanca lily*

Chief characteristics

Location: Full sun to light shade
Type: Bulb
Size: 4 feet (1.2 m)
Conditions: Good, deep, well-drained soil
Flowering time: July to August
Zone: 3

There are almost as many types of lily as there are roses. It is an enormous family. If you get into a conversation with a lily expert, you are going to hear about American hybrids, Harlequin hybrids, Aurelian hybrids. It is perfectly understandable if you feel overwhelmed. The lily family is vast and full of exotic specimens, producing some of the most dazzling, fragrant, exotic and tropical-looking flowers in the summer garden.

Selection usually comes down to a matter of color and style. Height can also be a factor. Lilies can be tiny and delicate, or gigantic. Most of the popular ones range in size from 3 to 6 feet (90 to 180 cm). There are three main flower forms: trumpet-shaped, bowl-shaped (with petals curved slightly back) and turk's-cap (petals curved fully back on themselves). Colors range from orange to pink, from white to purple. Some lilies have two-tone speckled flowers like the familiar tiger lily (*Lilium lancifolium*), which has orange petals with black spots. (It is also known as *L. tigrinum*.)

Increasingly popular are the Asiatic hybrids, of which the pure white 'Casa Blanca' lily is one of the best. It is fragrant, grows 4 feet (120 cm) high, and is a very easy color to place in the garden. It is one of the show-stopping bloomers that gives the garden a much-needed lift of drama and scent in late summer. Other outstanding Asiatic cultivars include 'Stargazer' (fragrant, strawberry-pink throat with a creamy white edge), 'Monte Negro' (dark red), 'Enchantment' (orange), 'Elite' (orange), 'Connecticut King' (yellow), 'Citronella' (yellow), 'Paprika' (red), 'Cote d'Azur' (pink) and 'Apollo' (white).

Trumpet lilies (*Aurelians*) are midsummer bloomers with large flowers that can easily stretch to 8 inches (20 cm) long. One of the best is 'African Queen' (apricot-orange). Other quality performers include 'Pink Perfection' (pink), 'Golden Splendour' (pure yellow) and 'Regale' (white).

Where to plant it

Grow lilies among perennials or alone in pots on the patio. They are one of the plants that really should be used more to add color to the midsummer garden.

Lilies will tolerate average soil, but they always need good drainage. For the best effect, plant in large groups in the middle or at the back of the perennial border in full sun or light shade. Like clematis, lilies prefer to have their heads in the sun and their roots in the shade. You will keep your lilies happy if they are shielded at the base from the hot afternoon sun.

How to care for it

Plant bulbs 6 to 9 inches (15 to 23 cm) deep. The rule of thumb is to put them down to a depth three times the thickness of the bulb. Lilies are not bothered by cold, wet winters, but they will rot in poorly drained ground. However, they will also not do well if left without moisture in fast-draining, dry, sandy soil.

Taller plants need to be staked or they will flop over the moment the flowers appear. They are really not as temperamental as all this sounds and can be used to make a spectacular showing throughout the growing season.

Good companions

Contrast is the name of the game with lilies. They can be planted to provide striking color combinations with roses, hydrangeas, peonies and perennials such as late-flowering astilbes, *Phlox paniculata*, white gooseneck loosestrife, echinacea or *Monarda* 'Marshall's Delight', 'Prairie Night' or 'Gardenview Scarlet'. Use lilies to inject color into those areas of the perennial border that need a lift in midsummer.

For your collection

🐦 Lily connoisseurs delight in the reasonably hard-to-find Martagon Hybrids because of their distinctive turk's cap flowers that are displayed in graceful, nodding clusters. Look for the pure white *Lilium martagon album*, which has escaped the family curse of rank odor and has a very pleasant smell.

🐦 The Madonna lily (*Lilium candidum*) has very fragrant white flowers with yellow stamens in the center. It grows 4 or 5 feet (1.2 to 1.5 m) high and thrives in soil sweetened by wood ashes. You can also achieve a similar scent by growing *Hosta plantaginea*, which has fragrant white flowers in late summer.

🐦 There are three pollen-free lilies now available for growing in pots on balconies and decks. They are 'White Kiss' (white), 'Aphrodite' (pale pink) and 'Fata Morgana' (golden yellow). They all grow about 2 feet (60 cm) tall.

🐦 Lily-turf (*Liriope spicata*) is not a lily at all, but a grass-like ground-cover. It has short lavender flower spikes from July to August. Hardy to Zone 6, it grows to 8 inches (20 cm).

*L*onicera japonica 'Halliana'

Common name: *Hall's honeysuckle*

Chief characteristics

Location: Sun or part shade
Type: Deciduous vine
Size: 15 feet (4.5 m)
Conditions: Ordinary, well-drained soil
Flowering time: June to October
Zone: 4

Every English-style garden has honeysuckle. It is as important to the total garden picture as roses, clematis, shrubs or perennials. Without a freewheeling tangle of bright-flowered honeysuckle, a summer garden seems somehow incomplete. The vine not only saturates the air with delectable perfume, it brings a relaxed balance to the stiffer, more formal structures of the garden. Honeysuckle is a reliable worker, vigorously smothering walls or fences, trellises and arbors with attractive, soft green foliage. The heavily scented flowers, ranging from creamy white to reddish-purple to pale yellow, are a wonderful added bonus.

The most popular is *Lonicera japonica* 'Halliana', better known as Hall's honeysuckle. It is the best all-purpose honeysuckle, quickly scampering to 15 feet (4.5 m) high by 10 feet (3 m) wide and producing extremely fragrant white flowers that eventually turn a golden yellow.

Other species, such as the yellow-flowering *L.* × *tellmanniana* and red-flowering *L.* × *brownii*, have excellent flower color, but no scent.

Other top forms of honeysuckle include scarlet-trumpet honeysuckle (*Lonicera* × *brownii* 'Dropmore Scarlet'), which has rich red blooms; *L.* × *heckrottii* 'Goldflame', which has yellow-pink flowers; purple-leafed Japanese honeysuckle (*L. japonica* 'Purpurea'), a semi-evergreen cultivar valued for its foliage rather than its purple-red flowers; and late-blooming Dutch honeysuckle (*L. periclymenum* 'Serotina'), which produces blooms that are red-purple on the outside and pinkish-yellow on the inside. Any of these attractive vines will do well in medium-sized gardens.

Where to plant it

Ideal for growing on fences, trellises, arbors and arches, honeysuckle can also be used to cover banks as a groundcover. Plant vines in spring to early summer. Honeysuckle needs six hours of sun but, like clematis, they also prefer to have shaded roots. The sugary scent of honeysuckle can travel on the night air right across the garden, so there is no need to have the vine situated directly under windows or next to doorways.

How to care for it

Young shoots of a new plant need support to get started up a trellis or fence. You can use canes or wires or sturdy black thread. Prune severely in spring and lightly in summer to keep it in bounds. Left unpruned, honeysuckle will suffer dieback in the center because of the lack of air flow and light. Aphids can be a problem, particularly in hot, dry summers. Use a strong jet of water to knock them off or bring in some ladybugs. Frequent visits by hummingbirds are a major compensation.

Good companions

Early-flowering clematis, *Clematis alpina* 'Jacqueline du Pre' or 'Pamela Jackman', or *C. macropetala* 'Bluebird', can be encouraged to intermingle with honeysuckle and put on an early spring flowering, leading into honeysuckle's summer performance. To provide shade for roots, you could use *Geranium macrorrhizum* or *Corydalis lutea* as a groundcover.

For your collection

There are many types of honeysuckles worth trying.

🌣 *Lonicera* 'Mandarin'. This new introduction is hardy to Zone 4 and has large, intensely orange flowers in July. It is a cross between *L. tragophylla* and the popular 'Dropmore Scarlet', drawing vigor and beauty from both parents.

- 🐌 *Lonicera periclymenum* 'Graham Thomas'— another late-blooming Dutch honeysuckle—has yellow blooms and a spicy fragrance.
- 🐌 *Lonicera tragophylla* (Chinese honeysuckle) is also highly regarded as one of the most outstanding, producing extra large golden-yellow flowers in June and July.

upinus Russell Hybrids

Common name: *Russell lupins*

Chief characteristics

There was a time when lupins were regarded as coarse, wild flowers, not suitable for the civilized flower garden. That changed with George Russell, a patient Yorkshire gardener who earlier this century took time to grow all kinds of wild lupins, allowing them to freely mix and mingle. That experiment resulted in a whole new generation of exciting hybrids. Today, many gardeners consider lupins necessary in their planting scheme.

Location: Sun or semi-shade
Type: Perennial
Size: 3 feet (90 cm)
Conditions: Moist, well-drained, neutral soil
Flowering time: June to July
Zone: 4

Like delphiniums and foxgloves, lupins add height, color and attractive architectural form to the perennial border. They are particularly outstanding when planted in large, sweeping drifts. Their tall, distinctive, tapering spikes of tightly clustered flowers have a classical, well-behaved elegance that makes them the very model of a border plant. The range of colors extends from rose, pink and red to white, yellow and assorted vibrant bicolors. The Russell Hybrids are still among the best and most reliable. Top hybrids include 'Mrs. Micklethwaite' (named after the woman whose garden George Russell tended), 'Elsie Waters', 'La Chatelaine', 'Magnificence', 'My Castle' and 'Limelight'.

Where to plant it

Grow lupins in neutral to slightly acidic, well-drained, sandy soil in clumps at the front or in the middle of the perennial border or in dense sweeping drifts. They are spectacular in the late spring/early summer garden, but can look a little tatty once they have finished flowering. It is best to associate them with plants that will grow up in front of them and flower in midsummer.

How to care for it

Short-lived, lupins last no longer than a couple of seasons. To ensure you always have a few, it is usually necessary to grow standby plants from seed or get into the habit of picking up new plants every spring.

Slugs and snails can be a nuisance, so watch for them, especially when the plants are emerging in spring. Mildew can be a problem in hot, humid summers. You can minimize it by not allowing the soil to dry out and by thinning the foliage to improve air circulation.

Cut off the flower stems before the seed pods develop and you can often stimulate a second flush of blooms later in the summer.

Good companions

A generous clump of lupins can share ground with poppies and phlox, penstemon and campanulas. They mix well with the blue flowers of baptisia and contrast warmly against the golden yellow foliage of hostas or rising up behind the silver leaves of lamb's ears.

For your collection

- *Lupinus arboreus* (tree lupin) is a short-lived semi-evergreen shrub that grows to between 5 and 7 feet (1.5 to 2.1 m) high and produces fragrant primrose-yellow blooms from July to October.
- *Lupinus polyphyllus*. You may want to find room for one of North America's own indigenous species, which was one of the species George Russell (and other top hybridizers) used to raise some of his best modern hybrids. This lupin has deep blue to reddish-purple flowers and can grow as high as 5 feet (1.5 m).

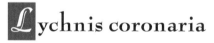ychnis coronaria

Common name: *Rose campion, catchfly*

Chief characteristics

New gardeners always fall in love with *Lychnis coronaria* when they see it for the first time. What they like best are the lovely rose-magenta or white flowers, displayed in loose sprays at the ends of slender pale gray stems. The word *Lychnis* is derived from the Greek *lychnos*, which means lamp and refers to the brightness of the flowers. The plant is now as common in many gardens as

Location: Full sun or light shade
Type: Perennial
Size: 2 feet (60 cm)
Conditions: Average, well-drained soil
Flowering time: June to August
Zone: 3

foxgloves and roses. In a mass planting scheme, the silver-gray foliage of rose campion provides a pleasing canvas of color on which to exhibit the deep pink flowers. A relative of carnation (*Dianthus*), the best-known campion is Maltese cross or cross of Jerusalem (*Lychnis chalcedonica*), which has dazzling clusters of scarlet flowers and grows 3 to 4 feet (90 to 120 cm) high. But *L. coronaria*, especially the white version, 'Alba', is now being seen more often in private gardens.

Where to plant it

The dainty rose-magenta flowers of *Lychnis coronaria* catch the eye wherever they appear. The plant looks best tucked behind other plants in the perennial border, such as short forms of yarrow, blue centaurea or lavender, or popping up from behind a low boxwood hedge or dotted among the green foliage of still-developing perennials.

How to care for it

Campion needs to be regularly deadheaded in order to keep it blooming. It grows best in full sun and prefers ordinary, or even poor, soil, as long as it is well drained. It will also flourish reasonably well in light shade.

It is easy to propagate from seed. Not a long-lived plant, it often self-sows and succeeds in propagating itself around the garden. If you don't want it to self-sow, snip off the dead flowerheads before they turn to seed. Cut the stems down once flowering has finished.

Good companions

The vivid blue spikes of *Salvia farinacea* or *Nepeta* 'Dropmore Blue' offer an interesting contrast to campion's small red-magenta flowers. The blooms look striking set against the burgundy-plum leaves of a smoke bush (*Cotinus coggygria*) or mingled with the feathery silver foliage of *Artemisia ludoviciana* 'Valerie Finnis' or 'Silver King'. It can also be harmonized with penstemons and shrub roses.

For your collection

- *Lychnis alpina* (Arctic campion) is ideal for the spring rockery, growing only 6 inches (15 cm) high and producing tufts of green leaves and pink flowers from May to June.
- *Lychnis × arkwrightii* 'Vesuvius' has red-orange flowers, grows 18 inches (45 cm) tall and is a good cut flower.
- *Lychnis flos-jovis* (Jove's flower) has small clusters of purple or red flowers. It grows 24 inches (60 cm) high, quickly naturalizes and combines well with mock orange and hydrangeas.

ℒysimachia clethroides

Common name: *Gooseneck loosestrife, Chinese loosestrife*

Chief characteristics

Location: Sun or part shade
Type: Perennial
Size: 3 feet (90 cm)
Conditions: Ordinary, moist soil
Flowering time: July to September
Zone: 3

A superb cut flower, *Lysimachia clethroides* is admired for its distinctive white blooms that resemble the head and neck of a goose. A substantial clump in the summer garden can be quite dramatic, especially when there is a slight breeze that causes the shapely goosenecks to nod gently in unison in the same direction. The spectacle is enchanting.

Lysimachia clethroides should not be confused with purple loosestrife (*Lythrum*), which is a terrible imported weed that has taken over many of our lake and marsh areas. The cheerful gooseneck loosestrife does, however, have one downside—it is an incorrigible colonizer. But it can be restrained in the most basic way—dig the clump back into bounds the same way you do with a rampant clump of mint when it starts to get out of hand. Gooseneck loosestrife first appears in spring as tiny red shoots in the ground. It quickly jumps up 2 or 3 feet (60 to 90 cm) to form a lush patch of leaves. The white flowers, which are actually composed of hundreds of smaller star-shaped flowers with black centers, appear from early July to the end of September. A native of China and Japan, *L. clethroides* found its way to Europe many years ago and has now become a part of the natural landscape.

Where to plant it

Grow *Lysimachia clethroides* in fertile, moist garden soil in full or partial shade. It has even been used in water gardens, but it probably prefers being on the banks of a stream, pond or brook.

How to care for it

It will reward you if you dig in lots of compost when you plant it. Divide clumps every 3 or 4 years or whenever you feel your loosestrife is getting carried away with itself. The flowers can be cut any time. They do look exquisite indoors mixed with hosta leaves, liatris, summer phlox, roses and daylilies. In the fall, the leaves will die back and you will know it is time to clean up. But what a fun party it was.

Good companions

The plants you pick to mix with *Lysimachia clethroides* will need to have height and solid form if they are going to hold their own. The lovely white-flowering *Campanula lactiflora* will blend nicely, flower earlier while the lysimachia is still developing, and disappear before the gooseneck flowers appear. This gives you continuity of color. Blue bellflower (*Campanula persicifolia*), *Helleborus argutifolius* and peonies also bloom before lysimachia. For direct contrast, use the blue flowers of aconitum, the yellow blooms of rudbeckia or the pink flowers of *Lavatera thuringiaca* 'Bredon Springs' or 'Kew Rose'. The solid form of *Sedum spectabile* 'Brilliant' or *Sedum* 'Autumn Joy' can provide structure and a cover for the uninteresting lower part of loosestrife's flower stems.

For your collection

- *Lysimachia nummularia* (moneywort or creeping jenny) is a trailing, groundcovering plant that can also be used in window boxes and hanging baskets. It is a natural cover for moist, light shade areas.
- *Lysimachia punctata* is a bushy plant that produces masses of yellow flowers from June to August and grows about 2 feet (60 cm) high. It also likes moist soil and is an excellent choice for growing in sunny spots at the side of a pond or stream, although it will also perform perfectly well in light shade.

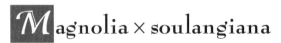

*M*agnolia × soulangiana

Common name: *Saucer magnolia*

Chief characteristics

English garden guru Christopher Lloyd called magnolias "the most glamorous and effective of all shrubs or trees." He added: "There is room for at least one specimen in every garden." There is no arguing with that. Magnolias have long been regarded by garden authorities everywhere as classy, aristocratic plants with exquisite flowers and handsome foliage. There is a record of magnolias being grown extensively in gardens as early as 650 A.D. when Buddhist monks planted *Magnolia denudata*, with its striking white flowers, at temples to symbolize purity.

Location: Sun or light shade

Type: Deciduous tree or shrub

Size: 15 to 25 feet (4.5 to 7.5 m)

Conditions: Ordinary, well-drained soil

Flowering time: May to June

Zone: 5

There are many popular magnolias. We all have our favorite. The saucer magnolia (*M.* × *soulangiana*) is one of the most reliable. It flowers for four weeks in late spring with creamy white, goblet-shaped blooms, flushed with purplish-pink. It can be grown as a bush in the mixed border or as a stand-alone tree. The foliage, which is a lush and pleasant green, comes after the flowers. It is sometimes called "tulip tree" because of the shape and color of the flowers. Popular cultivars include 'Alexandrina', 'Coates' and 'Rustica Rubra'.

Where to plant it

Magnolia × *soulangiana* grows happily in moisture-retentive, well-drained soil, where it can enjoy full sun in the mornings and semi-shade after lunch. Once established, magnolias can be difficult to relocate, so it is important to take your time picking the right spot. The flowers of *M.* × *soulangiana* are beautiful against the dark background of a yew or cedar hedge. They last longer if given some protection from wind and driving rains. *M.* × *soulangiana* can be worked into a mixed border or planted as a special feature in a formal lawn.

How to care for it

Grow magnolias in fast-draining soil and water well in the summer. They also like to be fed well, so add enriching organic material—fertilizer or well-rotted compost—to the soil every spring, but be sure not to disturb the magnolia's roots. Heavy pruning is discouraged because magnolias bleed and have a problem bouncing back, but light pruning can be done after flowering in midsummer.

Good companions

In the mixed border, magnolias harmonize with rhododendrons, evergreen azaleas and *Pieris japonica*.

For your collection

- The Little Girl Hybrids, developed at the U.S. National Arboretum in the mid-'50s, are gaining popularity because their compact size makes them useful in small gardens. They are hardy to Zone 5 and all have a sturdy frame, reaching 6 to 8 feet (1.8 to 2.4 m) at maturity. Look for 'Randy' (reddish-purple flowers) or 'Ricki', which has similar flowers to 'Randy' only larger and slightly twisted. To complete your Little Girl series, you will also need 'Susan' and 'Betty'.
- *Magnolia denudata* 'White Yulan' (Yulan magnolia) is a small, rounded tree with very fragrant, white, cup-shaped flowers in May and striking fall foliage. The buds need some protection from late frost.

- Magnolias with bright white star-like flowers include Kobus magnolia (*M. kobus*), which produces slightly more substantial flowers, although they have been described as "dirty white" compared to the clear white blooms of the more familiar *M. stellata* and the graceful anise magnolia (*M. salicifolia*). The cultivar 'Wada's Memory' has a very high rating for the whiteness and abundance of its blooms.

- *Magnolia* × *loebneri* 'Leonard Messel' has masses of 12-petaled purple-pink flowers in early May and attractive green foliage all summer, turning yellow in fall. It grows to 15 feet (4.5 m) at maturity. Also consider *Magnolia* × *loebneri* 'Merrill', which has a similar growth habit as *M. stellata* but is slightly more vigorous and has larger, 15-petaled white flowers in May.

- *Magnolia sieboldii* is loved by plant connoisseurs because of its classy, pure white, lightly fragrant, cup-shaped blooms. It also has delicately colored green leaves. You can grow it as a tree or a shrub but since it has a spread of 15 feet (4.5 m) high and wide, you need a fair amount of space in your garden to accommodate it properly. The fragrance of the flowers has been described as being like a flavorsome bouquet of pineapple-orange lilies.

- *Magnolia stellata* (star magnolia) has a profusion of pure white, multi-petaled flowers in early spring. A small tree, it grows 10 feet (3 m) and is a good choice for gardens where space is limited. Look for 'Royal Star'.

*M*iscanthus sinensis 'Gracillimus'

Common name: *Maiden grass*

Chief characteristics

Miscanthus is not an ornamental grass to trifle with. It can be big and bold and dramatic and you need to find the right spot for it to look its best. In the right place, this very expressive grass will make a powerful architectural statement. One of the tidiest and most versatile forms is *Miscanthus sinensis* 'Gracillimus'. It can be easily accommodated in a medium-sized garden and will quickly form a magnificent cascading clump of thin, straplike blades. The dwarf form, 'Yaku Jima',

Location: Full sun to light shade
Type: Ornamental grass
Size: 4 to 6 feet (1.2 to 1.8 m)
Conditions: Good, moist soil
Flowering time: August to September
Zone: 5

grows to only 3 or 4 feet (90 to 120 cm) and has silvery plumes in late summer. This is a good choice for gardens where space is limited.

Other top cultivars of *Miscanthus sinensis* include the novel 'Zebrinus' (zebra grass), which has bright green leaves with golden, horizontal zebra-like stripes; 'Silver Feather' (silver feather grass), which has tall, white plumes, very much like pampas grass; and 'Variegatus' (Japanese silver grass), which forms a striking fountain of silver-green cascading leaves. All these are worth experimenting with, although you will probably only want one.

Where to plant it

'Gracillimus' is best used to give the garden a special accent or focal point. It can punctuate the flow in a perennial border, or it can be placed at measured intervals to create a recurring theme. It can also be useful for screening less attractive corners of the garden.

The idea of incorporating ornamental grasses into your planting scheme is primarily to provide visual and textural relief. Grasses bring movement as they sway in the breeze and they refract sunlight in ways that add unexpected dimensions to the overall look and atmosphere of the garden.

How to care for it

Maiden grass can grow over 6 feet (1.8 m) tall but it is quite capable of standing without support. Grow it in full sun or semi-shade in moist soil and it will flourish. Leave it untouched at the end of summer and by winter many of the cascading blades will be the color of straw. After a heavy frost or light snowfall, it will look astonishingly ethereal with a pale, ghostly beauty.

Good companions

Maiden grass combines well with other hardy grasses, such as the equally decorative *Pennisetum* 'Hameln', short clumping dwarf moor grass (*Molinia caerulea*), the eye-catching blue grass *Festuca glauca* 'Elijah Blue' or blue oat grass (*Helictotrichon sempervirens*). The bold, swordlike leaves of *Crocosmia* 'Lucifer' make an exciting foliage contrast and the bright red flowers add an engaging theatrical touch. Consider using big-leafed hostas like 'Sum and Substance' or vase-shaped forms like 'Krossa Regal', again for textural tension and focal interest.

For color, yellow rudbeckia and stonecrop make ideal partners. For more subtle colors, try the blues of *Iris sibirica* 'Caesar's Brother', the purples of liatris or the gentle hues of late-flowering Japanese anemones like 'September Charm' or 'Honorine Jobert'.

For your collection

- Other excellent cultivars of *Miscanthus sinensis* include 'Strictus' (porcupine grass), which grows to 5 feet (1.5 m); 'Silberpfeil' (silver arrow miscanthus); and 'Variegatus', which grows to 5 to 6 feet (1.5 to 1.8 m) tall and has distinctive green-and-white-striped, arching foliage.
- *Miscanthus floridulus* (giant Chinese silver grass) produces a massive towering fountain of leaves that can form a very effective screen 10 feet (3 m) tall or large grassy hedge if mass planted. If you have acreage, this is an awesome plant to have.
- *Hakonechloa macra* 'Aureola' is a particularly striking grass to try in a pot. It is slow-growing, mounding to 18 to 24 inches (45 to 60 cm), with two-tone green-yellow leaves that turn reddish-brown in fall.

Monarda 'Gardenview Scarlet'

Common name: *Bee balm, bergamot*

Chief characteristics

The flowers of monarda—bright red, candy pink or purplish-blue—are extraordinary works of art. They are displayed, very confidently, at the top of sturdy, 3- or 4-foot (90- to 120-cm) stems. The leaves are mildly aromatic when rubbed and have been used for generations in potpourris. But the main reason you should grow bee balm is for the flowers that add color and verve to the garden in July and August. A mature clump of monarda looks fantastic, especially contrasted with other spectacular summer-flowering perennials, such as shasta daisies, phlox, lavatera or blue globe thistle. The flower clusters of bee balm first begin to appear in early to mid-July and continue blooming into September. Each bloom is a masterpiece of creative design. Each flower is formed by more than a dozen smaller, open-throated, tubular flowers that look rather like snapping (or singing) crocodiles. These individual flowers form a cluster and explode in a fountain of color from a central crown that has small, downward-pointed leaves forming a decorative collar.

Location: Full to part sun
Type: Perennial
Size: 3 to 4 feet (90 to 120 cm)
Conditions: Good, moist, well-drained soil
Flowering time: July to September
Zone: 3

There are several fine cultivars available but *Monarda* 'Gardenview Scarlet' is an old tried-and-tested favorite with bright scarlet-red flowers.

A similar form called 'Cambridge Scarlet' is also an established favorite, but 'Gardenview Scarlet' is considered the superior performer. Two other top cultivars are 'Marshall's Delight', a Canadian hybrid with handsome candy pink flowers, and 'Prairie Night', which has dark purple flowers.

All the blooms make fine cut flowers and look rather exotic and tropical when combined with liatris, echinops and ligularia. Put the four together in a vase and you have brilliant red (*Monarda* 'Gardenview Scarlet'), lilac-purple (*Liatris spicata*), steel blue (*Echinops ritro*) and golden yellow (*Ligularia stenocephala*). It may sound like a jarring clash of colors, but each flower has the strength to maintain its own presence and individuality without detracting from that of the others, in a remarkable example of harmony and diversity.

Where to plant it

Grow monarda in large clumps in good, moist, well-drained soil, in full or part sun along with other sun-loving mid- to late summer–flowering perennials. It will flourish very happily in full sun next to a stream or on the edge of a bog garden.

Bee balm is not tall enough to go right at the back of the border, and it's far too tall for the front, so the middle of the border is the ideal location. This also allows you to grow shorter perennials or shrubs in front to hide bee balm's spindly stems.

As its name suggests, bee balm attracts bees. It also will catch the attention of butterflies and hummingbirds. Herbalists used its leaves to treat sore throats and bronchitis and to make a soothing tea. Bergamot is what gives Earl Grey tea its distinctive smell.

How to care for it

Don't let your bee balm go without water, especially in the hot days of summer. Make sure you mulch around the plants in spring as a moisture-conserving device, and water copiously during dry spells. Bee balm is also notorious for gobbling up all the nutrients in the soil. The solution is to mulch with well-rotted compost or manure in spring and again in late fall to replenish the soil. This is a good plant for reminding us that soil needs to be repeatedly amended and nourished with new organic material. The plant's greedy feeding habit can actually work for the good of all the other plants in the flower bed if it gets us into a routine of regular soil amendment.

Like *Phlox paniculata* and delphiniums, bee balm can be prone to mildew in late summer after a spell of hot weather. The problem is made much worse if the plants are not watered adequately at soil level and if there is poor air circulation. You can spray with a fungicide, but you may find mildew will only be a minor problem if you water carefully and plentifully and take a little time to thin out clumps to allow greater air flow. Cut down stems at the end of the season. Clumps can be easily divided every few years.

Good companions

In full bloom in July and August, bee balm combines well with delphiniums, globe thistle, sea holly, echinacea, daylilies, crocosmia and shasta daisies, all of which like similar conditions—lots of sun and soil that is well drained without drying out completely. The red flowers of 'Gardenview Scarlet' can be heightened by combining them with the deep purple foliage of *Cimicifuga* 'Brunette' or the blues of *Salvia farinacea*, *Nepeta* 'Six Hills Giant', *Scabiosa* 'Butterfly Blue' or *Aster* 'Lady-in-Blue'. The bright yellows of rudbeckia would be too harsh but the soft pale yellow of *Coreopsis verticillata* 'Moonbeam' would work.

For your collection

Other good *Monarda* cultivars for your collection include 'Snow Maiden' (white flowers), 'Blue Stocking' (violet-blue), ' Pink Tourmaline' (dark pink), and 'Adam' (bright red).

Morus alba 'Pendula'

Common name: *Weeping mulberry*

Chief characteristics

There is clearly a big demand for small, well-behaved, weeping trees for compact, urban gardens. Take a quick drive around any urban neighborhood in southern Ontario and you'll see garden after garden with either a weeping mulberry (*Morus alba* 'Pendula') or weeping peashrub (*Caragana arborescens* 'Pendula'). At one time, neatly pruned lollipop-style catalpa trees were all the rage for decorating entranceways or for edging driveways. Today it's top-grafted peashrub or white mulberry trees. And what's wrong with that? Size and structure is always an important issue when planting a tree or shrub, but it becomes a crucial consideration in situations where space is limited and a low-maintenance, formal landscape is desired. Both weeping mulberry and

Location: Full sun to light shade
Type: Deciduous tree
Size: 8 feet (2.4 m)
Conditions: Fertile, well-drained soil
Zone: 4

weeping caragana trees do a marvelous job. They are dependable, drought resistant, trouble-free, thrive even in mediocre soil, and they deliver just what many homeowners want from their front-garden landscape—balance, formality, elegance, simplicity.

Both dwarf trees are desirable, but the weeping mulberry has a little more character, to my eye. It has lush, cascading, shiny green foliage, a cleanly defined mushroom shape and a short, stocky stem that becomes gnarled with age. The two top varieties of weeping mulberry to look for are 'Teas', which has blackberry-shaped reddish-purple fruit in July, and the more popular 'Chaparral', which is a non-fruiting cultivar. They both grow 8 to 9 feet (2.4 to 3 m) tall.

The weeping peashrub is at its best planted next to black wrought-iron railings or against brick steps. Look for *Caragana arborescens* 'Walker', which has finely cut foliage, yellow flowers in May and grows 5 feet (1.5 m) tall.

Where to plant it

Weeping mulberry thrives in full sun or light shade in ordinary soil that stays moist in summer. It can tolerate hot, dry spells, but it will look its best if not deprived of water for too long.

If you plan to plant your tree next to a driveway, remember it will eventually grow quite wide, perhaps even 14 to 16 feet (4.2 to 5 m). This is not the tree to plant in the middle of a lawn or in a spot where you want to impress. It is a practical, little workhorse tree for a functional, no-nonsense landscape. It has charm, but don't expect it to turn heads or arouse much passion from avid gardeners.

How to care for it

Prune *Morus alba* 'Pendula' every April to keep it looking neat and trim. Without its annual haircut it will quickly turn into a monster of a mound, unattractive and dumpy-looking. The fruit of 'Teas' can be messy if it is allowed to drop and stain the sidewalk or driveway.

Good companions

Plant summer annuals such as pansies, nicotiana or petunias under the sheared canopy of your weeping mulberry or consider a more permanent perennial planting of hostas, astilbes or hardy geraniums. Since these trees tend to stand alone, there is not much point thinking about foliage contrast, but such shrubs as pink-flowering potentilla or red-flowering spiraea would make happy companions.

For your collection

Here's a list of other outstanding weeping trees.

- 🐾 *Salix caprea* 'Pendula' A small, slow-growing, umbrella-shaped tree, this has silvery catkins that turn yellow in April followed by gray-green foliage. Grows 5 feet (1.5 m) high.
- 🐾 *Salix alba* 'Tristis' (golden weeping willow). This looks spectacular in an estate garden or park planted next to a lake or stream. It has lime-green foliage on yellow weeping branches and grows 45 to 50 feet (13 to 15 m).
- 🐾 *Malus* 'Louisa' (Louisa weeping crabapple). A small weeping tree, growing to 16 feet (5 m) at maturity, this has dark green leaves, pink flowers in May, and yellow fruit in September.
- 🐾 *Malus* 'Red Jade'. One of the most popular small weeping crabapples, this has pink buds that open to pure white flowers in May. It grows only 13 feet (4 m) tall. It gets its name from the bright red color of the fruit, which first appears in September but continues into late fall.
- 🐾 *Prunus subhirtella* 'Pendula' (weeping Japanese cherry). This fine specimen has a graceful umbrella form and produces masses of deep rose-pink flowers in May. One of the first Japanese cherries to be brought to North America from Japan, 'Pendula' is a modest grower, reaching 20 feet (6 m) high.
- 🐾 *Pyrus salicifolia* 'Silver Cascade' (weeping willow-leafed pear, ornamental pear). This delightful tree for the medium-sized garden has silver-gray leaves and a weeping form. It is slowly becoming more appreciated as gardeners discover its virtues and versatility.
- 🐾 *Betula pendula* 'Youngii' (Young's weeping birch). Ideal for the courtyard or small garden because it is short and compact. It is usually sold as a weeping standard, top-grafted onto a trunk about 6 to 8 feet (1.8 to 2.4 m) off the ground.
- 🐾 *Acer palmatum* 'Crimson Queen' (laceleaf Japanese maple). This is distinguished by its finely cut, almost feathery, reddish-purple foliage that cascades over twisted and contorted branches to form an extremely graceful and compact weeping shape. Hardy to Zone 6. Also look for 'Red Dragon', 'Garnet' and 'Atropurpureum'.
- 🐾 Wisteria and buddleia can also be trained into a weeping, small tree and look very attractive tucked into a perennial border.

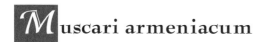uscari armeniacum

Common name: Grape hyacinth

Chief characteristics

After winter, we crave color in the garden. Snowdrops, the traditional harbingers of spring, are a welcome sight. But few early spring–flowering bulbs are as long-lasting or as useful throughout the garden as the simple grape hyacinth. Its lack of complexity and pretension makes it all the more likeable. It is without doubt a true garden classic with a subtle sophistication that many of the showier stars of the garden lack.

Location: Full sun
Type: Bulb
Size: 6 to 8 inches (15 to 20 cm)
Conditions: Moist, but well-drained soil
Flowering time: March to May
Zone: 4

Muscari gets its common name, grape hyacinth, because its tiny blue flowers are tightly gathered in grapelike clusters at the top of the short 6-inch (15-cm) stems. The faintly fragrant flowers last a long time. They can usually be found in the garden from early March through to the middle of May.

Native to southeast Europe and western Asia, where it flourishes on grassy hillsides, muscari naturalizes effortlessly when scattered throughout the garden under trees and shrubs and in clumps intermingled in the perennial border. It does particularly well in rockeries, probably because of the sunshine and good drainage. A member of the lily family, muscari is indifferent to frost, being able to cope with temperatures several degrees below freezing.

Where to plant it

Where not to plant grape hyacinths? There's the question. They fit in every corner of the garden and are especially useful for providing color while other perennials are waking up from winter.

Grow muscari in full sun or light shade in average, well-drained soil. The bulbs should be planted to a depth of 3 times their height—3 to 4 inches (7.5 to 10 cm)—any time from September to October. They are not expensive, so plant lots of them and watch them multiply as the years go by. You can also grow muscari in pots. They are impressive mass-planted in a simple terra cotta pot or shallow dish. Bring the pot into a warm room in the middle of winter and you can have a colorful show in January or February to whet your appetite for the coming season.

How to care for it

Muscari is a reasonably rapid self-propagator. Thick clumps should be divided every few years and replanted immediately. When the flowers fade and the strap-like leaves turn yellow, mow or shear them to the ground. They will bounce back as good as new the following spring.

Good companions

Violas and primulas combine well with muscari, which are usually up and out of the ground long before most perennials have begun to stir. This is really one of their great attributes. While hostas, astilbes, bleeding hearts and daylilies are slow risers, grape hyacinths can cover the ground with their rich green leaves and brighten the earth with their vivid blue flowers. They should be mixed with other spring-flowering bulbs like *Iris reticulata*, snowflakes (*Leucojum vernum*), bluebells (*Scilla non-scripta*) and the yellow flowers of trout lily (*Erythronium* 'Pagoda'), all of which flower around the same time. An excellent combination is to marry the pale blues of *Puschkinia scilloides* with glory-of-the-snow and grape hyacinth.

For your collection

 White-flowering *Muscari azureum* 'Album' or *M. botryoides* 'Album' are a nice change of pace from the popular deep blue *M. azureum* 'Blue Spike'. Another cultivar is 'Sky Blue', which has pale blue flowers with a white rim.

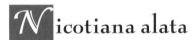icotiana alata

Common name: *Tobacco plant*

Chief characteristics

When you first discover this remarkable plant (and there has to be a first time, even though it has been in gardens for generations), you are bound to be impressed by its perpetual and reliable flowering habit and the exceptional fragrance of its blooms at twilight. The trumpet-shaped flowers not only come in great colors—warm reds, clear whites and a classy lime-green—they also have the knack of attracting hummingbirds. Native to South America, *Nicotiana alata* is also structurally impressive.

Location: Full sun to light shade
Type: Annual
Size: 2 feet (60 cm)
Conditions: Good, well-drained soil
Flowering time: June to September

The taller forms may need staking, but the more popular, shorter hybrids are perfectly able to stand upright without support in a border or flower pot. That is a quality much appreciated by gardeners who like plants that behave themselves and do not interfere too much with their neighbors.

Outstanding cultivars to seek out include 'Havana Appleblossom', the bushy 'Nikki' Hybrids and the dwarf 'Starship', 'Domino' and 'Merlin' series, ideal for using in tubs, pots and window boxes. When you start to garden, it is satisfying (and necessary) to have some undisputed successes. Nicotiana lets you express a certain amount of creativity and also put on a great show of color on your patio or deck. When gaps appear in the perennial border, you can rely on the sweetly scented tobacco plant to restore harmony.

Where to plant it

You will see the 'Nikki' Hybrids mass-planted in city parks. That might put you off doing the same in your own garden, but it can be great fun to "paint" with it. There are tasteful white and lime-green forms, and a solid clump of red can be exceptionally vibrant and eye-catching. Use nicotiana in pots on your deck or patio where the sweet scent can be enjoyed when you sit out with friends on a summer's evening.

How to care for it

Nicotiana grows best in rich, well-drained soil in a sunny location. Deadheading the spent flowers will encourage plants to keep on blooming. Leaves are slightly sticky with sap, so this is best done with a pair of scissors. Watch out for aphids.

Nicotiana produces tiny brown seeds in tiny baked pods at the end of summer. Collect the seeds in an envelope. They germinate very easily indoors in February and will provide you with a massive crop of new plants for the next season.

Good companions

Nicotiana has many and varied uses. Use it in combination with any other annuals in tubs and pots. You could trim a pot, for example, with lobelia, alyssum, or verbena and dusty miller (*Cineraria maritima*) for a touch of soft gray. The best companions for nicotiana in the open garden are plain, green-leafed perennials like lady's mantle, hardy geraniums or a backdrop of peony foliage. For color contrasts, try white *Cosmos bipinnatus* 'Sonata', the orange-yellow flowers of California poppies (*Eschscholzia californica*) or the purple, fragrant flowers of *Heliotropium peruvianum*.

For your collection

- *Nicotiana tabacum.* Pick this up if you fancy trying your hand at growing the true tobacco plant. It will grow 5 feet (1.5 m) tall with a strong stem, large leaves and rose-pink flowers at the top. Quite a conversation piece for your next garden party.
- A better bet is *Nicotiana sylvestris*, which is also somewhat towering at 5 feet (1.5 m) but has exceptionally perfumed white trumpet-shaped flowers. Or try *N. langsdorffii*, which produces apple-green flowers and is a particular favorite of floral artists. Both of these are praised to the hilt by plant connoisseurs, but weekend gardeners are not so easily impressed. These more obscure nicotianas are an acquired taste.

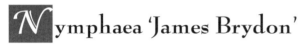

*N*ymphaea 'James Brydon'

Common name: *Hardy water lily*

Chief characteristics

Location: Full sun

Type: Perennial water plant

Size: 6 to 12 feet (1.8 to 3.6 m)

Conditions: Fertile soil

Flowering time: June to July

Zone: 3

There is always room in a garden, no matter how small, for a water feature and a few water plants. It doesn't matter if you live in an apartment with a small balcony or a townhouse with a tiny patio, you can still have at least a ceramic pot or half-barrel with a few well-chosen water plants and a small fountain or bubbler. The look and sound of a water feature is immensely relaxing. Water features are easy to install, take little time to maintain, and can make a world of difference to the atmosphere of your outdoor living space.

You can now buy easy-to-assemble pond kits that come complete with everything you need—pump, rubber liner, filter, fountain and plants. Some suppliers even throw in Japanese trapdoor snails to gobble up any algae that might form. Oval-shaped ponds are popular, but simple, rectangular ponds have a special charm and elegance.

Most people start small and then expand. It is very common to hear people lament that they didn't install a bigger pond in the first place. So if you have plenty of room, consider putting in at least a 1,000-gallon (3,800-litre), 9- by 10-foot (2.7- by 3-m) pond with a 700-gallon (2,660-litre) submersible pump. (With pumps, the rule of thumb is that you need one that will move at least half the water in your pond every hour. Many people install larger pumps than are required in order to create dramatic waterfalls or a rushing stream.)

You don't need a lot of plants to start. You will certainly want some water lilies. They are, after all, the quintessential pond plant. They mostly need five or six hours of sun to bloom properly, though the flat, floating lily pad has charm with or without flowers.

Water lilies are not cheap. Expect to pay $30 to $40 for one plant. And there are thousands from which to choose. There are tropical and hardy water lilies, so be sure you know which kind you are buying. One will overwinter, the other won't. Tropical lilies should be treated as annuals—they bloom for a single season. Hardy water lilies will bounce back every year and will go through the winter safely.

Water lilies can be separated into three basic sizes: large, medium and small. For a tub, trough or small pond, look at the miniature plants, which spread only a few feet and don't require deep water.

An outstanding all-round specimen for formal or informal ponds and water features in average-sized gardens is *Nymphaea* 'James Brydon'. It has deep red flowers and pads that spread 6 to 12 feet (1.8 to 3.6 m). It looks perfectly at home in the small pond and is the ideal size to create a cluster without covering the entire water surface.

Other top-performing hardy water lilies to look for are 'Joey Tomocik' (canary yellow) 'Burgundy Princess' (pink-red), 'Comanche' (apricot-yellow) and 'Mayla' (bright red).

Best of the tropical water lilies are 'Emily Grant Hutchings' (pink), 'Blue Beauty' (lilac-mauve), 'Red Cup' (fuchsia-red) and 'Albert Greenberg' (pink-orange). For patios, the fragrant, early-blooming dwarf Chinese varieties are a good choice. They thrive in hot, sunny spots and are hardy to Zone 5.

Where to plant it

Grow lilies in a small pond, rectangular pool or even in a 3-foot (90-cm) square planter box or large ceramic pot with black plastic liner to make it watertight. Water lilies are not the least expensive of plants, so it is important to think about the color you want when you go to buy one. Also ask about the "spread" when you buy: lilies are listed as small, 1 to 6 feet (30 cm to 1.8 m); medium, 6 to 12 feet (1.8 to 3.6 m); or large, 12 feet plus (3.6 m plus) according to how far the leaves spread. The more water surface you have, the bigger the lily you can place. In a small pond you probably don't need more than a couple. In a tub or barrel, you definitely need only one.

How to care for it

Water lilies will flower reliably provided they are planted in rich soil in warm, shallow water and get at least five hours of direct sunlight. The more sun they get the more flowers they produce. They are heavy feeders and need to be well fertilized before being plonked in the water. To do this without polluting the water, use heavy clay to sandwich slow-release fertilizer in the soil in the pot. You can also get water-lily food in powdered tablets or sachets. The same technique can be used for other plants that are grown in water.

Dead and decaying leaves should be removed to prevent any buildup of rotting vegetation in the water. Water lilies thrive best when they don't have to compete too vigorously with other plants. The oxygenators will do a great job of keeping the water clean and free of algae, but you should also change the water in small tubs and troughs regularly. Water that is pumped through a fountain or a spouting ornament also gains oxygen, which is a way to keep it fresh and clear.

Good companions

Many moisture-loving perennials, such as astilbes, hostas, polygonum, rodgersia and ligularia, can be grown in the moist soil at the edge of a pond. Creeping jenny (*Lysimachia nummularia*) makes a charming golden green foliage plant for creeping over rocks at the side of a pond. And the water forget-me-not 'Mermaid' (*Myosotis palustris*) is growing in popularity as more people fall in love with its delicate, sky-blue flowers. *Houttuynia cordata* (chameleon plant) is very useful as a groundcover plant for the side of a pond. Be sure not to let it get out of bounds.

For your collection

To complete your water garden, you'll need a variety of reliable shallow water and marginal plants. A mixture of rushes, irises and reeds and tropical and hardy plants will give your pond a natural and exotic look. Here's what you need.

- Oxygenating plants are nature's water purifiers. They float on the surface or sink under the water and help to keep a pond free of algae. Excellent oxygenators include the water violet (*Hottonia palustris*), hornwort (*Ceratophyllum demersum*), parrot's feather (*Myriophyllum aquaticum*) and Canadian pondweed (*Elodea canadensis*).

- For visual interest, consider *Colocasia antiquorum* (imperial taro), which has green leaves, blotched with bold purple markings; *C. esculenta* 'Black Magic' or 'Jet Black Wonder', both of which have deep purple foliage; or *C. esculenta* (common green taro), which has plain green leaves. There are also spectacular water cannas now available, some of which can soar 6 feet (1.8 m) high. Look for 'Bengal Tiger' (variegated foliage and orange flower), 'Black Knight' (purple with bright red flowers), and the Longwood Hybrids (pink, red and yellow). The cannas are all tender and need to be brought into a frost-free place over winter.

- ❦ *Cyperus papyrus* (Egyptian papyrus) will give you a lovely spray of green foliage atop 4-foot (1.2-m) stems. Arrowheads (*Sagittaria*) are now regarded as prerequisite pond plants along with hard-flowering marginals such as marsh marigold (*Caltha palustris*) and the sky-blue flowers of water forget-me-nots (*Myosotis palustris*), hardy to Zone 5.
- ❦ Rushes and reeds to try are zebra rush (*Scirpus* 'Zebrinus') or dwarf cattail (*Typha minima*), two wonderful decorative specimens. Also consider blue rush (*Juncus glaucus*), goldrush reed (*Phragmites australis*) and flowering rush (*Butomus umbellatus*).
- ❦ Aquatic irises have bold, upright, broad, sword-like leaves. Yellow flag iris (*Iris pseudacorus*) is very popular, producing a bright yellow flower at the top of a stem that can reach 4 or 5 feet (1.2 to 1.5 m) high. A more manageable option is the blue flag iris (*Iris versicolor*), which grows only 3 feet (90 cm) high. Variegated iris (*Iris pseudacorus* 'Variegata'), is another good choice.
- ❦ *Eichhornia crassipes* (water hyacinths) are a reliable floating plant with thick succulent-like leaves. Two other first-rate floating plants are fairy moss (*Azolla filiculoides*) and water lettuce (*Pistia stratiotes*).

*O*phiopogon planiscapus 'Nigrescens'

Common name: *Black mondo grass, black lilyturf, black spider grass*

Chief characteristics

Location: Part shade
Type: Perennial
Size: 6 to 8 inches (15 to 20 cm)
Conditions: Fertile, moist soil
Flowering time: July to August
Zone: 6

Black is a fun color to play with in the garden. It adds a sense of drama, novelty and curiosity, and it allows you to show the dark side of your imagination. There is really no true black in nature. What appears black to our eyes is actually the deepest shade of purple. But why spoil the fun? If it looks black, let's call it black.

One of the best black plants is black mondo grass (*Ophiopogon planiscapus* 'Nigrescens'). Its botanical name, *Ophiopogon*, roughly translated means "snake beard." Originating in Japan, it produces a spidery clump of thin, jet-black, strap-like leaves. In late summer, it has tiny mauve flowers, which are soon followed by minute, rather insignificant black berries that last most of winter. The plant is evergreen and keeps its black foliage all winter.

Mondo grass is especially useful for creating bold contrasts. For shockingly effective results, marry it up with the yellow leaves of creeping jenny (*Lysimachia nummularia*) or the silver foliage of *Lamium maculatum*, or allow it to creep up through white fairy thimble bellflowers (*Campanula cochleariifolia*). Mondo grass is often planted under birch trees to contrast against the white bark. My son has made use of it in his black-and-purple garden along with purple ajuga, black hollyhocks, purple sage, black daylily, purple liatris, black pansies (*Viola cornuta* 'Black Magic') and purplish-black *Euphorbia dulcis* 'Chameleon'. You can have even more fun with black mondo grass by using it to give "hair" to a Greek-styled terracotta wall sconce.

You might also like to experiment with *Liriope muscari*, another compact, grasslike perennial with blackish tones. It has dark, grassy leaves and short, spiky, violet flowers.

Where to plant it

Grow black mondo grass in moist, well-drained soil in partial shade, although it will tolerate full sun if kept reasonably well watered. It is best used as an accent plant. It may look like a useful groundcover but it doesn't spread rapidly enough to provide extensive cover. Like its spidery nature, it tends to creep here and there and turn up in unexpected places. It does, however, work well as an edging plant next to paths and it can be very effective planted between stepping stones.

How to care for it

Mondo grass is trouble-free and indifferent to wet winters provided it has good drainage. Thick clumps can be divided in spring.

Good companions

There is no shortage of good companions for *Ophiopogon planiscapus* 'Nigrescens'. It contrasts beautifully with any of the following: Japanese blood grass (*Imperata cylindrica* 'Red Baron'), blue grass (*Festuca glauca*), spurge (*Euphorbia myrsinites*), dead nettle (*Lamium maculatum*), creeping jenny (*Lysimachia nummularia*) and *Ajuga reptans* 'Purpurea'.

For your collection

🐾 Other black plants worth pursuing include black snapdragon (*Antirrhinum* 'Black Prince'), black sweet william (*Dianthus barbatus* 'Nigrescens') and the hardy mourning widow geranium (*Geranium phaeum*), which has small black flowers.

Acer palmatum 'Bloodgood'
(Japanese maple)

Actinidia kolomikta
(Kolomicta vine, super-hardy kiwi vine)

Acer palmatum dissectum
'Crimson Queen' (laceleaf Japanese maple)

Ajuga reptans 'Bronze Beauty'
(common bugleweed)

Adiantum aleuticum (western or five-fingered maidenhair fern)

Akebia quinata (chocolate vine)

Alchemilla mollis (lady's mantle)

Allium aflatunense (ornamental onion)

Aquilegia (columbine)

Artemisia schmidtiana 'Silver Mound'
(wormwood)

Aster × *frikartii* 'Monch'
(michaelmas daisy)

Astilbe × arendsii 'Fanal' (false spiraea)

Astrantia major (masterwort)

Betula utilis jacquemontii (himalayan birch)

Brugmansia × candida (angel's trumpet)

Buddleia davidii (butterfly bush)

Buxus microphylla koreana
(Korean boxwood)

Van Bleem Gardens

Campanula persicifolia (bellflower)

Ryan McNair

Campsis radicans (trumpet vine)

Ryan McNair

Camassia (quamash)

Heritage Perennials

Cimicifuga 'Brunette' (bugbane, snakeroot)

Coreopsis verticillata 'Moonbeam' (tickseed)

Ryan McNair

Clematis × *jackmanii*
(Virgin's bower)

Ryan McNair

Cornus alba 'Elegantissima' (silverleaf dogwood)

Corydalis lutea
(yellow corydalis)

Cotinus coggygria
'Royal Purple' (smoke tree,
smoke bush)

Crocosmia 'Lucifer'
(montbretia)

Delphinium Pacific Hybrids (larkspur)

Dicentra spectabilis 'Alba' (bleeding heart)

Digitalis purpurea (foxglove)

Elaeagnus angustifolia
(Russian olive, oleaster)

Ryan McNair

Euonymus fortunei 'Emerald Gaiety'
(emerald gaiety euonymus)

Euphorbia griffithii 'Fireglow' (spurge)

Echinacea purpurea (purple coneflower)

Foeniculum vulgare 'Purpureum'
(bronze fennel)

Geranium cinereum 'Ballerina'
(cranesbill, hardy geranium)

Gleditsia triacanthos 'Sunburst'
(thornless gold honey locust)

Hamamelis × *intermedia* 'Diane'
(witch hazel)

Helictotrichon sempervirens (blue oat grass)

Helleborus orientalis (lenten rose)

Ryan McNair

Heliotropium arborescens (heliotrope,
cherry-pie plant)

Hemerocallis 'Stella de Oro' (daylily)

Ryan McNair

Heuchera micrantha
'Bressingham Bronze' (coral bells)

Hibiscus syriacus 'Blue Bird'
(rose of Sharon)

Hydrangea arborescens 'Annabelle'
(Annabelle hydrangea)

Ryan McNair

Hydrangea petiolaris (climbing hydrangea)

Ryan McNair

Hosta 'Frances Williams'
(Frances Williams hosta)

Iris sibirica (Siberian iris, water iris,
Siberian flag)

Juniperus scopulorum
'Wichita Blue'
(blue column juniper)

Steve Whysall

Kniphofia (red-hot poker,
torch lily)

Ryan McNair

Lavandula angustifolia
(English lavender)

Lavatera trimestris 'Mont Blanc'
(annual mallow)

Ligularia stenocephala 'The Rocket'
(ligularia)

Liatris spicata (gayfeather, blazing star)

Lilium 'Casa Blanca' (Casa Blanca lily)

Lupinus Russell Hybrids (Russell lupins)

Lonicera japonica 'Halliana'
(Hall's honeysuckle)

Lychnis coronaria
(rose campion, catchfly)

Lysimachia clethroides
(gooseneck loosestrife)

Magnolia × soulangiana
(saucer magnolia)

Monarda 'Gardenview Scarlet'
(bergamot, bee balm)

Miscanthus sinensis 'Gracillimus'
(maiden grass)

Morus alba 'Pendula' (weeping mulberry)

Muscari armeniacum (grape hyacinth)

Nymphaea 'James Brydon'
(hardy water lily)

Nicotiana alata (tobacco plant)

Ophiopogon planiscapus 'Nigrescens'
(black mondo grass, black lilyturf,
black spider grass)

Paeonia lactiflora 'Karl Rosenfeld' (peony)

Papaver orientale 'Mrs. Perry'
(oriental poppy)

Pelargonium (geranium, zonal geranium)

Pennisetum alopecuroides (fountain grass)

Philadelphus coronarius 'Aureus'
(mock orange)

Picea pungens 'Hoopsii' (colorado blue
spruce, hoop's blue spruce)

Phlox paniculata 'Fujiama' (phlox)

Polemonium caeruleum 'Brise d'Anjou'
(variegated Jacob's ladder)

Ryan McNair

Polygonum bistorta 'Superbum'
(fleece flower, knotweed)

Potentilla fruticosa 'Abbotswood'
(potentilla, cinquefoil)

Prunus cistena (purple-leaf sand cherry)

Primula japonica 'Miller's Crimson'
(candelabra primula)

Rhododendron 'Hi-Light'
(Northern Lights azalea)

Rosa 'Ballerina' (Ballerina rose)

Rosa 'Elina' (Elina rose)

Rosa 'Mary Rose' (Mary rose)

Rosa 'Morden Blush' (Parkland rose)

Rosa 'New Dawn' (New Dawn rose)

Salvia × *sylvestris* 'May Night'
(perennial salvia, sage)

Rosa 'Souvenir de la Malmaison'
(Souvenir de la Malmaison rose)

Ryan McNair

Scabiosa columbaria 'Butterfly Blue'
(pincushion flower)

Van Bloem Gardens

Scilla (Hyacinthoides) non-scripta
(English bluebell, squill)

Ryan McNair

Sedum × 'Autumn Joy' (stonecrop)

Spiraea bumalda 'Gold Flame' (spiraea)

Stachys byzantina 'Silver Carpet'
(lamb's ears)

Styrax japonica (Japanese snowbell or
snowdrop tree)

Syringa vulgaris 'Mme. Lemoine'
(French lilacs)

Ryan McNair

Taxus × *media* 'Hicksii' (Hick's yew)

Ryan McNair

Thymus × *citriodorus* 'Doone Valley'
(creeping lemon-scented thyme)

Tilia cordata 'Greenspire'
(little-leaf linden, lime or basswood)

Ryan McNair

Viburnum plicatum 'Summer Snowflake'
(summer snowflake)

Wisteria sinesis (Chinese wisteria)

Weigela florida 'Red Prince'
(Red Prince weigela)

Paeonia lactiflora 'Karl Rosenfeld'

Common name: *Peony*

Chief characteristics

We all know and admire peonies; they have been firm favorites in gardens for years. They are a plant even non-gardeners have little difficulty identifying. We love them for their large, fragrant flowers, which appear from May to June, and for their lush foliage, which stays a pleasant, restful shade of green all summer long. Yet how many of us can name the peony we are besotted with?

Location: Full sun
Type: Perennial
Size: 3 to 4 feet (90 to 120 cm)
Conditions: Fertile, well-drained soil
Flowering time: June to July
Zone: 3

Not all garden centers can be bothered to label them with their full name, preferring to tag them by color. They have great names like 'Hot Chocolate', 'Sorbet', 'White Sands', 'Festiva Maxima', 'Butterbowl' and 'Sword Dance'. But most people wouldn't know them by those names if they saw them. Even some expert gardeners, when pressed, can do no better than describe a peony by its color. This is a dishonor peonies share with daylilies, which are also extremely useful in the garden landscape and universally loved, but which are rarely referred to by their proper and complete botanical name.

Peonies also have a reputation for sulking when moved or planted too deeply or messed with. They flower their best after being left undisturbed for several years. And they don't bloom for very long. Their magnificent multi-petaled blooms, some with a fragrance that rivals that of old garden roses, appear in the middle of spring and are over and done within a month. By the time we start to notice them, they have run their course and our attention quickly gets diverted to other showy early summer performers. Despite all of this, peonies are still superb plants and no garden can afford to be without them.

There are three key groups: early flowering hybrids; Japanese or anemone-form peonies, which have large, graceful blooms; and double peonies, which have tightly packed, multi-petaled, chrysanthemum-like flowers or cup-shaped blooms like roses that are wide open.

The basic garden peony is *Paeonia lactiflora*. It comes in a wide range of colors, including assorted shades and combinations of pink, red, white and yellow. One of the most reliable all-round performers is 'Karl Rosenfeld', which produces brilliant, fragrant red flowers in June. It has handsome foliage and is a trouble-free plant with excellent resistance to pests and diseases.

Other star performers to look for include 'Sarah Bernhardt' (apple-blossom pink), 'Bowl of Beauty' (pale pink with white center), 'Mons Jules Elie' (double pink), 'Shirley Temple' (double white-pink), 'Lady Alexandra Duff' (pale pink) and 'Duchess de Nemours' (pure white).

Where to plant it

Grow peonies in full sun in fertile, well-drained soil with a mixture of other perennials and flowering shrubs. Peonies are best combined with other plant material rather than grown in mass groups. When flowering is over, they form a great backdrop with their soft, shapely leaves. Before planting your new peony, think carefully about where you are placing it. Once it is in the ground, it does not like to be disturbed. Plant in late September, then leave it alone to establish itself. This could take more than one season. Don't be alarmed if you see weak or few flowers the first year after planting.

How to care for it

There are a few rules about looking after peonies that if followed make them a lot more enjoyable to grow. Peonies hold themselves up perfectly well while they are developing in early spring, but after they start to flower, especially if they get hit by heavy rain, the stems can topple sideways and the bush will begin to look ragged and unkempt. The secret is to set link-stakes around the emerging stems to give the bush the support it will need later on when it reaches its peak blooming period.

Ants can seem like a problem. They can often be found running all over the plant, especially over unopened flower buds. Some gardeners say this actually stimulates the buds to open more rapidly. The consensus of opinion, however, is that ants do neither harm nor good; they just busy themselves and disappear.

The most important thing to remember about peonies is that they should not be disturbed. They don't like being moved or having their roots interfered with in any way. If you divide a clump, expect the plants to sulk for a season.

Good companions

Since peonies vanish completely back into the ground over winter, the space they occupied can look barren in early spring. Surround the peony crown with various spring-flowering bulbs. Bluebells, dog's tooth violet, grape hyacinth, crocus, glory-of-the-snow and dwarf narcissi are all good choices. They will provide color and cover while the new pink-red peony shoots are slowly rising. Once the leaves have formed, the peony will need some supporting neighbors. Try campanula, centaurea, euphorbia, aquilegia, salvia, lupin, foxglove, shrub roses, lychnis and allium.

For your collection

- Gardeners looking for more unusual colors have been particularly impressed by early flowering hybrids such as 'Cytherea' (cherry-peach mix), 'Red Charm' (rich red), 'Coral 'n' Gold' and 'Coral Charm' (coral-peach).
- Also growing in popularity are the Japanese peonies, notably 'Leto' (pure white), 'Snow Swan' (ivory) and 'White Cap' (raspberry). Doubles with outstanding color include 'Angel Cheeks' (pink with red freckles), 'Dinner Plate' (shell pink), 'Jeannot' (rose-pink) and 'Mary Eddy Jones' (light pink).
- Another very popular peony is *P. lutea*, which has single, vivid yellow flowers and attractive foliage. It grows to 6 feet (1.8 m).
- *Paeonia tenuifolia* (fernleaf peony) is unlike any other peony. It has elegant, finely cut, fernlike leaves and produces dark crimson flowers in May.

*P*apaver orientale 'Mrs. Perry'

Common name: *Oriental poppy*

Chief characteristics

Poppies are like cherries on a cake. They don't add a lot of substance, but they inject a special beauty and charm. In the early summer garden, poppies hover like butterflies, their delicate flower petals appearing as fragile as tissue paper. Think of poppies as a garden's jewelry and you will immediately understand how to use them to the best effect—as decorative finishing touches, decadent indulgences, the carnation in the buttonhole. The opposite of hostas and rhododendrons, they are flowers we flirt with—just don't expect a long-term relationship from them. They are full of frivolity and gaiety and have nothing to offer in terms of structural longevity.

The Oriental poppy (*Papaver orientale*) is one of the most popular

Location: Full sun

Type: Perennial

Size: 2 to 3 feet (60 to 90 cm)

Conditions: Light, well-drained soil

Flowering time: May to June

Zone: 3

poppies. It has rough, hairy foliage and soft, satiny flowers that come in a wide range of colors from blood-red to salmon-pink to pure white. The peachy pink 'Mrs. Perry' is an old-fashioned hybrid, a favorite of cottage gardeners. Other top Oriental poppies include 'Perry's White' (white with black spot), 'Goliath' (deep red with dark center), 'Allegro' (scarlet), 'Brilliant' (red), 'Carneum' (salmon-pink) and 'Picotee' (salmon-pink with white edges). They all grow 2 to 3 feet (60 to 90 cm) high.

Where to plant it

Grow Oriental poppies mixed with perennials in full sun in well-drained, light soil. They won't flourish in heavy, clay soils and will die even faster in waterlogged or overly wet soil.

The main drawback to growing poppies is the gaping holes left in your garden once they have finished flowering. The solution is to plant them among late-flowering perennials that will rise up once the poppies are done and fill the gaps. Another idea is to have perennials standing by in pots that can be moved into gaps. This is not a bad idea to use throughout the garden to keep it looking in great shape all year. You would be amazed how many gardeners do this and no one knows because their borders always look so seamless.

How to care for it

Make sure you grow poppies in well-drained, fertile soil. Pick the seed pods and sow seed where you would like flowers the following year. Once plants have finished flowering, don't allow the foliage to become an eyesore. Cut it down or take the plants out completely and replace them with perennials in pots or fill-in annuals like nicotiana, pelargoniums or red salvia.

Good companions

Grow Oriental poppies with perennials that flower from July to September. Good choices are *Phlox paniculata*, ornamental grasses, daylilies, veronica, fall asters and Japanese anemones. For companions in late spring/early summer, think about lupins, alliums, forget-me-nots, campanulas, hardy geraniums and shrub roses.

For your collection

- *Eschscholzia californica* (California poppy). This is the poppy that most new gardeners fall in love with. It has yellow to deep orange flowers and distinctive feathery foliage and grows 8 to 15 inches (20 to 38 cm) high on sunny, well-drained hillsides or banks. Easy to grow from seed, the California poppy will self-sow and return year after year. Efforts to transplant rarely succeed, even when the poppies are lifted in a whole clump of earth.

🐾 Two other poppies, the passion of plant connoisseurs, are the Himalayan blue poppy (*Meconopsis betonicifolia*) and the Welsh poppy (*M. cambrica*). The Himalayan poppy grows 3 to 4 feet (90 to 120 cm) high in cool, semi-shade locations and has light, sky-blue flowers. The Welsh poppy has small yellow or orange flowers atop 12-inch (30-cm) stems. If you do grow the Himalayan blue poppy, be aware of the popular belief that you should prevent it flowering the first year. This seems to have some truth in it as the plant will put out more foliage growth if it is not putting energy into flower production—and a more robust plant is better able to survive winter.

🐾 *Papaver atlanticum* (atlas poppy) grows to 12 inches (30 cm) and has soft orange flowers. Although a short-lived perennial, it does self-seed quite freely and is best sown randomly in a sunny border.

🐾 *Papaver nudicaule* (Iceland poppy) comes in shades of yellow, red, pink and white and grows to 18 inches (45 cm). It is a self-seeding biennial, growing leaves one year, flowering the next.

🐾 *Papaver rhoeas* (the famous Flander's field poppy) is also known as the Shirley poppy. It grows 12 inches (30 cm) high in a range of colors. It is grown as an annual, sown in early spring.

𝒫elargonium

Common name: *Geranium, zonal geranium*

Chief characteristics

Most people, even those who don't garden, know the name of these plants. Or at least they think they do. Pelargoniums are a standard in all summer gardens. You see them everywhere, adding cheerful, long-lasting color to patios and decks, window boxes and hanging baskets. They are also used to inject a festive splash of color into large-scale planting schemes in public parks. The majority of people call them geraniums. This is technically (botanically) incorrect. True geraniums are equally wonderful plants, actually hardy perennials, commonly called in informed horticultural circles, "cranesbills."

Unlike the true geranium, pelargoniums are tender and are grown

Location: Full sun
Type: Annual
Size: 12 to 18 inches (30 to 45 cm)
Conditions: Fertile soil
Flowering time: June to September

as summer annuals. Although native to South Africa, they are not considered rare or terribly exotic. Unfortunately, like the lowly marigold, they are sometimes rejected as loud and common. Nevertheless, they are a vital player in the summer garden. Drought-tolerant and pest-free, they are marvelously dependable and forgiving plants. They are certainly among the world's most-loved flowers. All gardeners should find a place for at least a pot or two on their patio or porch.

The most familiar pelargoniums are the ones known as zonal geraniums. They come in a wide variety of colors from deep red to hot pink, to bright white, to salmon, to orange. There are far too many to mention by name here. It really comes down to picking out what you like most when you visit the garden center in April.

Within this category, you will also find "fancy-leaf" types, which literally have fancy, decorative leaves, most variegated creamy yellows and purplish maroons.

There are a few other types of pelargoniums worth knowing. Ivy-leafed geraniums (cultivars of *Pelargonium peltatum*) have ivy-shaped leaves and a cascading habit. They are especially useful for hanging baskets or for trailing over the edges of large pots. Angel pelargoniums (*Pelargonium × dumosum*), with lovely delicate flowers that resemble angel wings, are great for hanging baskets and window boxes. These are immensely popular in England, thanks to the work of hybridizers who have produced exciting new cultivars that have caught the eye of gardeners at the Chelsea Flower Show. Regal geraniums (*Pelargonium × domesticum*) are also known as Martha Washington pelargoniums. They have large, showy flowers with ruffled, overlapping petals. Colors range from soft white to raspberry-red, to dark purple, to magenta-pink.

Where to plant it

Pelargoniums like rich, porous soil. They like heat, so they should be planted where they will get full sun. They'll tolerate some shade, but too much shade will produce leggy growth and feeble flowers. They don't like to be watered too generously. In fact, overwatering is one way to kill them. But they have no objection to being potted with other annuals. They like it when their roots are somewhat restricted by space.

How to care for it

Feed pelargoniums every couple of weeks during their flowering period with a half-strength solution of 20-20-20. Water regularly but sparingly. Pinch-prune the top of the plant to make it bushier and more floriferous. Remove faded flowerheads regularly to keep the plant tidy and encourage blooming.

If you like, take cuttings in late summer to maintain a supply of your favorite plants, but don't bother to overwinter whole plants. In most cases, all you end up overwintering is fungal or viral diseases. The cost and effort are not really worth the trouble, especially when you know inexpensive plants are available every spring.

Good companions

The beauty of pelargoniums is that they provide a stable foundation for imaginative container-planting schemes. Trailing verbena, petunia, alyssum, diascia, brachycome, anagallis, argyranthemum all make excellent companions for pelargoniums in pots. Red salvia and lime-green nicotiana can be combined with canna lilies and red or white pelargoniums for outstanding container plantings.

For your collection

🐿 Scented geraniums are always fun to have around in the summer. Grown for their aromatic leaves, which need to be touched or brushed to release their scent, these collectible geraniums offer a surprising range of fragrances including lemon (*Pelargonium crispum*), apple (*P. odoratissimum*) or peppermint (*P. tomentosum*). While ordinary pelargoniums are not worth overwintering—it is best to grow new plants from seed or cuttings or buy new plants in spring— scented geraniums are a little more special and can be kept for many years by bringing them into a frost-free environment during winter.

*P*ennisetum alopecuroides

Common name: *Fountain grass*

Chief characteristics

Fountain grass produces a generous cascade of sandy-colored foxtails at the end of graceful arching stems in late summer. It gets its name because it resembles water splashing out from a fountain. It can be used as a feature plant to create a focal point or to add foliage interest to the perennial border. Whether planted in substantial drifts or alone in a container, it performs outstandingly, growing about 2 feet (60 cm) high. Its main function, however, is to provide a light,

Location: Full sun

Type: Ornamental grass

Size: 2 to 3 feet (60 to 90 cm)

Conditions: Fertile, moist soil

Flowering time: July to September

Zone: 5

airy textural contrast to neighboring plants. Starting out green, *Pennisetum alopecuroides* slowly turns yellow at the end of summer and becomes a delightful barnyard-tan color in fall. The graceful bottlebrush-like foxtails start out creamy white and turn more almond as the season progresses.

The cultivar 'Hameln' is a more compact, early flowering, dwarf form that grows about 2 feet (60 cm) high, while the slightly taller 'Moudry' produces dark, almost black, bottlebrush spikes. A miniature cultivar called 'Little Bunny' grows 10 to 12 inches (25 to 30 cm), which makes it quite suitable for use in a rockery.

Oriental fountain grass (*Pennisetum orientale*) is less hardy but is considered by some to be one of the most handsome fountain grasses because of its glossy, blue-green, compact leaves and its silky, soft pink plumes, which last a long time and gradually fade to gray. It grows about 18 inches (45 cm) high.

Where to plant it

Fountain grass grows naturally in open meadows and beside streams in open woodland areas. It is best planted in the middle or back of the perennial border, although the shorter forms can be located more to the front. Use fountain grass to soften the hard edges of rock walls or to provide some textural relief to hard brick or slate patios.

How to care for it

Fountain grass has no pest or disease problems. To thrive, it needs plenty of sun. Plant it in moist, well-drained soil. If you can find a sunny, sheltered, frost-free part of the garden in which to plant it, all the better. Divide the clumps in spring.

Good companions

The bright yellow flowers of rudbeckia and the salmon-colored, broccoli-like heads of stonecrop are traditional partners for ornamental grasses. These combos, while classic, have become a bit of a cliché and gardeners are hungry for new matches.

For late summer contrast, the tender purple-leafed fountain grass (*Pennisetum* 'Rubrum'), with its beautiful burgundy foliage and pink bottlebrush plumes, is worth considering. Butterfly gaura (*Gaura lindheimeri*), which produces a myriad of pinkish-white flowers at the end of tall waving stems, would also make a good partner. The red-magenta flowers of *Lychnis coronaria* could be mixed in for fun and the dark moody blues of *Caryopteris* × *clandonensis* 'Dark Knight' are worth experimenting with.

For your collection

- 🐾 *Pennisetum* 'Burgundy Giant'. If you have room on your sunny deck, you could try growing this in a large container. It will soar to 5 feet (1.5 m) and produce thick, tropical-looking, beet-colored, straplike leaves. It is very tender, officially designated a Zone 9–10 plant— which means it needs plenty of sun to do its stuff.
- 🐾 *Sesleria caerulea* (moor grass). This hardy, clumping grass with metallic blue-gray foliage is useful as an edging or in perennial borders and rock gardens. It does well in the shade of trees and shrubs. It grows 6 to 12 inches (15 to 30 cm) and is hardy to Zone 5.

*P*hiladelphus coronarius 'Aureus'

Common name: *Mock orange*

Chief characteristics

Location: Full sun to light shade
Type: Deciduous shrub
Size: 10 feet (3 m)
Conditions: Fertile, well-drained soil
Flowering time: June to July
Zone: 3

The great value of having a mock orange in the garden is that it has masses of white flowers in July. This helps to bridge the gap at the critical time of midsummer and provides a smooth transition in the shrub border between spring and autumn. The other marvelous attribute of a mock orange bush is its highly scented blooms, which have a clear, refreshing orange-blossom perfume. There are many cultivars to choose from. One of my favorites is *Philadelphus coronarius* 'Aureus', which has golden-yellow leaves that provide excellent foliage contrast, especially alongside the purple leaves of smoke bush. 'Aureus' is a medium-sized shrub that grows about 6 to 8 feet (1.8 to 2.4 m) high and produces abundant clusters of fragrant, creamy white flowers in early summer.

The most commonly planted mock orange is *Philadelphus × virginalis*, which is hardy to Zone 4 and has large, pure white flowers in late June with excellent fragrance and attractive green foliage. 'Glacier' has fragrant, double white flowers and grows to 5 feet (1.5 m). The outstanding cultivar 'Miniature Snowflake' grows only 4 feet (1.2 m) high and also has very fragrant double white blooms. *Philadelphus* 'Buckley's Quill' is a semi-dwarf variety, growing to 5 feet (1.5 m), with double white flowers in early summer. Other kinds of mock orange you may come across include 'Beauclerk', 'Belle Etoile' and 'Sybille'.

Where to plant it

An excellent choice for the back of the mixed shrub border, the golden-leafed *Philadelphus coronarius* 'Aureus' is good for foliage contrast. Place it in a spot where the fruity orange scent can be appreciated and permitted to mingle with the other pleasant aromas of the summer garden. Mock orange can be grown close to a back gate or next to an arbor or gazebo. The smaller forms will fit very nicely in a garden with limited space.

How to care for it

An easy-care shrub, mock orange likes sun. It will tolerate light shade, but does not like dense shade. The soil does not have to be exceptional but it should be well drained without drying out in summer.

Prune mock orange in late summer after flowering or in spring before flowers appear. A third of the old stems can be comfortably snipped out, especially in the taller shrubs. This will keep the bush from becoming too dense and will promote new growth.

Good companions

Dark backgrounds are best to bring out the foliage color of *Philadelphus coronarius*. A bank of conifers, or yew or cedar hedging, will also accent the white flowers. Lily-of-the-valley shrub (*Pieris japonica* 'Temple Bells') makes a good partner since it will kick off the season with impressive clusters of white flowers in spring, paving the way for mock orange in the summer. *Pieris japonica* 'Valley Valentine' does a similar job, growing 7 feet (2.1 m) tall at maturity and producing deep red flowers. These are both, however, slightly less hardy than *Pieris japonica* 'Forest Flame' and 'Mountain Fire', both of which have flame-red new foliage in spring that turns green with maturity. You could also consider *Pieris* 'Brouwer's Beauty', which has yellow new foliage that turns dark green in summer.

Other suitable partners for mock orange include magnolias, rhododendrons, old garden roses, peonies, purple smoke bush (*Cotinus coggygria*) and buddleia. Rose of Sharon (*Hibiscus syriacus*) is another possibility; top cultivars include 'Double Blue', 'Ardens' (purple), 'Aphrodite' (rose-pink), 'Morningstar' (white with red centers), 'Rubis' (red), 'Coelestis' (sky blue) and 'Blushing Bride' (pink carnation-type bloom). They all grow about 10 feet (3 m).

For your collection

- *Philadelphus coronarius* 'Variegatus' has white flowers and light white and green leaves that add striking foliage interest to the shrub border. It is a medium-sized shrub, growing about 8 feet (2.4 m).

$\mathcal{P}$hlox paniculata 'Fujiama'

Common name: *Phlox*

Chief characteristics

You don't need a wall calender or a digital watch to know what time of year it is. Your garden is just as accurate a guide to the seasons. You know, for instance, that summer is definitely at its peak when you see tall, majestic clumps of *Phlox paniculata* holding up sweetly scented bright red, white, pink and purple flowers. It is an understatement to say phlox is a stalwart of the summer garden or even to describe it as a workhorse or a popular perennial. It is much more. It is one of the plants you cannot do without if you want to lift your garden in July and August to the zenith of its glory. Before people torment you with tall tales of how prone phlox is to mildew and aphids, scorched leaves and leaf-munching snails, hold on to this: whatever the problems, you can overcome them, and you will be glad you didn't turn your back on phlox. The rewards far outweigh the piddling drawbacks.

Location: Full sun
Type: Perennial
Size: 3 to 4 feet (90 to 120 cm)
Conditions: Good, moist, well-drained soil
Flowering time: July to September
Zone: 4

There are several excellent cultivars of *Phlox paniculata* to consider. One of the best white forms is ' Fujiama'. It has pure white flowers in mid- to late summer and is much more disease resistant than most other garden phlox. Its flowers are slightly smaller than those of other cultivars but they last a lot longer. Other top performers include 'Nora Leigh' (creamy-white variegated foliage with near white flowers with pink eye), 'Darwin's Joyce' (almost identical to 'Nora Leigh'), 'Starfire' (cherry-red), 'Amethyst' (lavender-violet), 'Elizabeth Arden' (pink), 'Eva Cullum' (pink with red eye), 'Europa' (white with pink eye) and 'Bright Eyes' (pink with a cerise eye).

Where to plant it

Phlox paniculata looks its best grown in large groups in full sun in the middle or back of the flower bed. It flourishes in soil that is free-draining but also capable of retaining moisture. Top names like 'Fujiama' and 'David' are sturdy plants that hold themselves perfectly erect and do not require staking. Other kinds may need a helping hand to look their best and should be carefully staked as they rise from the ground in spring.

Color preferences are personal. You may find the single-color cultivars form less jarring associations. They can also present the most striking image. If you are going to use the vivid two-tone or orange phlox, you will need to give more thought to potential color clashes.

How to care for it

Put down a good layer of mulch, either well-rotted compost or manure, in spring as the plants reappear and start their climb upward. Water copiously in dry spells. Thin out clumps to improve air circulation and prevent mildew and leaf rot closer to the ground. As a last resort, spray with a mild solution of fungicide. You can spray your delphiniums and bee balm at the same time. But keeping the soil moist, the air flowing and the plants healthy are your three best forms of defense against mildew. It is not nearly as big a problem as some people say.

Good companions

There is no shortage of partners for phlox. Try bee balm, globe thistle, shasta daisies, daylilies, stachys, liatris, crocosmia, penstemon, ornamental grasses, Russian sage (*Perovskia*), baby's breath, lavatera, alliums, asters, rudbeckia and second-flush campanulas and delphiniums.

For your collection

Phlox also offers some excellent low-growing, evergreen plants for the sunny rockery garden or for tumbling over a low retaining wall.

- *Phlox subulata*. The creeping type of phlox is worth getting to know. Look for 'Emerald Blue' (pale lilac), 'Emerald Pink' (soft pink), 'Benita' (lavender-pink) or 'Atropurpurea' (rose-red).
- *Phlox douglasii* is so similar to the cultivars of *P. subulata* just mentioned, it is hard to tell them apart. They flower around the same time. Top performers are 'Red Admiral' (soft red), 'Crackerjack' (bright red), and 'Rose Cushion' (pink). All are very useful as mat forming plants for filling spaces in the rockery or edging or softening the sharp corners of walls.
- *Phlox maculata* (meadow phlox). There are some lovely forms worth trying. They are supposed to be slightly more mildew resistant than some of the more popular summer phlox. *P. maculata* 'Alpha' has lilac-pink flowers with a darker pink eye in the center; 'Omega' and 'Miss Lingard' have white flowers; and 'Rosalinde' has bright pink blooms.

$\mathcal{P}$icea pungens 'Hoopsii'

Common name: *Colorado blue spruce, Hoop's blue spruce*

Chief characteristics

Location: Full sun to part shade
Type: Evergreen tree
Size: 30 feet (9 m)
Conditions: Ordinary, well-drained soil
Zone: 3

Conifers are not essential in a garden, but they are useful for structure and winter color. The Colorado blue spruce is exceptional in January against white snow or with frost on its bright, steel-blue needles. There are many different cultivars from which to choose but Hoop's blue spruce (*Picea pungens* 'Hoopsii'), is the bluest of the spruces and one of the most desirable. It has stiff horizontal branches and dense, silver-blue needles. It is relatively slow-growing, reaching only 8 feet (2.4 m) after 10 years, and its growth can be somewhat irregular for the first few years, but the spectacular blue needles easily make up for any perceived flaws.

Other popular forms of *Picea pungens* to look for include 'Fat Albert', a compact, slow-growing, upright pyramidal tree that requires no pruning to maintain its shape; 'Hoto', which has bright, blue-gray needles; 'Fastigiata', which is very narrow and has vivid blue needles; and 'Moerheimii', which has dark blue needles. *P. pungens* 'Glauca Pendula' has blue-green needles and can be used to add special architectural interest to your garden. *P. pungens* 'Glauca Bakeri', the dwarf globe blue spruce, is a slow-growing, compact bush with gray-blue needles. It is a good specimen for the rockery since it grows only 2 to 3 feet (60 to 90 cm).

Where to plant it

Grow blue spruces in the mixed shrub border as contrast foliage plants or alone as a special specimen. The role of conifers in the garden is to provide structural "bones" and year-round color. Use them to tie your garden landscape together so there is some structure even in the dead of winter.

How to care for it

Blue spruces get their color from a powder that is formed on the outside of the needles. If you rub a needle, it will turn green. Iron trace elements in the soil are very important in the formation of the powder. A trick to keep your blue spruce blue is to add some aluminum sulfate—the same chemical used to keep hydrangeas blue—to the soil. This makes the soil more acidic, which helps the plant absorb more iron and produce more blue powder.

Conifers need to be well watered when they are establishing themselves. They require routine pruning the rest of the time to maintain their shape. Some forms of blue spruce are not always willing to grow a single leader shoot, so you may have to prune carefully to achieve the shape you want. The popular cultivars 'Hoopsii' and 'Fat Albert' are less demanding.

Good companions

Rhododendrons, azaleas, magnolias, pieris, mahonia, corkscrew hazel, hollies, yellow- and red-twig dogwoods, ornamental grasses and witch hazels are all good companions. Groundcover plants include euonymus, euphorbia, cotoneaster, sedum, creeping phlox, juniper and potentilla.

For your collection

These popular evergreens are also excellent performers.

- *Larix decidua* 'Pendula' (weeping European larch) has soft green weeping foliage that turns golden in October. It can be used as a mounding groundcover or you can stake it to whatever height you desire to establish an upright specimen.
- *Thuja occidentalis* 'Rheingold' is a popular, slow-growing, dwarf conifer with golden yellow foliage that turns bronze in winter. It combines well with heathers, especially the winter-flowering species. It grows 10 feet (3 m) high by 6 feet (1.8 m) wide in 10 to 12 years.
- *Thuja occidentalis* 'Smaragd' has emerald-green foliage that requires minimal pruning and retains its color year-round. It is better known as the "emerald cedar," perhaps because people have a hard time pronouncing 'Smaragd.'
- *Ginkgo biloba* (maidenhair tree). One of the world's oldest trees, there is fossil evidence that this dates back to dinosaur times. It has lovely, yellow, butterfly-like leaves in fall. It stays a teenager for the longest time, growing slowly to 25 feet (7.5 m) after 20 years or more. It has the potential to go higher.

Polemonium caeruleum 'Brise d'Anjou'

Common name: *Variegated Jacob's ladder*

Chief characteristics

It is always fun to walk with friends around the garden and point to a plant that has an interesting story to tell. Variegated Jacob's ladder is just such a plant. The story goes that the plant vanished for almost a century before resurfacing in a small nursery in France. It was spotted by an alert gardener and has since been propagated and circulated around the world.

Location: Part sun to light shade
Type: Perennial
Size: 18 to 24 inches (45 to 60 cm)
Conditions: Moist, well-drained soil
Flowering time: May to June
Zone: 2

The beauty of this handsome cultivar of Jacob's ladder is its striking, cream-and-green-striped foliage. It has delicate blue flowers, which are produced at the top of erect stems. The plant gets its name from the ladder-like appearance of its leaves. 'Brise d'Anjou' looks good in the perennial border but really grabs attention when it is combined in a pot with *Scabiosa columbaria* 'Butterfly Blue'. The two shades of blue flowers interact very well together and the more rigid structure of Jacob's ladder contrasts effectively with the looser foliage of scabiosa.

The more common form of Jacob's ladder is the plain, green-leafed, cottage-garden inhabitant, *Polemonium caeruleum* It also produces rosettes of small blue flowers on tall, erect stems in June. A beautiful fragrant white-flowering cultivar, *P. caeruleum* 'Album', is available, as well as a more compact plant called 'Blue Pearl'.

Where to plant it

Grow Jacob's ladder in sunny or semi-shaded sites in good, slightly moist soil. It will perform better if given some shade in the afternoon. The middle of a mixed perennial border is a good place for it. And 'Brise d'Anjou' looks splendid in a pot on a patio and can be used as a feature plant in the garden.

How to care for it

Polemonium has a reputation for seeding itself here, there and everywhere. To eliminate the problem, clip the flowerheads before they get into full seed production. Keep plants well watered in the dry days of summer. If the leaves show signs of scorching, move plants to a shadier site. Divide clumps in fall or early spring.

Good companions

The busy cream-and-green-striped foliage of 'Brise d'Anjou' makes it stand out, but it also means you have to be careful where you place it or you could end up with a riotous scene. Surround it with the foliage of plants like astrantia, polygonatum, and *Aconitum napellus*. The calm, cool blue flowers look spectacular above the warmer, purple-blue, crown-like flowers of *Centaurea montana*. Blue hostas, like 'Halcyon', 'Hadspen Blue' and 'Blue Belle', will echo the soft blue flowers of Jacob's ladder.

The white plumes of astilbes like 'Snowdrift', 'Bridal Veil' or 'Washington' would not cause too much alarm, and the dark flowers of mourning widow cranesbill (*Geranium phaeum*) could be thrown in behind.

For your collection

Other fine polemoniums and blue-flowering plants include the following.

- *Polemonium carneum* has pink flowers and grows about 15 inches (38 cm) tall while *P. pulcherrimum*, (skunkleaf Jacob's ladder) gets only 12 inches (30 cm) high and has blue flowers with a yellow throat.
- Another outstanding blue-flowering perennial worth getting to know is the Chinese balloon flower (*Platycodon grandiflorus*), which grows 24 to 30 inches (60 to 75 cm).
- *Caryopteris* × *clandonensis* 'Dark Knight' is a woody shrub that grows 2 to 3 feet (60 to 90 cm) high and is generally sold as a perennial. It produces deep purple flowers from August to October in a full-sun location.
- *Corydalis flexuosa* 'Blue Panda', 'China Blue' and 'Purple Leaf' are three exciting blue-flowering plants that caused quite a fuss when they first became available. They are still very much admired for their blue blooms. Grows about 12 inches (30 cm) tall.
- *Aconitum carmichaelii* 'Arendsii' is a fall-blooming monkshood, with clusters of deep violet-blue blooms displayed on sturdy stems about 3 feet (90 cm) tall.

Polygonum bistorta 'Superbum'

Common name: *Fleece flower, knotweed*

Chief characteristics

'Superbum' produces pink bottlebrush flowers for about a month starting around the middle of May. The flowers are formed at the top of slender, 2-foot (60-cm) stems. Insignificant on their own, the flowers become an impressive spectacle, especially when combined with purple alliums. The blooms of 'Superbum' make an excellent cut flower, combining well in tall vases with blue or lilac aquilegias, purple-speckled foxgloves, pale blue bearded irises, red peonies and coral bells to form a natural, seasonally correct bouquet. The only drawback to 'Superbum' is that it flowers in spring and has little to offer in the summer months. With thoughtful planting this need not be a problem.

> **Location:** Full sun to part shade
> **Type:** Perennial
> **Size:** 24 to 30 inches (60 to 75 cm)
> **Conditions:** Ordinary, moist, well-drained soil
> **Flowering time:** May to June
> **Zone:** 3

Botanists changed the name of the plant a while ago. You'll now find it labeled *Persicaria bistorta* 'Superba', although a lot of garden centers have stayed with the old name. By the way, the name 'Superbum' is pronounced "Superb-um," although some people have fun pronouncing it "Super-bum." Either way is perfectly acceptable.

Another popular cultivar is *Polygonum affine* 'Dimity', which grows only 6 to 8 inches (15 to 20 cm) high and has short red flower spikes that turn to pink as they age. This dwarf knotweed (now officially *Persicaria affinis*) is considered by some to be the most useful of the lot because it is compact and has a mat-forming habit.

There is one other type—*Polygonum amplexicaule*—which is a much taller, bushier plant that produces crimson poker-like flowers on 3- to 4-foot (90- to 120-cm) stems most of summer. Varieties to look for include 'Firetail' (salmon-red) and 'Taurus' (scarlet red).

Where to plant it

The key to placing 'Superbum' in the right spot is to remember that once it has finished flowering and you have cut down the faded flower spikes, all that is left is the low carpet of green leaves. So you need to think about what to plant with it to create a sequence of color. It will fit nicely under trees or shrubs that have a couple of feet (60 cm) of open space at their base. It can also be used in pots.

Knotweed grows best in moist soil in full sun or light shade. The ideal spot is where it receives morning sun and afternoon shade.

How to care for it

Cut 'Superbum' right down to the ground the moment it finishes flowering. This will seem rather dramatic, but in no time at all, fresh new leaves will appear as the plant quickly rejuvenates itself. It sometimes even starts to flower a second time, but the idea here is to avoid the unsightly mess of the old first leaves.

Divide clumps every few years. If the plant starts to become invasive, simply take a shovel and dig it back to its boundaries or give the excess away to friends and neighbors. Leaves can scorch badly in direct afternoon sun. Water in dry summers.

Good companions

Ornamental onion (*Allium aflatunense*) makes an excellent partner for 'Superbum'. The round purple heads of allium harmonize perfectly with knotweed's pink bottlebrush spikes. Camassias will also push up through the leaves if you like a pink and blue flower contrast. Astilbe, astrantia, hardy geranium, and hosta are all excellent partners for maintaining a sequence of blooms.

An interesting companion (but not on the shelf at every garden center) is *Mukdenia rossii* (also known as *Aceriphyllum*), which looks something like a miniature umbrella plant (*Peltaphyllum*) because of its dense clusters of maple-like leaves. It grows only 12 inches (30 cm) high and likes rich but not boggy ground in light shade. It is considered a first-class woodland landscape plant and is hardy to Zone 5.

For your collection

- *Polygonum cuspidatum,* now *Fallopia japonica* (Japanese fleece flower). This is a somewhat invasive groundcover for mass planting around trees and shrubs.

Potentilla fruticosa 'Abbotswood'

Common name: *Potentilla, cinquefoil*

Chief characteristics

Gardeners often want the impossible— a plant that flowers beautifully and perpetually, yet requires minimal or no maintenance, has no pest or disease problems, and grows only 2 feet (60 cm) high. There is no perfect plant, but this little bushy decidous shrub is about as good as it gets. Here you have a plant that has the longest flowering period of all garden shrubs, pumping out yellow, orange, red, white or pink blooms (depending on the variety) from June right through to fall. It is immune to most pests and disease and it will thrive happily in sun or light shade in the poorest of soils.

Location: Full sun or light shade
Type: Deciduous shrub
Size: 2 to 4 feet (60 to 120 cm)
Conditions: Average, semi-moist, well-drained soils
Flowering time: June to September
Zone: 2

A member of the massive rose family (Rosaceae), which includes apples, raspberries and strawberries, *Potentilla* gets its common name, cinquefoil, from its leaves, which are often divided into five lobes or fingers. However, most us call potentilla by its botanical rather than common name. A remarkable little shrub, it has one other outstanding quality: it is relatively slow-growing, putting on less than 12 inches (30 cm) a year, and will keep its nicely rounded shape with minimal pruning. It is also drought tolerant and will not sulk if planted in heavy soil.

Choosing the right potentilla for your garden is a matter of personal taste. There are several excellent cultivars available. 'Abbotswood' is the best of the white-flowering cinquefoils. It has attractive blue-green foliage and it can be used both as a feature plant or for hedging. Two white-flowering types are 'Snowbird' (double white) and 'McKay's White' (creamy white), but 'Abbotswood' is number one in my book.

The best of the reds is 'Red Robin', which has fiery, brick-red flowers that hold their color in full sun instead of turning orange as some red- and pink-flowering types have a tendency to do.

Other popular performers include 'Goldfinger' (golden yellow), 'Pink Princess' (light pink), 'Goldstar' (yellow), 'Primrose Beauty' (pale yellow, silvery gray foliage), 'Tangerine' (orange-yellow), 'Pink Beauty' (clear pink), 'Royal Flush' (rosy pink) and 'Red Ace' (red).

Where to plant it

Use *Potentilla fruticosa* as a feature, front-of-the border plant in a perennial or mixed scheme, or as part of the foundation planting in a rockery or planted in a row to form a low-growing, informal hedge. It thrives in full sun or light shade in average or poor sandy soil, more alkaline than acidic. Although drought tolerant, potentilla does require a reasonably moist, yet well-drained site.

The top red cultivars—'Red Robin' and 'Red Ace'—maintain their color best if given protection from hot afternoon sun, which can fade the red flowers to orange. The white- and yellow-flowering varieties also tend to lose their crisp tones, but less noticeably, in the heat of summer, returning to their old form in the cool days of September.

How to care for it

The beauty of potentilla is that it has no enemies. Pests and disease pass over it in search for more vulnerable prey. You may hear talk about cinquefoil being prone to leaf spot and strawberry weevils but it rarely happens.

Pruning is not recommended, but can be done simply to maintain the plant's shape. You will probably find it necessary to prune your plant every few years to remove old dead wood and promote new healthy growth. When you prune, take out a complete branch, rather than using hedging shears to trim it back. The best time to do this is the first moment of spring or in fall.

If you decide to try your hand at propagating potentilla, you'll find it generally roots very easily from softwood or semi-ripe cuttings taken from June to August.

Good companions

Lavender, *Spirea bumalda* and *Artemisia* 'Silver Mound' all make good partners for potentilla. Also consider sun-loving, long-flowering perennials such as *Geranium* 'Ballerina', *Helenium autumnale* and *Salvia* 'Butterfly Blue' for companions. In light shade, mix in some hostas, ornamental grasses and impatiens. Potentilla also looks good planted in front of hydrangeas or sharing ground with dwarf conifers and yuccas.

For your collection

The many cultivars of *Potentilla fruticosa* are the most widely grown, but there are a few other species worth finding a place for in your garden.

🐾 *Potentilla megalantha* (strawberry-leaved cinquefoil) has leaves covered with silvery hairs as well as cheerful yellow flowers. It grows

6 to 8 inches (15 to 20 cm) tall and forms a low mat at the front of the border.

- *Potentilla nepalensis* 'Miss Willmott' is named after the infamous British gardener who went about scattering *Erigeron* seeds everywhere. This is a reliable performer, growing to 12 inches (30 cm) and producing crimson-pink flowers in June.
- *Potentilla tonguei* (staghorn cinquefoil) has apricot flowers with red centers in July and August. A good evergreen plant for late-summer color, it grows 12 inches (30 cm) high, making it a useful pick for the front of the border.

*P*rimula japonica 'Miller's Crimson'

Common name: *Candelabra primula*

Chief characteristics

There are really only two kinds of primula: the garish, multi-colored hybrids you see for sale outside supermarkets in spring, and the rest, which are generally far more beautiful and elegant. These simple-flowered plants are a joy to have in the garden. It is all in the eye of the beholder, of course, but once you have seen an exhibition of the subtle, soft pastel shades of primula, you will never go back to the jarring "supermarket specials." These supermarket plants seem to escape criticism because they are marketed as the chosen "cheerful" heralds of spring and have been deemed the appropriate symbol for displaying in pots on doorsteps to signal the end of winter.

Location: Full sun to semi-shade
Type: Perennial
Size: 2 to 3 feet (60 to 90 cm)
Conditions: Fertile, moist, well-drained soil
Flowering time: March to May
Zone: 5

You can do a lot better. There is, for example, the common English primrose (*Primula vulgaris*), which has superbly simple, soft yellow flowers on modest 6-inch (15-cm) stems in March to April. Or how about one of the oldest and most enduring primulas of all, 'Wanda', which has plain purple flowers and has since been used to produce a wide range of colorful hybrids? There are many other classy performers such as 'Evonne', which has dark red flowers with golden yellow edges, making it look rather like a stylish necklace. 'Mahogany Sunrise' is very similar, with each petal edged with gold. These were bred by Dr. John Kerridge of B.C. He has also introduced a number of other worthy primulas, including 'Velvet Moon' (red with yellow center). The drumstick primrose (*P. denticulata*) is among the first to appear in spring and is also very lovely, growing only 12 inches (30 cm) high and coming in a range of subdued colors from blue to lilac, white to pink. It gets its name "drumstick" from the shape of the tightly clustered flowerhead. Names to look for include 'Alba' (white), 'Rubin' (rose) and 'Blue Selection' (lilac to deep blue). You will easily spot them because of their distinctive shape.

But of all the primulas, the most classy, to my mind, are the candelabra primulas (*Primula japonica*), which also just happen to be among the easiest to grow. In moist soil, especially by the banks of streams or ponds, they will quickly colonize to present a magnificent picture in late spring. The flowers are beautifully arranged in neat tiers (hence candelabra) along stems that can stretch 18 to 24 inches (45 to 60 cm) high. Colors range from white to pink, red to apricot. Despite being next to one another in mass plantings, the colors never jar. 'Miller's Crimson' is sensational. It has intense crimson-pink flowers and large leaves. It is especially attractive when mass-planted. 'Postford White' is one of the most famous candelabra primulas, not only because of its pure white flowers but because it comes true from seed.

The old-fashioned double English primroses, which have multi-petaled, rose-like flowers, are also now more available. They thrive in moist, rich soil, and must be protected from scorching sun. Top names include 'Alan Robb' (pale apricot), 'April Rose' (deep red), 'Dawn Ansell' (white), 'Lilian Harvey' (rose-pink), 'Sunshine Susie' (golden yellow), 'Sue Jervis' (muted peach), 'Miss Indigo' (purple with white edges) and 'Quaker's Bonnet' (lavender-violet).

Where to plant it

The primula family is enormous. Some like wet, boggy ground; others like growing in cool rockeries. *Primula japonica* 'Miller's Crimson' is happiest in moist soil. The ideal location to grow most primulas is the east side of the house in a cool, shady spot, perhaps under rhododendrons, deciduous trees and shrubs, where they can flower safely in spring and enjoy foliage protected from the sun in summer. In the spring, primulas will take all the sun you can give them. In the summer, the morning sun won't hurt them, but the midday or afternoon sun will burn them.

They are not as long-lived as other perennials, but in the right location they usually manage to self-seed.

How to care for it

Primulas need moist shade. Give them a shot of 20-20-20 liquid fertilizer to wake them up in spring and 0-10-10 to put them to bed in fall. They like moist soil but good drainage. When you plant them, dig in some sand or crushed rock or peat moss to get the soil right. Don't make your soil too rich in organic matter or it can become compact and soggy in winter and your primulas will rot.

Watch for slugs, snails, cutworms, weevils and aphids—they can all be a problem.

Good companions

Primulas are happiest tucked under rhododendrons or deciduous shrubs and trees. They combine well with spring-flowering bulbs like muscari, scillas, chionodoxa, leucojum and narcissus, as well as spring-flowering perennials like *Helleborus orientalis*. To achieve a sequence of blooms, put *Primula florindae* together with *Primula japonica*.

For your collection

- *Primula florindae* (giant cowslip). If you're lucky enough to have a woodland brook or stream or pond in your garden, you could grow the giant cowslip, which flowers in summer with fragrant yellow blooms on stems 2 to 3 feet (60 to 90 cm) high. Everything about this primula is oversized. Its perfume is heavy rather than delicate, and the leaves grow bigger according to the degree of moisture in the soil. There are also red and orange shades of *P. florindae* available.
- *Primula sieboldii* (Japanese star primrose). Another collector's item, this plant grows 9 inches (23 cm) tall and produces fabulous white or pink, magenta or purple flowers. Top names are 'Geisha Girl' (shocking pink), 'Mikado' (purple) and 'Snowflakes' (pure white).
- *Primula vialii* (Chinese pagoda primrose). Everyone falls in love with this primula when they see it for the first time. It has short pink bottlebrush flower spikes with a distinctive red cone on top that makes it look rather like a miniature red-hot poker plant. It does self-seed and if you get it in the right spot—a cool, well-drained, semi-shaded, woodland-type setting—you might have it for years to come.
- One other important group of primulas is the Auricula Hybrids, regarded by some as the "aristocrats of the primrose world" because of their showy, decorative flowers. Names to look for include 'The Baron' (yellow), 'Matthew Yates' (deep red), 'Camelot' (purple) and 'Chorister' (white).

$\mathcal{P}$runus × cistena

Common name: *Purple-leaf sand cherry*

Chief characteristics

Location: Full sun
Type: Deciduous tree
Size: 13 feet (4 m)
Conditions: Average, well-drained soil
Flowering time: May
Zone: 2

The explosion of cheerful pink cherry blossoms in spring always lifts my spirits and gives me a renewed sense of optimism and enthusiasm. If gardening is about anything, it is about knowing and valuing the inherent power of nature to overcome winter and bounce back to life. For me, gardening is often more about surrendering and responding to the beauty of a landscape than it is about the effort and skill required to create and maintain it. This is especially true when I stand looking in silent admiration at the exquisite blooms of flowering Japanese cherry trees.

There are many excellent cultivars for your garden or boulevard, but for the small garden, there is something especially charming about the purple-leaf sand cherry (*Prunus × cistena*). Perhaps it is the plum-colored foliage that makes it so appealing. Or perhaps the elegance and simplicity of the single, soft light-pink flowers in May. It is a popular tree and can be grown as a bushy foliage shrub as well.

The Kwanzan cherry (*Prunus serrulata* 'Kwanzan') is another first-rate pick with its sturdy, upright, vase-shaped, showy, double pink flowers in May. The copper-red young leaves turn green in summer and an impressive yellow in fall. Sometimes listed as 'Kanzan' or 'Hisakura', 'Kwanzan' will grow to about 25 feet (7.5 m).

Weeping Japanese cherry (*Prunus subhirtella* 'Pendula') is also a fine specimen with its graceful umbrella form. It produces masses of deep rose-pink flowers in May. One of the first Japanese cherries to be brought to North America from Japan, 'Pendula' is a modest grower, reaching 20 feet (6 m) high. Another cherry you should know about is the weeping Kiku-Shidare Japanese cherry (*Prunus subhirtella* 'Kiku-Shidare'), which grows to 13 feet (4 m). It has pink blossoms in May and tiny black fruit in September.

Where to plant it

Ornamental cherry trees are one of the great symbols of spring. Some call them the "queen of trees" and the "champion of spring bloomers." They all thrive in a sunny location in rich, well-drained soil. Plant your tree in September or as soon as the ground is workable in April.

If you are unsure of what kind you want, it is a good idea to take time in spring to look around before you pick out the one you like best. If you buy in late summer for fall planting you need to know how the tree will perform in spring.

The plum-colored leaves of *Prunus × cistena* provide excellent foliage contrast in the mixed shrub border. Or it can be grown alone to add delicacy and charm to a courtyard corner. The pink blossoms of a weeping cherry look particularly lovely next to a pond, where the flowers can cast a reflection in the water.

How to care for it

Watch out for aphids, borers, fungus leaf spots and powdery mildew. Apart from that, ornamental cherries require little maintenance. Prune them for shape when young, taking out crossing branches and routinely removing any branches killed or damaged in winter. Once trees are more mature, prune as soon as they finish flowering or wait until early winter. It is best not to prune them in the dead of winter for fear of creating wounds that could leave the tree open to disease.

Good companions

The blues of forget-me-nots and spring-flowering bulbs like bluebells and grape hyacinth will provide beautiful color contrast to the purple leaves of your little sand cherry. Underplant weeping cherry trees with early tulips and dwarf narcissus. Think about planting other trees or shrubs nearby that will provide a natural continuity and sequence of color. Lilacs, rhododendrons, deciduous azaleas, magnolias and weigela are all good partners.

For your collection

Crabapple trees offer a similar burst of pink blossoms in spring with the added bonus of fruit in fall. If you go looking for a crabapple, choose one of the following star performers.

- *Malus* 'Dolgo'. The large red fruit of this crabapple is renowned for making excellent jelly. The tree grows to 20 feet (6 m) and has white flowers in May.
- *Malus* 'Louisa'. A small weeping tree, growing to 16 feet (5 m) at maturity, this has dark green leaves, pink flowers in May, and yellow fruit in September.
- *Malus moerlandsii* 'Profusion'. Rose-pink flowers appear in May on this crabapple, which has bronze leaves and grows to 20 feet (6 m). It produces small red fruit in September.

🐦 *Malus* 'Red Jade'. One of the most popular small weeping crabapples, this has pink buds that open to pure white flowers in May. It grows only 13 feet (4 m) tall. It gets its name from the bright red color of the fruit, which first appear in September but continue coming into late fall.

🐦 *Malus* 'Royalty'. The regal red foliage of this tree turns bronze in late summer just as the red fruit begins to appear. 'Royalty' grows 20 feet (6 m) tall and has red-purple blooms in spring.

Rhododendron Northern Lights Series

Common name: *Northern Lights azalea*

Chief characteristics

It is a challenge to grow rhododendrons and azaleas successfully in Ontario gardens. First, there are extremely cold winter temperatures to contend with. Most rhododendrons thrive best in temperate climate zones, where winters are mild and temperatures occasionally dip below freezing. Second, there is the problem of establishing ideal soil conditions. Rhodos prefer acidic rather than alkaline soil, which is why they flourish so well in the Pacific Northwest where heavy rains wash any trace of lime from the soil and leave it perfectly acidic—ideal for plants such as kalmia and pieris and for turning the flowers of mophead hydrangeas an intense shade of blue. There are, however, rhodos and azaleas that flourish very nicely in colder climates. Some have been bred specifically for that purpose. The important issue here is to make the right selection.

> **Location:** Light, dappled shade
> **Type:** Deciduous shrub
> **Size:** 3 to 5 feet (1 to 1.5 m)
> **Conditions:** Average, slightly acidic soil
> **Flowering time:** May to June
> **Zone:** 3

You won't go wrong if you pick one of the Northern Lights azaleas. These top-performance hybrids were developed at the University of Minnesota especially for growing in the coldest areas of Canada and the United States. There are seven popular cultivars in the series: 'Golden Lights' (reddish-orange buds, highly fragrant yellow flowers); 'Hi-Light' (white flowers with yellow blotch); 'Orchid Lights' (orchid-pink flowers); 'Spicy Lights' (apricot and peach blooms); 'White Lights' (milk-white flowers); 'Rosy Lights' (purplish-red with rose-red shadings); and 'Mandarin Lights' (lightly fragrant, bright red-orange blooms). They are all hardy, even in chilly areas, flower in late May and grow between

5 and 6 feet (1.5 to 2 m) high, except for 'Orchid Lights', which is compact, growing to only 20 inches (50 cm).

Here are a few other helpful facts about these outstanding plants. 'Golden Lights' is particularly resistant to mildew; extremely hardy 'Orchid Lights' can survive being buried in deep snow and is a good plant for a rock garden or perennial border; 'Spicy Lights' has blooms with a spicy, fruity fragrance; 'White Lights' produces flowers that last several weeks.

Where to plant it

You will often find Northern Lights azaleas tagged with the name *Rhododendon*. Don't let this confuse you. Azaleas and rhodos are members of the same botanical family—azaleas are technically rhododendrons. What this means in practical terms is that they both thrive in the same soil conditions. They prefer well-drained, acidic soil, rich in organic matter. Rhodos and azaleas flourish in light, dappled shade where they are protected from direct sun in the afternoon, but they can be grown in full sun, provided you give them plenty of nitrogen and adequate water.

The bright flowers of the Northern Lights azaleas give a lift to any shrub border in spring, but they need to be placed so they don't compete or clash with other spring-flowering shrubs. They look best when set against a solid backdrop of dark green conifers.

How to care for it

Make sure the soil is right at the time of planting your azalea. It needs to be fertile, well drained, loamy and slightly acidic (with a pH of 4 or 5). Be careful how you water. More azaleas and rhododendrons are killed by overwatering than by cold weather. It is important not to water too little or too much.

Rhodos have a shallow root system, so don't use a hoe around the rootball and mulch well in winter to provide a little protection from cold and enrich the soil. To encourage a bushier plant, pinch-prune the ends of branches when the shrub is young to promote more lateral shoots.

Good companions

Euonymus, Japanese pieris, blue star juniper, heathers, boxwood, enkianthus, and white-flowered magnolias can all provide interest, either through foliage texture or with bright flowers.

Other rhodondendrons can also be worked into the landscape to create layers of foliage and bloom. Consider using one or more hybrids of *Rhododendron yakushimanum* or the new Finnish rhodos, 'Hellikki' or 'Peter Tigerstedt'. Spring-flowering bulbs can create a natural sequence of color or you could group all the Northern Lights series together in one area along with some of the famous Exbury and Knap Hill Hybrids— notably 'Strawberry', (soft pink), 'Gibraltar' (orange), 'Cockatoo' (orange-yellow) and 'Avocet' (creamy white with pink tinge)—to create a dynamic splash of color from May to June.

For your collection

Here is a guide to the hardiest of the hardy rhododendrons.

- The Finnish rhododendrons were developed at the University of Helsinki to withstand winter temperatures of –30°F (–34°C). Look for 'Hellikki', which grows to about 5 feet (1.5 m) and has dark violet-red trusses; and 'Peter Tigerstedt', which grows 5 feet (1.5 m) high and has white flowers with violet specks.
- *Rhododendron yakushimanum* hybrids are distinctive because of their very attactive, compact shape and the thick coating of brown suede-like hair (called indumentum) on the underside of the leaves. All "yaks" are extremely floriferous and very hardy. Look for 'Crete' (magenta-rose buds opening to light purple with yellow spots); 'Mardi Gras' (pale pink flowers fading to white); and 'Mist Maiden' (deep pink buds opening to apple-bossom pink and eventually fading to white).
- Other desirable rhodos that are reliable, hardy performers include: 'P.J.M.' (bright lavender-pink); *R. catawbiense* 'Album' (pure white), *R. catawbiense* 'Boursault' (lavender-violet); 'Olga Mezitt' (phlox pink); *R. ponticum* 'Variegatum' (green and white foliage and small lavender-pink flowers); 'Party Pink' (purple-pink); 'Nova Zembla' (striking red); 'Cotton Candy' (pastel pink); 'Casanova' (pink and yellow); 'Black Satin' (red-purple). They all bloom from late April to mid-May and grow between 4 to 6 feet (1.2 to 1.5 m) high.

osa 'Ballerina'

Common name: *Ballerina rose*

Chief characteristics

A terrific shrub rose, 'Ballerina' comes with excellent credentials. It flowers profusely, producing abundant clusters of small, pale-pink, single blooms with white centers. It is disease resistant and has a long history of consistent and problem-free performances in a variety of gardens in more than five different climate zones. It is not temperamental about the quality of the soil in which it is planted, and it is not the kind of rose to sulk and refuse to flower if it gets less than six hours of direct sunlight. 'Ballerina' grows to a manageable size, reaching 4 feet (1.2 m) high by 2 feet (60 cm) wide at maturity. Its flowers are similar in color to apple blossoms and have a pleasant, musklike, sweet-pea scent.

> **Location:** Full sun
> **Type:** Modern shrub rose
> **Size:** 4 feet (1.2 m)
> **Conditions:** Fertile, well-drained soil
> **Flowering time:** June to July
> **Zone:** 5

It is not difficult to figure out how 'Ballerina' comes by its name once you see the flowers. With their white centers and pink trim, they resemble a ballerina's skirt. As an added bonus, the rose has few thorns and its foliage is a soft light green that blends in well with other plants in the garden. This is the kind of rose that is so versatile you can work it into virtually any situation. Use it in the shrub border or as a general mixer in your perennial border. It can make a modest hedge or be trained into a small tree. You can, of course, use it a focal piece in your rose border.

Plant more than one and you'll fool visitors to your garden into thinking it is an even more prolific performer than it already is. 'Ballerina' is considered by some rose experts to be an old garden rose even though it was only introduced in 1937. That is partly because it can hold its own against top Gallica shrub roses such as 'Complicata', 'Charles de Mills', and 'Cardinal de Richelieu'.

Where to plant it

'Ballerina' will tolerate a variety of locations but it performs best in a sunny spot where it is protected from the intense heat of the afternoon sun. Give it room, if you want it to spread unhindered to its mature size of 4 feet (1.2 m) after a couple of years.

How to care for it

Resistant to most typical rose problems, 'Ballerina' rarely needs to be sprayed for black spot and seems able to repel other pests. However, don't leave it to starve, especially if it is in competition with heavy feeders in a perennial or shrub border. If you decide to grow it in a pot, make sure that it is a large one and don't forget to water routinely. See *Rosa* 'Elina', "How to care for it," for general pruning recommendations.

Good companions

Other shrub roses make excellent partners for 'Ballerina'. Check out the red form of 'Marjorie Fair', which has many of the same characteristics as 'Ballerina'. Another smashing companion would be 'Mary Rose', one of David Austin's new English roses, which is equally hardy and disease resistant.

For your collection

Buying shrub roses can become an addiction. Many gardeners enjoy them far more than hybrids, teas and floribundas because they blend in so naturally with other plants in the garden and have a high resistance to pests and disease. Here are a few other first-rate shrub roses to consider.

- 'Blanc Double de Coubert'. A tough and hardy French-bred rugosa rose that flowers in June and grows to 5 feet (1.5 m). Very fragrant.
- 'The Fairy'. Popular ever since its introduction in 1932, this profusely flowering rose has light pink blooms. It grows to 30 inches (75 cm).
- 'Fantin-Latour'. This famous centifolia rose has fragrant pinkish-white blooms and grows to about 5 feet (1.5 m).
- 'Hansa'. A medium-sized bushy rose with deep mauve to red blooms. It grows to 4 feet (1.2 m) and can be used for making a hedge.

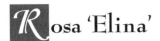osa 'Elina'

Common name: *Elina or Peaudouce rose*

Chief characteristics

Location: Full sun

Type: Hybrid tea rose

Size: 4 feet (1.2 m)

Conditions: Rich, well-drained soil

Flowering time: June to September

Zone: 5

It is a curious thing that so many avid gardeners look down their noses at hybrid tea roses. They will talk enthusiastically about the virtues of obscure and esoteric varieties of old garden roses, but give hybrid teas short shrift. Part of the problem is that many modern roses have a reputation for being excessively prone to pests and disease. There is also a kind of disdain for the high-strung, thoroughbred nature of hybrid teas and their hectic, high-powered life of perpetual flower production. It all seems so unnatural to some gardeners.

Nevertheless, gardens need roses and no garden is really complete without a few hybrid teas, the celebrity flowers of summer. The challenge is to pick the best of the best. 'Elina' is certainly an unbeatable star performer. It is more disease and drought tolerant and flowers more abundantly than most hybrid teas. Its large, white-primrose, lightly scented blooms are exquisite and make excellent cut flowers.

Bred in Ireland, 'Elina' was first introduced in 1984 and immediately began winning awards. It has been held up as a perfect example of what a hybrid tea should be: hardy, vigorous and beautiful. It was originally called 'Peaudouce' (French for "soft skin"). That turned out to be a big mistake. The breeders found the name did not help the rose make friends, so the name was changed to 'Elina'. The American Rose Society rates it 8.6 out of 10.

Where to plant it

Hybrid teas are the racehorses of the rose family, but they are not as temperamental or hard to care for as is sometimes suggested. They need full sun, at least six hours a day, and nutrient-rich, well-drained soil to flower properly. They also like to be fed well and watered deeply without being drowned. 'Elina' is one of the easier hybrid teas to care for. It is less prone to black spot and probably because of its robust healthiness and subtle scent, it doesn't attract insect pests. Grow it close to the house where you can appreciate it all the time rather than at the end of the garden where you have to travel to see it.

How to care for it

Roses are killed by extremes—either neglect or overzealousness. Too much fertilizer or too little fertilizer, too much water or no water at all can all be lethal. Moderation is a good rule of thumb in caring for roses.

Pruning always seems like the biggest hassle. There is so much talk about how to prune, when to prune and what to prune, most average gardeners end up too confused and scared to do anything. The golden rule is to first prune out all dead, diseased or damaged stems. Then remove thin, wiry stems that look unlikely to produce flowers. Prune out stems that rub against each other or cross one another. Keep in mind the overall shape of the bush. Finally, to promote good roots and healthy new growth in hybrid teas, prune healthy stems to about 18 inches (45 cm) from the ground. Do all this when the rose is dormant, at the end of winter or in early spring just before the buds break. If you are still nervous, follow the Easy Care Method devised by Britain's Royal National Rose Society. Prune your rose bush to half its height and then take out any dead wood. The society conducted experiments and found, in most cases, this method worked as well as more complicated methods.

Good companions

Lavender, santolina and purple allium all go well with roses. A low boxwood hedge can provide a formal border to your rose bed and it also serves to hide the less interesting lower parts of roses without interfering with air circulation.

For your collection

- Here's a list of the top-performing hybrid teas. 'Rosemary Harkness' (a mixture of orange, yellow and salmon), 'Double Delight' (creamy white petals with raspberry rims), 'Pink Peace' (fragrant pink blooms), 'Just Joey' (scented, coppery orange) and 'Sexy Rexy' (camellia-like pink flowers).
- Other star performers include 'Alexander' (cherry-red), 'Grandpa Dickson' (yellow), 'L'Oréal Trophy' (orange), 'Ingrid Bergman' (red), 'Pascali' (white), 'Heart Throb' (pink), 'Peace' (yellow), 'Piccadilly' (scarlet-yellow), 'Elizabeth Taylor' (pink), 'Silver Jubilee' (pink-peach) and 'Tropicana' (orange-pink).
- For outstanding fragrance, choose 'Pink Peace', 'Double Delight', 'Chrysler Imperial', 'Mister Lincoln', 'Fragrant Cloud', 'Ena Harkness', 'Granada', 'Lady Rose', 'Princesse de Monaco', 'Sterling Silver', 'Tropicana', 'Sutter's Gold' and 'Ingrid Bergman'.

osa 'Mary Rose'

Common name: *Mary rose*

Chief characteristics

Named after Henry VIII's flagship, 'Mary Rose' is one of the most regal hybrids in David Austin's celebrated stable of English roses. Austin, an English rose breeder, made a name for himself internationally by combining the exquisite, multi-petaled beauty of famous old garden roses with the prolific flowering power of top-performing modern hybrid teas and floribundas. The result is a new class of roses called "English roses."

> **Location:** Full sun
> **Type:** David Austin rose
> **Size:** 4 feet (1.2 m)
> **Conditions:** Rich, well-drained soil
> **Flowering time:** June to September
> **Zone:** 4

Everyone has his or her favorite Austin rose. 'Mary Rose' is mine. I have tried an assortment of others, but few performed as consistently or as beautifully as 'Mary Rose'. It has cheerful, fragrant, rose-pink blooms that start to appear in early June and continue sporadically to the end of summer. Austin describes the rose's growth habit as "near to ideal—bushy, twiggy and vigorous without being unruly."

Part of my satisfaction with 'Mary Rose' is that it fits so perfectly into the perennial border, effortlessly harmonizing with the feathery silver foliage of artemisia and the lacy foliage of bronze fennel. 'Mary Rose' is impressively disease resistant and it does not object to having its blooms clipped off at their peak to fill vases. The American Rose Society gave it an 8.7 rating out of 10.

There are other great roses in the Austin series you should also consider. 'Constance Spry' (soft pink) was the first to be introduced in 1961, while 'Evelyn' (apricot-yellow) is one of Austin's newer hybrids. Both are excellent. The most popular are the powerfully scented 'Gertrude Jekyll' (deep pink), 'Heritage' (light pink) and the dependable 'Graham Thomas' (yellow). One of the newest Austin roses is a fragrant pink called 'Geoff Hamilton'. It was first introduced at the Chelsea Flower Show in 1997 and is named after one of the most beloved English gardeners, who hosted a much-watched television show called "Gardener's World." Certainly a rose to look out for.

Where to plant it

Like all roses, 'Mary Rose' requires full sun, but will not complain if it gets a little shade in the afternoon. It is the perfect rose for slipping into the perennial border. It will mix happily with foxgloves and campanula and give you a very relaxed, free-flowing, English cottage garden look. Consider planting more than one for a more substantial display of flowers.

How to care for it

Roses need six hours of sun a day. If you don't get a lot of blooms it could be because the rose is not getting enough sun. Deadhead spent blooms regularly to encourage flowering. See Rosa 'Elina', "How to care for it," for general pruning recommendations.

English roses and modern floribundas and hybrid teas don't seem to get along very well. If you plant an English rose, try to find a place for it outside your more formal rose bed.

Good companions

The silvery foliage of *Artemisia* 'Powis Castle', the blue spikes of *Veronica spicata* or the bright white flowers of *Aconitum napellus* 'Albidum' all make great partners for planting around 'Mary Rose'. Pink foxgloves, blue or white campanulas and white sweet williams also make happy companions.

For your collection

If you become serious about roses, you will want to investigate more of David Austin's English roses. Austin is a fairly hard critic of his own roses, rating them with a star from 1 to 4. His own 4-star picks include the following.

Name	Color	Height
'Abraham Darby'	coppery apricot	4 feet (1.2 m)
'The Alexandra Rose'	coppery pink with pale yellow centre	4 feet (1.2 m)
'Brother Cadfael'	medium pink	3 feet (90 cm)
'Charles Rennie Mackintosh'	dusky lilac-pink	30 inches (75 cm)
'Chianti'	crimson to maroon	5 feet (1.5 m)
'Constance Spry'	soft pink	6 feet (1.8 m)
'Cottage Rose'	pink	30 inches (75 cm)
'The Countryman'	clear pink	2 feet (60 cm)
'The Dark Lady'	dusky crimson	3 feet (90 cm)
'Francine Austin'	white	4 feet (1.2 m)
'Gertrude Jekyll'	deep pink	4 feet (1.2 m)
'Glamis Castle'	white	30 inches (75 cm)
'Golden Celebrations'	coppery yellow	4 feet (1.2 m)
'Graham Thomas'	warm yellow	4 feet (1.2 m)

Name	Color	Height
'Heritage'	clear pink	4 feet (1.2 m)
'Jayne Austin'	soft yellow	42 inches (1 m)
'Kathryn Morley'	soft pink	3 feet (90 cm)
'L.D. Braithwaite'	crimson	42 inches (1 m)
'Leander'	deep apricot	5 feet (1.5 m)
'Lilian Austin'	salmon-pink	4 feet (1.2 m)
'Perdita'	soft pink	30 inches (75 cm)
'The Pilgrim'	yellow	3 feet (90 cm)
'The Prince'	crimson turning purple	3 feet (90 cm)
'Redoute'	soft pink	4 feet (1.2 m)
'St. Cecilia'	buff-apricot	30 inches (75 cm)
'St. Swithun'	soft pink	3 feet (90 cm)
'Sharifa Asma'	soft pink with gold	30 inches (75 cm)
'Shropshire Lass'	blush pink to white	6 feet (1.8 m)
'Winchester Cathedral'	white	4 feet (1.2 m)

osa 'Morden Blush'

Common name: *Parkland rose*

Chief characteristics

There are two special groups of hardy roses all Canadian gardeners, especially those gardening in Zones 5 and down, need to know about: the Parkland Series and Explorer Series. These are all extremely hardy, disease-resistant, long-blooming roses, specifically developed for cool northern gardens. 'Morden Blush' is one of the best of the Parkland roses, all of which came out over the last 30 years as the result of a breeding program that began in Morden, Manitoba, in the 1940s.

Location: Full sun
Type: Hardy shrub rose
Size: 2 to 3 feet (60 to 90 cm)
Conditions: Fertile, well-drained soil
Flowering time: June to July
Zone: 2

A proven winner, 'Morden Blush' has peachy pink, old-fashioned blooms that slowly fade to a soft shade of ivory. Extremely floriferous, it also has a reputation for flowering continuously for at least six weeks—the longest of any of the roses in the series. Compact, with gray-green foliage, it grows 2 to 3 feet (60 to 90 cm) high and the flowers have a delicate, refined perfume. There are stories of gardeners discovering this rose and then rushing back to the garden center to buy more once they have seen it in action. Other outstanding Parkland roses include 'Morden

Centennial' (medium pink), 'Morden Fireglow' (flaming orange-red), 'Morden Ruby' (ruby red), 'Winnipeg Parks' (scarlet red) and 'Morden Amorette' (bright red).

The Explorer Series of roses came out of a breeding program started at the Ottawa Experimental Farm in the 1960s. Seedlings were tested in Prince George, B.C., and Kapuskasing, Ontario, and amazed everyone by surviving temperatures of –30°F (–35°C) with minimal winter kill.

Named after Canadian explorers, the roses are mostly blends of rugosa roses, which have always been noted for their hardiness and immunity to pests and diseases. Popular hybrids include the neat, low-growing, white-flowering 'Henry Hudson', which scored a 9.1 out of 10 rating (outstanding) from the America Rose Society, and the fragrant red 'John Cabot', which scored 8.2.

Other dependable Explorer shrub roses include 'Martin Frobisher' (light pink), 'Alexander Mackenzie' (red), 'Frontenac' (deep pink), 'Champlain' (bright red), 'Charles Albanel' (red), 'Jens Munk' (clear pink) and 'Simon Fraser' (dark pink); and climbers 'John Davis' (pink), 'William Baffin' (pink), 'Henry Kelsey' (red), 'Captain Samuel Holland' (medium red) and 'Louis Jolliet' (medium pink).

Where to plant it

'Morden Blush' will thrive in fertile, well-drained soil in full sun. To get the best effect, plant two or three bushes in a close grouping. Try to arrange for a little shade in the afternoon to preserve the delicate color of the blooms, which can fade if exposed to intense sunlight all day.

There are Parkland and Explorer roses suitable for all purposes. For making a rose pillar, try 'Captain Samuel Holland' or 'John Davis'. The best of the climbers is 'William Baffin', but 'Louis Jolliet' is being touted as the new star in the wings. For hedging, 'Jens Munk' is dense and strongly fragrant, while 'Frontenac' produces a sustained display of pleasantly scented, deep pink blooms from June to September.

How to care for it

Make sure you buy Explorer and Parkland roses that have been grown on their own roots. Some rose growers, eager to get stock to garden centers, will graft these roses onto rootstock that is less hardy. It is not a rude question to ask if the roses are own-root grown, which means they will have all the qualities of disease resistance and hardiness you want. 'Morden Blush' and all the Explorer/Parkland roses require minimal maintenance. Plant them, water them well the first year, mulch to replenish the soil, and prune away dead or damaged wood in spring.

Good companions

Other Parkland roses make good companions for 'Morden Blush'. Plant them in groups of three to create a special rose garden. For shrub partners, use spiraea, euonymus and potentilla. For perennials, use lavender, artemisia, daylilies, blue grass, liatris and delphiniums. For bulb support, use alliums, camassia and scilla.

For your collection

- There are many old-fashioned roses that are also extremely hardy. Alba, centifolia, damask, gallica and moss roses are all hardy in cool climates. Great roses to consider include 'Maiden's Blush' (pink; alba), 'Fantin Latour' (pink; centifolia), 'Madame Hardy' (white; damask), 'Cardinal de Richelieu' (purple; gallica) and 'Henri Martin' (crimson; moss).

- Meidiland Series. The Meidiland roses, of California, have gained a lot of respect over the years as "landscape roses" because of their dependable flower power and resistance to mildew and black spot. Six top varieties, all hardy to Zone 4, include 'Bonica Meidiland' (pastel pink), 'Carefree Delight' (vivid pink), 'Fuchsia Meidiland' (mauve-pink), 'Sevillana' (scarlet-red), 'Pink Meidiland' (clear pink), and 'White Meidiland' (pure white).

- Pavement roses. Compact, low-growing shrubs (6 to 9 feet/1.8 to 2.7 m), these extremely hardy and disease-resistant roses were developed in Germany. They have proven popular with both novice and expert rose growers for lining sidewalks and boulevards, hence the name "pavement." There are seven varieties in the series: 'Scarlet Pavement' (fuchsia-red), 'Snow Pavement' (apple-blossom pink), 'Pierrette Pavement' (dark pink, exceptional fragrance), 'Showy Pavement' (pink), ' Foxi Pavement' (purple-pink), 'Dwarf Pavement' (bright pink') and 'Purple Pavement' (purplish-red).

- Groundcover roses. These exceptionally floriferous and disease-resistant roses can be used as low-growing, border plants or mass-planted to cover a large area. The 'Flower Carpet' series are all proven winners. You can get pink, yellow, white and appleblossom. They all grow 10 inches (25 cm) high.

ℛosa 'New Dawn'

Common name: *New Dawn rose, everblooming Doctor W. Van Fleet*

Chief characteristics

'New Dawn' is one of the most dependable and disease-resistant climbing roses. It can be relied upon to cover fences or walls and produce an outstanding flush of slightly fragrant, shell-pink blooms in early June. It will continue to flower throughout summer, although not nearly as profusely as at its peak.

Location: Full sun
Type: Climbing rose
Size: 15 to 20 feet (4.5 to 6 m)
Conditions: Fertile, well-drained soil
Flowering time: June
Zone: 4

First introduced in 1930 as the offspring of the famous rambling rose, 'Doctor W. Van Fleet', 'New Dawn' is less vigorous than its parent but is still considered by many to be the yardstick by which all other climbing roses are judged. The leaves have a healthy, shiny look while the light pink flowers, measuring 3 inches (7.5 cm) wide, are small, somewhat fragile, but plentiful. You can use 'New Dawn' to cover a fence between you and your neighbor and you can rest assured that it won't cause offense by leaving a mess or becoming too thorny or rampant.

Where to plant it

'New Dawn' will tolerate poor soil and some shade and can even be used to create a hedge or grown on the cold side of the house. Use it over an arch or arbor or fan it against a fence or brick wall.

How to care for it

Prune out anything that is dead, diseased, damaged or decadent (meaning weak and unproductive). The soil in which it is planted should be enriched every year with well-rotted compost or aged manure. Feed your rose with a balanced diet of granular rose fertilizer in early spring and once again in midsummer.

In extremely cold areas, consider using this overwintering technique: loosen the soil around the roots and gently tip over the canes and bury them in a shallow trench. Only the roots bend, not the stems or the bud union. Fill the trench with soil and cover it with leaves or straw. In April remove the mulch and raise the rose back into place. You can also use this technique to overwinter more tender floribundas and hybrid teas, or simply prune them back and mound 8 to12 inches (20 to 30 cm) around the base.

Good companions

Clematis is a perfect partner for 'New Dawn'. The purple forms, such as 'Jackmanii Superba', 'Polish Spirit', 'Etoile Violette' and 'The President', will bloom at the same time and provide a sensational contrast. When covering a fence, another climbing rose, such as the thornless 'Zephirine Drouhin', which has slightly larger, carmine-pink flowers that appear about the same time as 'New Dawn', can be interplanted for heightened color.

For your collection

There are many other fine climbing roses worth considering.

- 'Albertine'. Introduced in 1921, this has highly fragrant, pale coppery pink blooms. It is a fairly rampant rambler capable of covering a long fence or pergola.
- 'Altissimo'. This is not a tall climber, reaching only 10 feet (3 m), but it does produce large striking red flowers in small numbers over the whole summer rather than in one main flush. It is also a clean rose, resistant to mildew and black spot, making it a good choice for fixing against walls or fences.
- 'American Pillar'. This flowers profusely in July and still rates as one of the best climbers of all time. The flowers are deep pink with a white center. You do, however, need to plant it where the air circulates freely, because in stagnant air this rose is prone to mildew.
- 'Compassion'. A lovely, highly fragrant rose with pink- to salmon-colored blooms, this is one of the best from the Harkness Rose Company of England. It is ideal for walls and fences.
- 'Félicité Perpétue'. This has creamy fragrant white flowers and will happily clamber into trees. The "perpétue" reference does not mean it flowers perpetually—it has one burst of blooms.
- 'Francois Juranville'. This has fragrant, pale pink flowers in June and will easily scramble 20 feet (6 m). It is perfect for rose pillars, arches and arbors. It is a lot more pliable than other climbers, making it easier to bend it into place over structures.
- 'High Hopes'. An offspring of the more famous 'Compassion' rose, this climber has fragrant pale pink flowers and is a repeat bloomer. It is very disease resistant and a good choice for covering arches.
- 'Madame Gregoire Staechelin' ('Spanish Beauty'). This produces 5-inch (12.5-cm), very fragrant pink blooms in June. Its antique appearance gives it an old-fashioned charm.
- 'Rambling Rector'. An outstanding white, fragrant rambler, capable of covering large fences, reaching up into trees, and hiding eyesores.

🐾 'Zéphirine Drouhin'. This thornless climber is popular with British garden designers who often use it to cover arches along paths. It has vivid crimson-pink blooms that have been described as expressive of the "warmth of some old remembered days of summer, when roses innocently quartered their centers, and were expected to breathe a gentle fragrance into the air."

Rosa 'Souvenir de la Malmaison'

Common name: Souvenir de la Malmaison rose

Chief characteristics

Location: Full sun
Type: Bourbon rose
Size: 4 feet (1.2 m)
Conditions: Rich, well-drained soil
Flowering time: June to September
Zone: 5

A rose is a rose is a rose? Not so. Each one is different and we all have our favorites. There are, however, some roses that are definitely more disease resistant, floriferous or fragrant. One of the most superbly scented is 'Souvenir de la Malmaison'. It was named after the famous rose garden created by Empress Josephine, the wife of Napoleon Bonaparte, at the estate at la Malmaison, near Paris. The story goes that Josephine was so in love with roses, she tried to collect every known species. It was a natural and predictable consequence that she would eventually have a rose named to commemorate her ambitious undertaking and her passion for roses.

'Souvenir de la Malmaison' does not need an interesting history to make it desirable. It has lovely, creamy, white-pink, lushly petaled flowers that exude the most delicious fragrance. It is one of a group of roses known as bourbons, which were especially popular in Victorian England because of their repeat flowering characteristic. There are several excellent bourbons, but 'Souvenir de la Malmaison' is the most beautiful of them all. The scent has been described as an intoxicating mixture of cinnamon and ripe bananas with a hint of spice. Rain is this rose's only enemy. In drizzly, damp weather, the petals ball up because they get trapped by moisture and cannot expand properly.

Where to plant it

Grow 'Souvenir de la Malmaison' in a half-barrel or the rose bed, preferably where it gets some protection from rain. The advantage of growing it in a container is that it can be positioned close to the house where its fragance can be enjoyed more easily and where it is less exposed to downpours. Perhaps you have a front porch that faces west or south that gives you all the sun you need plus the required rain-shielding. This rose can, of course, be planted out in the open garden. An ideal position is below an open window.

How to care for it

Prune in late winter and don't worry if it seems to be a slow starter. See Rosa 'Elina', "How to care for it," for general pruning recommendations.

Flowering may not occur until later in June, but once it begins it will be prolific and continuous. Like all plants in containers, it will need a top-dressing of well-rotted compost in spring and a sprinkling of slow-release rose food.

Good companions

Excellent partners for 'Souvenir de la Malmaison' include other classic, old garden roses, such as the fabulous centifolia 'Fantin Latour' (blush pink), the outstanding 'Maiden's Blush' (soft pink) or the marvelous old portland rose, 'Jacques Cartier' (clear pink).

David Austin's English roses such as 'Gertrude Jekyll', 'Heritage' and 'Evelyn' also have the classy, old-garden rose look of 'Souvenir de la Malmaison' as well as delicious fragrance. Other heavenly scented roses worth investing in include the hybrid tea 'Double Delight' (cream, white and red) and the modern shrub roses 'Sarah van Fleet' (pink) and 'Jacqueline du Pre' (soft white).

For your collection

- There is a climbing form of 'Souvenir de la Malmaison' that will grow 6 to 8 feet (1.8 to 2.4 m) high. It flowers profusely in late June and thrives if planted on a sunny, south-facing wall in a spot where it gets protection from rain.
- Other great bourbons include the thornless 'Zephirine Drouhin' (rose-pink climber), which has a long flowering period; 'Madame Issac Pereire' (vivid crimson-pink), which has intense perfume and is considered the most fragrant of all roses; and 'Bourbon Queen' (rose-pink), a vigorous rose that will thrive in any soil, earning the title "Queen of the Bourbons."

Salvia × sylvestris 'May Night'

Common name: *Perennial salvia, sage*

Chief characteristics

'May Night' was voted Perennial Plant of the Year in 1997 by the Perennial Plant Association. It is a beautiful, compact plant that produces striking, indigo-blue flower spikes with a slight tinge of purple in early summer. It is very similar to its cousin, 'East Friesland', which flowers a little later in May. When they are planted side by side, it is hard to tell them apart. Both are excellent clump-forming plants, but 'May Night' has

Location: Full sun to part shade
Type: Perennial
Size: 18 to 24 inches (45 to 60 cm)
Conditions: Ordinary, well-drained soil
Flowering time: May to July
Zone: 3

a slight advantage because of the vivid beauty of its violet-blue flowers produced on stiff, upright stems. Drought tolerant and easy to care for, it can be used to create dense drifts of blue about 3 feet (90 cm) high at the front of the perennial border, hiding the feet of taller perennials such as lavatera. 'May Night' is also very desirable because of its resistance to drought; it won't sulk if left unwatered for a day or two in a dry spell.

Where to plant it

Grow 'May Night' in average, well-drained soil in full sun or a semi-shaded location. It can be combined with other kinds of sage, like *Salvia verticillata* 'Purple Rain' for foliage contrast and the annual *S. farinacea*, for continuous summer color.

How to care for it

An easy plant to care for, salvia only needs to be tidied up at the end of its flowering period. The key to growing it successfully is to make sure it is planted in a sunny, well-drained site. Add some sand to the base of the planting hole when you plant, to improve drainage. Wet soil and lack of sunlight is what kills most salvia. It is tough enough to deal with frost and snow.

Good companions

Reds and silvers are excellent color contrasts for the dark purple-blue flowers of 'May Night'. Good companions include daylilies, canna lilies, purple verbena, pastel shades of yarrow, red potentilla and blue ornamental grasses.

For your collection

- *Salvia argentea* (silver sage) is arguably the most aristocratic of the sage family. It has large, floppy, silver-gray leaves. It looks very classy when grown in a terra cotta pot as a simple decorative foliage plant for patio or porch.

- *Salvia farinacea* 'Victoria'. The deep purple-blue annual sage is another favorite for mass planting in the public landscape. However, this Texas native is a lot easier to work with. It flowers beautifully through the hot dry days of August and is one of the last flowers to go down in fall.

- *Salvia officinalis* 'Purpurascens'. Purple-leafed sage is an excellent plant for foliage contrast. Its soft purple-gray leaves heighten the feathery silver foliage of artemisia or stachys.

- *Salvia officinalis* 'Tricolor' is the variegated form of the common purple-leafed sage. It has green and white leaves, some with a reddish-pink tinge.

- *Salvia splendens* (scarlet sage) is used to brighten floral borders in city parks in summer. It is a powerful, attention-grabbing color that needs to be handled with care in the home garden. The hot red can appear too aggressive if it is allowed to stand alone without calmer hues.

- Salvias are coming back into popularity, and it is getting easier to find some of the rarer and more exotic forms, such as the following. *Salvia nipponica* 'Fuji Snow' has arrow-shaped leaves with variegated cream tips and butter-yellow flowers in midsummer. *S. sclarea*, the beautiful clary sage, grows 3 feet (90 cm) tall in warm sunny places and has lilac-purple flowers. *S. patens*, also known as gentian sage, grows 2 feet (60 cm) and has lovely, gentian-like, blue hooded flowers arranged sparingly along 2-foot (60-cm) spires.

- *Nepeta* 'Dropmore Blue' is another excellent blue-flowering, drought-tolerant plant for the front of the sunny border. Developed by a Canadian, it gets along very well with roses, grows 12 inches (30 cm) high and flowers freely from June to September.

Scabiosa columbaria 'Butterfly Blue'

Common name: *Pincushion flower*

Chief characteristics

The thing that makes 'Butterfly Blue' such a must-have plant is its astonishing flower power. Starting in spring, it will continue to produce delightful lilac-blue blooms about 1.5 inches (4 cm) wide, without pausing to catch a breath, right through to fall. Only *Geranium cinereum* 'Ballerina' and *Corydalis lutea* seem to be able to do that—flower repeatedly and consistently, producing top-quality blooms for at least three months. Scabiosa is also known as the pincushion flower because the center of each bloom looks like dozens of tiny pins pressed into a sewing cushion.

> **Location:** Full sun
> **Type:** Perennial
> **Size:** 15 inches (38 cm)
> **Conditions:** Good, well-drained soil
> **Flowering time:** June to September
> **Zone:** 3

Scabiosa makes an excellent cut flower and is available in lilac-blue, pink and white. There are dozens of kinds. *Scabiosa caucasica*, for instance, grows to almost 3 feet (90 cm) and has purple-blue flowers. There is also a white form. But the pick of the crop is *S. columbaria* 'Butterfly Blue', a shorter cultivar growing only 15 to 18 inches (38 to 45 cm) high, and its sister 'Pink Mist', an almost identical twin, except it has pale pink rather than blue flowers.

Where to plant it

Grow scabiosa in fertile, well-drained soil in full sun. It does brilliantly in containers, too. If you have a sunny driveway or front entrance where you need continual color all summer, either 'Butterfly Blue' or 'Pink Mist' will do the trick. In the perennial border, they should be grown at the front, but they need very good drainage if you are to keep them over the years, so make sure you add some sand to the planting hole to eliminate the possibility of waterlogging.

How to care for it

If aphids become a problem, wash them away with a strong jet of water or simply squish them off the stems. Deadhead the faded flowerheads regularly for the sake of neatness and to stimulate the plant to keep blooming. It is best to use scissors because the stems can get quite spindly and they also need to be pruned away. Fertilize every couple of weeks with a half-strength solution of 20-20-20.

Good companions

'Butterfly Blue' combines well with variegated Jacob's ladder, which has delicate, light blue flowers. The blues play off one another very nicely.

Geranium cinereum 'Ballerina' or 'Lawrence Flatman' make excellent partners. The geraniums also bloom perpetually all summer and need fast-draining soil in a full-sun location. Put 'Butterfly Blue' with either of these geraniums and throw in short clumping blue grass (*Festuca glauca*) and the purple spikes of *Liatris spicata*, and you have a winning association.

The taller types of scabiosa combine best in the perennial border with liatris, achillea, daylilies, *Phlox paniculata*, butterfly gaura, shasta daisies and crocosmia. You can also bring in ornamental grasses, especially the blue and burgundy ones. Place them in front of scabiosa, which allows the pincushion flowers to float high above the fountain-like foliage of the grasses.

For your collection

- *Scabiosa japonica* (dwarf pincushion flower) grows only 6 inches (15 cm) high, has mauve-blue flowers and can be used in the sunny rockery.
- *Scabiosa ochroleuca* grows to 3 feet (90 cm), has gray-green felty foliage and produces small, sulfur-yellow flowers in late summer. Unlike the species recommended above, it is not very long-lived, but the flowers can add interest to the perennial border.
- If you like the look of scabiosa, you will probably also like stokes's aster (*Stokesia laevis*), which has similarly shaped lavender-blue flowers.

Scilla (Hyacinthoides) non-scripta

Common name: English bluebell, squill

Chief characteristics

Nature uses color with immense subtlety. Yellow, purple and white flowers appear in perfect harmony and bob about on a great sea of green foliage. We can learn from this for our own gardens. It's always safe to play with colors as long as you follow nature's example and surround bright flowers with plenty of soothing, restful shades of green.

Location: Sun to light shade
Type: Bulb
Size: 18 inches (45 cm)
Conditions: Ordinary, well-drained soil
Flowering time: May
Zone: 3

Most of the problems with clashing colors occur because we ignore nature's green rule.

In the natural landscape, blue flowers play a significant role. There are few blue flowers, however, that have as much simple charm or lasting appeal as the plain, old-fashioned English bluebell (*Scilla non-scripta*). You will find bluebells in small woods and lanes all over England. As a boy growing up in Nottinghamshire, I remember a local copse that was known as Bluebell Wood because in spring the ground turned into a magnificent blue carpet of the magical bell-shaped flowers. I remember running through them, laughing and pulling up great bunches, without ever thinking about the destruction I was causing.

The most common of all bluebells, *Scilla non-scripta* bear deep violet-blue flowers with a distinctive bonnet shape in April and May. They are suspended in lovely, loose clusters on slightly arching 10-inch (25-cm) stems. They are easy to introduce into the garden and once you have found the right spot for them, you can enjoy their punctual arrival year after year.

When you go to buy bluebells, you may find them packaged under their new botanical name, *Hyacinthoides non-scripta*, or *Endymion non-scripta*, which can be confusing.

Where to plant it

Plant bluebells in ordinary, well-drained soil. They thrive in light or dappled shade under trees or shrubs, where they can naturalize. Resist the temptation to mix colors: squills look best in monochromatic drifts.

How to care for it

When colonies become too dense, divide the clumps and replant bulbs immediately.

Cut the flowerheads once they are finished. Watch to see that the flowering sequence works well with other plants. The ideal match is to have bluebells in bloom just ahead or just after their companions.

Good companions

Bluebells look good pushing up through groundcovers like epimedium or mingling with the lower branches of shrubs like rhododendrons.

They also work well with other semi-shade plants like bleeding heart, astilbe, polemonium, hardy geranium and hosta.

For your collection

🌢 How about a pink bluebell? Well, there is such a thing as a white bleeding heart and a yellow red-hot poker. You can get a pink form of the Spanish bluebell called *Hyacinthoides hispanica* 'Pink'. You can also get a pure white form. The Spanish bluebell (also called *Scilla campanula* or *Endymion hispanicus*) is larger than the English species.

🪶 *Scilla peruviana* (Cuban lily) is also part of the bluebell family and is loved for its spectacular hyacinth-sized blue flowerhead. It is very tender, which means it needs a frost-free environment. More of these are being marketed at Eastertime.

🪶 *Scilla siberica* is an excellent rockery bluebell. The Siberian or Prussian bluebell (*S. siberica* 'Spring Beauty') produces particularly lovely nodding blue flowers that dangle from short 5-inch (12.5-cm) stems. There is also a pretty white form, 'Alba'.

🪶 For the rockery, you could try the tiny blue Persian squill (*Scilla tubergeniana*), which grows only 4 inches (10 cm) high.

Sedum 'Autumn Joy'

Common name: *Stonecrop*

Chief characteristics

'Autumn Joy' is one of those rare plants that has value in the garden from the first moment it appears in spring to the end of fall when its sturdy broccoli-shaped flowerheads hang on defiantly in the heavy frost. Large perennial borders are often anchored at the corners with giant clumps of this plant. It flowers in late summer with tight clusters of salmon-pink flowers that appear about the same time as yellow black-eyed susans, the marvelous white and pink flowers of Japanese anemones and the stately feather-duster plumes of pampas grass.

Location: Full sun
Type: Perennial
Size: 3 feet (90 cm)
Conditions: Fertile, well-drained soil
Flowering time: September to October
Zone: 3

'Autumn Joy' certainly lives up to its name. One of the first perennials to appear in spring, it develops steadily through the summer, growing thick, fleshy, succulent-type leaves on erect stems. By late July to August, it will have formed large, attractive, flat-topped flowerheads. They not only offer a pleasing texture in the border, they provide valuable fall color and impressive structure that lasts into winter.

There are other cultivars similar to 'Autumn Joy', including 'Brilliant' and 'Stardust'. There are also some interesting types with bronze-red or purple foliage. Look for 'Atropurpureum', 'Matrona', 'Morchen', 'Vera

Jameson', 'Bertram Anderson' and 'Ruby Glow'. If in doubt, stick with 'Autumn Joy' or 'Brilliant', but it is worthwhile trying to work a few others into your planting scheme. These plants are also good for attracting bees and butterflies to the garden.

Where to plant it

Grow 'Autumn Joy' where it can quietly develop without demands for flowers or color during the summer and yet have a prominent place in the fall. This could be at the front of the perennial border, but it is probably best to locate it as a foliage plant behind shorter front-runners like *Salvia* × *sylvestris* 'May Night', *Geranium cinereum* 'Ballerina' or *Stachys* 'Countess Helene von Stein'. Wherever you plant 'Autumn Joy', don't just plant one. Plant three or five to create a substantial clump.

How to care for it

Sedums are long-lived, trouble-free plants. 'Autumn Joy' will divide easily but, like hostas, it is best left to mature into a mass of impressive foliage. Let the stems stay right into winter. They will stand up in the snow and can be part of the winter garden. By spring they will have turned soft and mushy and will give you a good reason to get outside in February or March to clean up for the spring explosion.

Good companions

'Autumn Joy' can also fill ground in front of rudbeckia, asters and euphorbias and shrubs like *Viburnum plicatum* 'Summer Snowflake'. Blue grasses and silver foliage plants like *Stachys byzantina* and *Artemisia schmidtiana* 'Silver Mound' make good neighbors. Also consider *Gaura lindheimeri*, which has delicate white-pink flowers at the top of long stems. It is quite drought tolerant and can even be grown successfully in gravel-covered areas.

For your collection

- *Sedum alboroseum* 'Mediovariegatum' is a variegated form. It is usually listed as *Sedum* 'Variegatum'. Not everyone likes foliage that is green with creamy white splotches in the center, but it has its place. It grows to 2 feet (60 cm), pulls in the bees and butterflies and has pale greenish-white flowers tinged with pink.
- There are a few worthy, low-growing sedums for the sunny rockery or fast-draining slope. *Sedum spathulifolium*, grows only 4 inches (10 cm) high and has tiny rosette-shaped, silver-gray leaves and bright yellow flowers. Names to look for are 'Cape Blanco' and 'Purpureum'. *S. spurium*, also known as dragon's blood, grows a little taller, about 6 inches (15 cm), and has pink, red or white flowers.

*S*piraea bumalda 'Goldflame'

Common name: *Spiraea*

Chief characteristics

There are two main groups of spiraea—
ones that have white flowers and ones that
have rose-pink flowers in June. You could
make room in your garden for one of each.
The white-flowering plants give you a
spectacular show of snowy flowers, while
the others are more valued for their yellow-
green foliage than their pinkish-red blooms.

Location: Full sun
Type: Deciduous shrub
Size: 40 inches (100 cm)
Conditions: Ordinary soil
Flowering time: June to
   July
Zone: 3

Most outstanding is *Spiraea bumalda* 'Goldflame', which produces
bronze leaves that turn golden yellow as they mature. The plant then
adds a few fireworks to its color show by producing rosy red flowers that
continue from June to fall.

The foliage is great for contrasting with other plants, and the flowers,
though not immensely significant, are an added bonus. 'Goldflame' is a
first-rate shrub for a small garden because it is compact and grows only
3 to 4 feet (90 to 120 cm) high. It also thrives in a container and is a
good plant for adding foliage interest to a patio, deck or sunny balcony.

Where to plant it

Spiraea thrives in a variety of soils and is not unhappy in full sun or
light shade. The summer-flowering spiraeas, such as 'Goldflame', can be
used as accent plants. Site them in a visible location where their pink
flowers and gold foliage can give texture and color contrast. You can, of
course, become overenthusiastic about summer-flowering spiraeas and
use them too abundantly. This invariably ends up giving the plant a bad
name and spoils the garden, making it look boring and unimaginative.

The "bridal wreath" spiraeas are especially useful for their exuberant
shower of white blooms. The challenge is to grow them in places where
they can be appreciated while in full bloom, then allowed to quietly
fade into the background and become part of the general foliage screen
for the rest of the year.

How to care for it

All spiraeas are ruggedly disease and pest resistant. The compact
summer-flowering forms require little more than tidying up in the
spring. If they look particularly tatty, you can chop them back more
severely. Prune the taller, cascading garland forms immediately after they

have flowered to promote new growth. The larger, twiggy, spring-flowering spiraeas also need to be pruned regularly to prevent dead wood from building up in the center of the bush.

Good companions

Some excellent companions for 'Goldflame' are blue grasses (*Festuca glauca, Helictotrichon*); the pink flowers and silver stems of *Lychnis coronaria*; and the stiff, succulent foliage and salmon flowerheads of *Sedum* 'Autumn Joy'.

Mix white-flowering spiraeas in the shrubbery with potentilla, *Pieris japonica* 'Forest Flame', lavatera, smoke bush, and white-flowering shrubs like *Philadelphus* and *Viburnum* 'Summer Snowflake' for continuous foliage and flower color.

For your collection

- *Spiraea japonica* 'Anthony Waterer' is called the dwarf pink spiraea. It has bright green leaves and produces rosy pink flowers from July to September. It grows only 2 or 3 feet (60 to 90 cm) high.
- *Spiraea japonica* 'Limemound' is less of a novelty, but also interesting. It has lemon-yellow leaves tinged with pink and produces light pink flowers in summer. This shrub grows only 3 feet (90 cm) high, but it mounds up to 6 feet (1.8 m) wide.
- *Spiraea japonica* 'Little Princess' has mint-green foliage and rose-pink flowers. There is a golden form called 'Golden Princess'.
- *Spiraea japonica* 'Shirobana' is something of a novelty plant. It blooms late in the summer, producing white, pink and red flowers simultaneously from July to September. It grows only 2 or 3 feet (60 to 90 cm) high and has bright green leaves.
- *Spiraea japonica* 'Snowmound' is a short shrub that grows 4 or 5 feet (1.2 to 1.5 m) high and displays masses of white flowers on long, graceful, arching stems in spring.
- *Spiraea thunbergii* 'Fujino Pink' has light pink clusters of flowers in June. It is a small, compact shrub with green leaves that turn bright yellow in autumn.
- *Spiraea* × *vanhouttei* is the best of the white-flowering spiraeas. Its dazzling cascade of snow-white flowers in May gives spring-flowering spiraea its common name—bridal wreath. The Vanhouttei spiraea is a compact, upright deciduous shrub. It grows into a fountain shape about 6 feet (1.8 m) high with diamond-shaped, dark green leaves. It is certainly one of the best spring performers.
- Other top performers worth checking out include 'Thor' (white flowers in June, dwarf), 'Goldmound' (pink flowers, bright yellow foliage in July) and 'Garland' (white flowers in June).

Stachys byzantina 'Silver Carpet'

Common name: *Lamb's ears*

Chief characteristics

Of all the great silver foliage plants available to gardeners, *Stachys byzantina* continues to be the most used in gardens— as a groundcover or decorative edging plant or simply to provide color and textural contrast in the perennial border. It is a 5-star perennial, a top performer. The soft, silver-gray leaves are aptly named, looking and feeling rather like the ears of lambs. In mid-June, the plant sends up solid silver spikes which by early July produce tiny lilac-purple flowers. These silver stems are not always completely rigid. At best, they all stand up in composed unison. But with rain and wind, they can flop around. Usually, the stems do not interfere too badly with other plants, but some gardeners don't care for them or their flowers and prefer to cut out both as soon as they appear, to focus attention squarely back on the lush carpet of soft, gray foliage.

> **Location:** Full sun
> **Type:** Perennial
> **Size:** 15 to 18 inches (38 to 45 cm)
> **Conditions:** Good, free-draining soil
> **Flowering time:** June to July
> **Zone:** 4

There are three main cultivars of *Stachys byzantina* from which to choose. 'Silver Carpet' is one of the best. It grows only 6 to 8 inches (15 to 20 cm) high, which makes it an excellent front-of-the-border edging plant. It has all the qualities we admire in lamb's ears—soft woolly gray leaves and low, mat-forming growth habit—but since it rarely flowers, the foliage tends to stay more compact and dense. 'Primrose Heron' grows to 12 to 18 inches (30 to 45 cm) tall, has pale yellow-green, felty leaves and insignificant magenta flowers, and is useful as a groundcover in dry sunny areas. 'Countess Helene Von Stein', 12 to 18 inches (30 to 45 cm), is gaining popularity because of its large leaves and non-flowering habit, which make it appealing to gardeners with a special interest in foliage colors and textures.

Where to plant it

Grow *Stachys byzantina* in fertile, well-drained soil in full sun. It is very drought tolerant, using its leaves to cling on to every drop of moisture. Use lamb's ears as a solitary specimen to add focus and textural interest, or plant it in a large drift to create a stream-of-silver look. It is best placed at the front of the border, even though the stems rise up almost 2 feet (60 cm). For the first two months it is very low to the ground.

Prune the spires away if they grow high enough to block your view of other flowers.

Lamb's ears look especially attractive next to stone walls or softening the edges of a concrete or gravel path.

How to care for it

Rain does the most damage. A plant that loves warm, rocky, fast-draining Mediterranean hillsides, *Stachys byzantina* is not at all happy if it has to put up with heavy rains in the growing season. The leaves become mushy and prone to disease, so good drainage is essential.

Tidy up the plant in spring. Remove all dead and diseased foliage, and take out the worst-looking stems once the peak flowering period is over in July. There are no pests to worry about. Aphids, slugs and snails have no interest in lamb's ears.

Good companions

Let your imagination fly. There are always new and imaginative combinations popping up. The purple flowers on the gray spikes of lamb's ears look great against the solid purple flower spikes of liatris. Scarlet bee balm can also provide a striking contrast. Lamb's ears will sit very comfortably at the foot of purple smoke bush or purple-leaf sand cherry. Blues of salvia and scabiosa, the purple varieties of stonecrop, and the magenta and white flowers of *Lychnis coronaria* all offer interesting possibilities.

For your collection

- *Stachys macrantha* has the same first name but is nothing like any of the others mentioned here. It has large, green, mintlike leaves, grows 2 feet (60 cm) high and produces lilac-purple flowers from June to July.
- If you like lamb's ears, you will probably also want *Ballota pseudo-dictamnus*, which has so many of the same fine characteristics—great gray foliage that is easy to care for, no pests or disease, evergreen if planted in a protected spot, and valuable structural and textural interest for the garden. Ballota grows about 2 feet (60 cm) tall and spreads a little wider. The small, oval-shaped, gray-green leaves look like tiny bowls and are arranged in pairs up the silver stems. In a clump, they have a highly patterned, very decorative look. Ballota will tolerate poor soil but don't make it suffer too much.
- The artemisias, of course, are regarded as the true aristocrats of gray foliage. Look for 'Powis Castle', 'Silver Mound' and 'Valerie Finnis'.

🐦 Another gray-foliage plant, *Verbascum bombyciferum* has a woolly stem and yellow flowers in June and July. It is a real show-stopper that will have all your visitors oohing and aahing over its theatrical impact. It can reach 6 feet (1.8 m) with very little effort.

🐦 *Phlomis fruticosa* (Jerusalem sage) has woolly gray-green foliage and yellow banana-like flowers.

Styrax japonica

Common name: *Japanese snowbell or snowdrop tree*

Chief characteristics

One of the worst gardening errors is to plant a big tree like a poplar, weeping willow or deodar cedar in a small front yard. Unfortunately, it is a mistake many have made and lived to regret. They don't, of course, start out as big trees. Deodar cedar (*Cedrus deodara*), for instance, looks like a perfectly charming, inoffensive creature as an infant in the nursery. But 10 years on and it will have outgrown its allotted space and become a headache with lanky branches full of razor-sharp needles.

Location: Full sun to part shade
Type: Deciduous tree
Size: 25 feet (7.5 m) at maturity
Conditions: Moist, well-drained soil
Flowering time: Mid-June
Zone: 6

If you're looking for a moderate-growing, small tree for your small- or medium-sized garden, you cannot do much better than to pick the graceful snowbell tree. It is relatively slow-growing, reaching only 25 to 30 feet (7.5 to 9 m) with a loosely rounded top at maturity. It takes about 10 years to reach 15 feet (4.5 m). An exceptionally handsome deciduous tree, it has masses of fragrant white snowdrop-like flowers with yellow centers in mid-June. They don't last very long, sometimes only a couple of weeks if rain comes along and knocks them about. When the tree is covered with dainty, drooping, bell-shaped flowers, it is a glorious picture. The flowers are best viewed from underneath, looking up into the tree. When it has finished flowering, the tree is still attractive, with soft leaves covering an elegant framework of arching branches. In late summer, clusters of tiny green nutlike seeds can be seen dangling from the branches. They eventually turn brown and drop to the ground before winter.

Where to plant it

The snowbell tree grows best in moist, free-draining, fertile soil in full sun or light shade. Plant in early spring in a sheltered location. Since the white flowers hang down, locate the tree where it is easy to look up into the branches. My snowbell tree is positioned at the top of a set of steps. This allows visitors, as they come to the house, to see the blooms from the best angle.

Styrax japonica is also well sited on a slope above a path or grown in a raised planter on a patio. The tree needs room on either side to expand, as it tends to grow out rather than up, although this habit can be managed with judicious pruning.

How to care for it

Water your tree well during the first year after planting. Mulch to keep the soil moist but not sodden. The snowbell tree is grown not only for its foliage and flowers but for its graceful form. It is important to maintain the integrity of the tree's shape when it comes time to prune. Wonder, ponder and prune wisely. The tree does not require heavy pruning; in fact, it rather dislikes it. If you have to prune, do it with intelligence and sensitivity to its natural form. No topping, please.

Good companions

Underplant with spring-flowering bulbs such as snowdrops, bluebells, crocus, grape hyacinths or daffodils. You can even use this tree in shrub form in the mixed border.

For your collection

- *Styrax obassia* (fragrant snowbell tree) produces similar flowers to *S. japonica*, but blooms a little earlier and has larger, oval leaves.
- *Halesia carolina* (Carolina silverbell tree) is also a member of the styrax family. It has attractive, white, bell-shaped flowers in May and could be more widely grown. It is more loosely structured than *Styrax japonica* but is still an excellent tree for the small garden. It grows to 20 to 30 feet (6 to 9 m).

$\mathcal{S}$yringa vulgaris French Hybrids

Common name: *French lilacs*

Chief characteristics

Lilacs have one great thing (and realistically, only one thing) going for them—super-fragrant, sensational-looking flowers. They don't have great foliage that turns spectacular shades of red and yellow in fall. They don't produce attractive fruit or berries. But there is really nothing to compare to the intoxicating perfume of their distinctive clusters of flowers in May and June. And that is certainly enough to establish them as one of the most popular flowering garden shrubs of all time.

Location: Full sun
Type: Deciduous shrub
Size: 8 to 10 feet (2.4 to 3 m)
Conditions: Average, well-drained, neutral soil
Flowering time: May to June
Zone: 3

The big question is which kind of lilac to grow. There are many from which to choose—small, medium and large varieties—and a delightful range of colors, everything from purple, lavender and lilac to blue, red and pink. At one time, the common lilac (*Syringa vulgaris*) was the only kind available, but then along came French nurseryman Victor Lemoine who bred an exciting collection of hybrids in the late 1800s. Suddenly gardeners discovered they had access to a whole new range of colors and forms. The French lilacs, as they are now known, are still all excellent, dependable plants. They grow 8 to 10 feet (2.4 to 3 m), require minimal maintainance and can be relied upon to put on an impressive display of perfumed blooms every spring.

Top performers include 'Charles Joly' (magenta), 'Sensation' (lilac-blue) and 'Madame Lemoine' (creamy yellow to white). Other popular ones are 'Monge' (single red), 'Belle de Nancy' (double pink), 'President Grevy' (lilac-blue), 'Olivier de Serres' (lavender-blue) and 'Montaigne' (light pink).

A Russian hybridizer named Kolesnikov picked up where Lemoine left off and produced an excellent variety called 'Krasavitsa Moskvy', which is sold in Canada under the name 'Beauty of Moscow'. It has pink buds turning a waxy white with a frilly, dense petaled look that is rather similar to noisette roses.

Where to plant it

Lilac thrives in full sun or light shade and prefers soil that is neutral, but tending towards the chalky, alkaline end of the spectrum. You can use lilac as a specimen plant to provide color and fragrance from May to June or you can plant a row of them to create an informal hedge or windbreak. There are now some excellent dwarf varieties available for growing as low hedges or in containers or borders where space is limited. Those grown in containers need to be repotted regularly and well watered in summer months.

To appreciate the scent of the bloom, locate your lilac close to a gate or next to a path, or consider training a bush at one side of an arbor. Use a taller variety of lilac to screen out an eyesore.

How to care for it

To keep your lilac healthy and happy and flowering profusely each year, always do these three things: 1) Deadhead regularly, removing the flower heads the moment they are finished. 2) Prune out dead or unproductive branches and thin, weak stems to make room for strong, new, flower-producing shoots. 3) Amend the soil every couple of years by adding well-rotted compost or cow manure as a top-dressing.

Good drainage is important. Heavy, clay soils can be improved by adding sand and grit and planting the lilac on a slightly raised mound. Don't be impatient for your lilac to produce flowers. New bushes often take two or three years to start flowering profusely.

Good companions

In England, garden after garden displays lilacs in full bloom in May along with the cascading golden-yellow flowers of laburnum trees. Other perfect partners for lilac include pink-flowering crabapple and cherry trees. Lilacs can also be underplanted very nicely with a variety of spring-flowering bulbs—grape hyacinths, scilla, erythronium and species crocus are all excellent choices—and blue- and yellow-leafed hostas are also reliable partners.

You can extend the flower season by combining a French lilac with one of the hardy Preston lilacs, which bloom later in June. If fragrance is what you are looking for, 'Beauty of Moscow', 'Katherine Havemeyer' and 'Michel Buchner' are worth hunting down. Two of the best white-flowering lilacs are 'Madame Lemoine' (also available in tree-form) and 'Maud Notcutt' (produced at the English nursery, Notcutts).

For your collection

- *Syringa meyeri* 'Palibin' (dwarf lilac). Useful for creating a compact, low hedge, this has purple-pink flowers in June and grows to 5 feet (1.5 m). It is also available in a patio-tree form.
- *Syringa patula* 'Miss Kim'. This dwarf Korean lilac has become a very

popular deciduous shrub because it can be used in gardens where space is limited. It grows about 6 feet (2 m) high and has fragrant clusters of icy purple flowers from May to June. The dark green foliage gets a burgundy tint in fall. It needs winter protection in areas where temperatures drop to –30°F (–34°C).

* *Syringa prestoniae* (Preston lilacs). These were specifically developed by Isabella Preston, of Ottawa, for fragrance, disease resistance and hardiness. They tolerate colder winter temperatures than most of the French lilacs and have a habit of flowering a little later, usually in June. Varieties to consider include 'Donald Wyman' (mauve), 'James McFarlane' (clear pink), 'Minuet' (pale pink), 'Isabella' (purple-pink) and 'Nocturne' (purple-pink).

* *Syringa reticulata* 'Ivory Silk' (Japanese tree lilac). This compact tree grows to 25 feet (7.5 m) and produces large clusters of creamy white flowers in June. It is gaining popularity because of its suitability for small gardens and because it requires little maintenance and can cope with pollution from car fumes and poor air quality in densely populated urban settings.

*T*axus × media 'Hicksii'

Common name: *Hick's yew*

Chief characteristics

Location: Full sun to light shade
Type: Evergreen shrub
Size: 10 feet (3 m)
Conditions: Ordinary, well-drained soil
Zone: 5

Privacy is an important element in a garden. Without privacy, it can be impossible to enjoy the benefit of your hard labor to create a garden paradise. If walls or fences won't do the job of defining borders and providing privacy, the task usually falls to a hedge of some sort. Yew makes a very classy hedge. It is slow-growing and you need patience, but in the long run it ends up being far more attractive than other types of hedging. Yew's dark foliage will provide a dramatic backdrop for the beautiful flowers and shrubs in your garden.

The common English yew is *Taxus baccata*. Left undisturbed, it would eventually grow to 40 feet (12 m) or more. However, the best kind of yew for hedging is *Taxus × media* 'Hicksii', which is a cross between English and Japanese species. Hick's yew produces a narrow, upright bush with lovely, dark green foliage that holds its color and requires minimal maintenance. It is slow-growing and it can take 10 years or more for it to reach 8 or 10 feet (2.4 to 3 m).

Golden yew (*Taxus baccata* 'Fastigiata Aurea') is another fine hedging plant. The new foliage in spring is golden yellow and then turns green, retaining touches of gold on the edges of the needles. It will grow to 5 feet (1.5 m) after 10 years, ultimately reaching 15 feet (4.5 m).

Where to plant it

Grow yew in reasonably well-drained soil. It thrives in deep shade to full sun and prefers soil that is not excessively acidic or alkaline. Plant yew as an accent plant or as a formal hedge to provide screening. The dark form of the more column-shaped yews can provide a very effective dramatic contrast in a cottage garden full of old-fashioned roses and flowering shrubs and perennials.

How to care for it

The beauty of yew is that once it is established it is very easy to maintain and does not mind being pruned into shape or cut back into place. It can handle heavy rains, cool winds and hot dry spells. It is also reasonably indifferent to air pollution.

Good companions

The best companion for a yew hedge is a perennial border. The dark foliage of a yew hedge is the perfect backdrop for the diversity of color you find in a richly planted herbaceous border. Yew contrasts well with the complex, twisted form of Harry Lauder's walking stick (*Corylus avellana* 'Contorta'), which produces pale yellow catkins in winter. You could also position a red- or yellow-flowering witch hazel—*Hamamelis* × *intermedia*—in front of or beside the dark shape of your yew.

For your collection

You are not likely to want to collect different forms of yew, even though there are many. There are yews that make useful groundcovers, such as the dwarf spreading English yew (*Taxus baccata* 'Repandens') and the dense, vase-shaped yew (*Taxus* × *media* 'Brownii'), both of which are hardy to Zone 5. But if you need a hedge and don't have time for a slow-growing yew, here are some other options.

- 🦌 *Thuja occidentalis* 'Smaragd' (emerald cedar) is an extremely popular hedging plant with a cleanly defined pyramidal shape and rich emerald-green foliage that holds its color through winter. It is hardy to Zone 3 and can reach 20 feet (6 m) if left unpruned. Other cultivars of *Thuja occidentalis* to consider include: 'Nigra' (dark green), 'Holmstrup' (bright green), 'Yellow Ribbon' (bright yellow), 'Unicorn' (deep green) and narrow 'Brandon' (bright green.)

- *Thuja plicata* (western red cedar) is also popular. It grows quickly, doesn't mind being sheared, bounces back from a cold winter and stays green all year.

- *Buxus koreana* 'Winter Beauty' (boxwood) is the right pick for a low hedge to define a rose bed or herb garden or simply to divide one part of the garden from another. It has blue-green foliage.

- *Tsuga canadensis* (hemlock) has a loose, feathery foliage, but reasonably formal look, which makes it a good candidate for a screen or windbreak.

- *Ilex crenata* is a member of the holly family and has tiny black berries in winter, but it has all the appearance of a box-type hedge and can be clipped into a formal-looking waist-high barrier.

- *Ligustrum amurense* (privet) is a most popular and attractive hedge used in many parts of England. It has soft, glossy leaves and can be sheared into a very tidy shape.

- *Forsythia intermedia*, a popular deciduous shrub, is one of the heralds of spring. It can be used to create a striking informal hedge of bright yellow flowers in March.

- Two other great deciduous hedging plants are common European beech (*Fagus sylvatica*) and hornbeam (*Carpinus betulus*). Hornbeam has such magnificent foliage it is surprising it is not used more for hedging, as well as for pleaching, a way of weaving the branches of a row of trees to form a hedge or a screen 5 or 6 feet (1.5 to 1.8 m) above the ground. Part of the problem with hornbeams, perhaps, is their tendency to hold on to their decaying leaves in winter. The European beech has a similar habit.

- In gardens where space is not limited, shrub roses can be used to form relaxed barriers in areas where neat, compact formality is not required.

- Other hedging possibilities are spiraea, berberis, eleagnus, and *Viburnum plicatum* 'Summer Snowflake'.

*T*hymus × citriodorus 'Doone Valley'

Common name: *Creeping lemon-scented thyme*

Chief characteristics

Thyme is a low-growing, sweet-scented perennial that is very useful as a colorful, compact groundcover, ideal for growing in sunny rockeries and for filling crevices between paving stones. It can also be grown in pots with spring-flowering bulbs like yellow crocuses and short blue irises.

Location: Full sun
Type: Perennial
Size: 4 inches (10 cm)
Conditions: Ordinary, well-drained soil
Flowering time: July to August
Zone: 4

Thymus × citriodorus 'Doone Valley' gives off a powerful lemon scent when the leaves are brushed. It grows 4 to 6 inches (10 to 15 cm) high and has dark green aromatic leaves tipped with gold. Other top names include 'Gold Edge', 'E. B. Anderson' and 'Argenteus'.

Common thyme (*Thymus vulgaris*) has aromatic gray-green leaves and tiny, pale lilac flowers in June. Creeping mother of thyme or wild thyme (*Thymus praecox*) grows 3 or 4 inches (7.5 to 10 cm) high, has purple, red or white flowers, and spreads to form an attractive matlike covering. You will sometimes find it in garden centers under the label *Thymus serpyllum*. Good cultivars include 'Purple Carpet' (light purple), 'Coccineus' (red), 'Elfin' (pink) and 'Albus' (white). Woolly thyme (*Thymus pseudolanuginosus*) has soft silvery foliage and bright pink flowers.

Where to plant it

Thyme is mostly useful as a groundcover in sunny rock or herb gardens. You can use it to make an aromatic lawn as long as it is not walked on all the time. Thyme does attract bees when in full flower, so you will want to watch where you put your bare feet! It is the perfect plant for filling in gaps, so grow it between slabs of slate to make a sitting area in a sunny corner of the garden, use it to fill crevices between stepping stones or let it tumble over the sides of raised beds.

How to care for it

Grow thyme in slightly alkaline soil. It must have well-drained soil if it is to survive a wet winter or spring. All thymes require sun to flower properly. If they get straggly, gently shear them back immediately after flowering. Divide clumps in spring or fall to make more plants.

Good companions

You can make a groundcovering tapestry of soft pink, lavender, white and red-purple flowers using a variety of thymes—'Doone Valley', woolly thyme, creeping thyme and so on. Blue *Iris reticulata*, scillas or yellow crocuses all look great flowering above the dense, compact green leaves of lemon-scented thyme.

For your collection

- Two excellent forms of variegated thyme are *Thymus caespititius* 'Aureus' (gold-green) and *Thymus* × *citriodorus* 'Silver Queen'.
- Other great low-growing plants that can gently mound to cover ground with a soft, cushion-like carpet include *Phlox subulata*, *Dianthus gratianopolitanus* and *Armeria maritima*.

*T*ilia cordata 'Greenspire'

Common name: Little-leaf linden, lime or basswood

Chief characteristics

Location: Full sun to light shade
Type: Deciduous tree
Size: 40 to 50 feet (12 to 15 m)
Conditions: Moist, well-drained soil
Zone: 3

It is wonderful that there is so much interest in growing feature trees such as Japanese maples and beautiful white- or purple-flowering magnolias, but to my mind there is still something truly majestic about a large, leafy-green shade tree. Ash and oak trees are outstanding shade specimens and mountain ash trees have a special, late-summer charm when they are covered by clusters of red berries, but for me, nothing compares to the classical conical form and elegant heart-shaped leaf of the little-leaf linden. Whenever I see a stately linden tree I immediately think of the Dorset I once knew and the poem "Linden Lea," which the late British composer Vaughan Williams set to such beautiful, romantic music.

Sublime in its symmetry, the linden looks superb standing alone at the end of a lawn, or pleached in rows to form an avenue of neat trunks and blended foliage, or evenly spaced along a quiet boulevard of a suburban street. Critics of the linden say it is boring and has been overplanted and lacks the flower power of more exotic trees like empress tree (*Paulownia*) or Japanese lilac tree (*Syringa reticulata*). Yet the linden remains one of the most popular trees for creating shade in summer and for providing a lovely show of color when the leaves turn yellow in the fall. The sweet scent of the tree's delicate yellow flowers in July have been described as "a fragrant treat as fine as any rose could give."

The best linden for the medium-sized garden is *Tilia cordata* 'Greenspire'. It remains beautifully compact and has a nice straight trunk. Another first-rate little-leaf linden is *Tilia cordata* 'Glenleven', which grows faster and is slightly taller and less dense than 'Greenspire'.

You won't want to plant the native American linden (*Tilia americana*) unless you have a large country estate. It is a fast-growing, enormous tree that will reach 60 feet (18 m) or more and has a reputation for being intolerant of air pollution. There is, however, a more manageable variety called 'Raymond' that grows to only 40 feet (12 m).

Where to grow it

Plant 'Greenspire' in full sun or light shade in fertile soil that stays moist without being wet or boggy. You can use a linden as a feature tree in a lawn, to create shade for the house, for pleaching and hedging, or as a tree for the boulevard. Bees will be attracted to the tree's tiny fragrant yellow flowers in July, and while this is rarely a problem you may want to take it into account when selecting the site for your new tree.

How to care for it

Little-leaf lindens are disease and pest resistant and require little pruning. They do not like severe drought, so make sure your tree is well watered in hot summers. Aphids and bark borer have been known to be a problem, but this usually occurs where too many trees have been planted, creating stress and poor air circulation.

Pruning is basically a matter of removing any damaged limbs in spring. Lower branches sometimes have to be removed to create more light for grass growing beneath the branches.

Good companions

Lindens stand alone and look beautiful in a solitary location, especially on a grassy boulevard or expanse of lawn. But the light shade a linden creates can allow an assortment of shade-loving shrubs, like rhododendrons and hydrangea, and perennials such as hostas and astrantia, to thrive in a mixed planting.

For your collection

Ash, oak and mountain ash are also excellent specimens for creating shade and giving the landscape strong botanical structure. Here's a list of the best cultivars for the job.

- *Fraxinus americana* 'Autumn Purple' is a handsome, oval-shaped, seedless ash with bright green leaves. It grows to 50 feet (15 m) tall.
- *Fraxinus pennsylvanica* 'Patmore'. The most popular of the ash shade trees, it has a graceful, oval form and medium green leaves. It grows to 50 feet (15 m) high.
- *Quercus robur* 'Fastigiata'. This form of English oak has an attractive columnar shape and deep green leaves that turn copper in fall. It grows to 40 feet (12 m).
- *Quercus rubra* (red oak). This fast-growing native oak develops a beautiful round canopy that turns brilliant scarlet in fall. It will grow to 80 feet (24 m).
- *Quercus palustris* (pin oak). The perfect pick for moist sites, pin oak, also known as swamp oak, has a stately pydramidal form, drooping lower branches and bright scarlet foliage in fall. It will grow to 50 feet (15 m).
- *Sorbus aucuparia* (European mountain ash) has white flowers in spring and large clusters of red berries in fall. It grows to 25 feet (7.5 m).
- *Sorbus aucuparia* 'Fastigiata'. This column-shaped European mountain ash has attractive dark green leaves and large orange berries in fall. It can be planted where space is limited, fairly close to the house, without becoming a problem. It grows to 30 feet (9 m).
- *Sorbus aucuparia* 'Rossica Major' (Russian mountain ash) has a very attractive pyramidal shape, produces clusters of large red berries in fall and grows to 35 feet (10 m).

Viburnum plicatum 'Summer Snowflake'

Common name: *Summer snowflake*

Chief characteristics

Most moderate-sized gardens have room for at least two or three different kinds of viburnum. It is an extremely versatile family of shrubs, especially useful for providing groundcover or winter color or fragrant white blooms in spring. 'Summer Snowflake', a plant introduced by the University of B.C. Botanical Garden, is ideal for a low-maintenance garden. It covers itself in April to May with a full flush of white, clover-shaped flowers. The rate of flowering slows in June and continues at a more modest tempo all summer. 'Summer Snowflake' has a compact form and slow-growing habit, making it very manageable and a good shrub for the small- or medium-sized city garden.

Location: Sun to semi-shade
Type: Deciduous shrub
Size: 8 feet (2.4 m)
Conditions: Good, moist soil
Flowering time: May to June
Zone: 5

Where to plant it

All viburnums thrive in full sun in good soil that stays moist but not soggy. Where you plant them depends on the variety and the function you want it to fulfil. 'Summer Snowflake' can be planted in groups to create a low hedge or screen, or individually in the mixed border.

How to care for it

Viburnums are fuss-free plants, rarely requiring attention to deal with pests or diseases. They only need pruning to clear out dead and damaged branches and routine pruning after flowering to keep them within their boundaries.

Good companions

'Summer Snowflake' and most of the other spring-flowering viburnums blend with magnolias, mock orange, rhododendrons and small trees. They can be underplanted with spring-flowering bulbs like scilla and grape hyacinths or various spring- and summer-blooming perennials.

For your collection

🌿 *Viburnum burkwoodii* (Burkwood viburnum) is a semi-evergreen shrub with white flowers in May. The shiny green leaves turn bronze-brown in fall. It grows 7 to 10 feet (2 to 3 m).

- *Viburnum carlcephalum* (fragrant snowball) is a compact shrub, 5 to 7 feet (1.5 to 2 m), with very fragrant dense clusters of waxy white "snowball" flowers in May.
- *Viburnum carlesii* (Korean spice viburnum) is an outstanding spring-flowering shrub. It grows into a small, rounded, 4- by 4-foot (1.2- by 1.2-m) bush with heavily scented white clusters of flowers in March and April.
- *Viburnum × juddii*. A mounding shrub about 5 feet (1.5 m) with fragrant white flowers in May. The lush green foliage turns an attractive shade of purple-red in October.
- *Viburnum opulus* 'Roseum' (European snowball). Commonly called the snowball bush, it is possibly the best-known viburnum because of its spectacular June display of dazzling creamy white, globular flowerheads that look like snowballs. It grows to 10 feet (3 m). *V. opulus* 'Compactum' (compact highbush cranberry) produces white flowers and has green leaves that turn purple-red in October.
- *Viburnum plicatum tomentosum* 'Mariesii' is a spectacular shrub if you have space. It grows to 8 feet (2.4 m) and in spring its pure white, flat, lacecap flowers are elegantly displayed along the entire length of its long horizontal, tiered branches. It has been planted to dramatic effect as the feature at the end of a large lawn, or as one of the stars of the shrub border.

Weigela florida 'Red Prince'

Common name: *Red Prince weigela*

Chief characteristics

In designing your garden, it is always important not only to think about shapes and structures, but to take time to plan a sequence of blooms throughout the year. It is very easy to ignore this aspect of gardening and end up with a landscape that is full of color and vitality in May but has little interest in August and September. *Weigela florida* 'Red Prince' is especially useful in this regard because as well as producing wonderful, crimson-red, tubular flowers for a six-week period from June to July, it also blooms sporadically in August. Moreover, this compact, low-maintenance, pest-free shrub attracts hummingbirds to your garden.

Location: Full sun to light shade

Type: Deciduous shrub

Size: 3 to 5 feet (1 to 1.5 m)

Conditions: Ordinary, well-drained soil

Flowering time: June

Zone: 5

They can't resist the sweet-scented clusters of foxglove-like flowers, which are further heightened by the bush's lush deep green foliage.

'Bristol Ruby' is the best known weigela. This is the variety every garden center stocks without question. But it does not always perform reliably in cooler northern gardens, where it often dies down to the ground and sometimes has difficulty recovering its structural beauty and flower-power. 'Red Prince', on the other hand, is one of a new, hardier breed of weigelas. It is acclaimed for its vigor, purity of color, winter toughness, and exuberant blooming habit. Since it grows to only 5 or 6 feet (1.5 to 2 m), it can easily be grown in small- and medium-sized gardens. Its cousin, 'Minuet', is an even more compact variety, growing less than 3 feet (90 cm) tall and producing light pink flowers against a background of green leaves with a purple tinge.

Where to plant it

Weigela will thrive in full sun or light shade in well-drained soil. It prefers rich, fertile soil, but it won't sulk too badly if you insist on planting it in average soil. 'Red Prince' can play a valuable role in the middle of the mixed border or shubbery, where its crimson flowers can be enjoyed in June, leaving other plants to hold the stage in May and July. You can also use 'Red Prince' to create an informal hedge or add lavish color to boring banks and berms. Although the newer, more compact forms of weigela do not grow very tall, the shrub still needs some space on either side to accommodate its thin, arching branches.

Variegated forms perform better when planted in light shade. The ideal time to plant weigela is in late September or as soon as the ground can be worked in April.

How to care for it

Pest and disease resistant, weigela asks for only two things: to have the soil in which it is planted enriched with well-rotted manure or compost every second year; and to be pruned regularly to maintain its shape and vigor. Prune branches as soon as the flowers fade. Older shrubs can be rejuvenated by thinning out branches and enriching the soil.

Don't let the soil dry out in summer months, especially if the shrub has just been planted in spring.

Good companions

Other spring- and summer-flowering shrubs make excellent companions for weigela. To create a sequence of blooms, consider French lilac, hydrangea, rhododendrons and azaleas, and viburnum for early spring to the end of May. To pick up where your weigela leaves off in June, consider potentilla, hibiscus, spiraea and some of the more compact modern shrub roses. Perennial partners could include daylilies, hardy geraniums, *Sedum* 'Autumn Joy', and well-behaved clumping grasses like *Festuca glauca*.

For your collection

- White-flowering weigela. 'White Knight' and 'Bristol Snowflake' both grow to about 5 feet (1.5 m) and have white flowers in June.
- Pink-flowering weigela. Look for 'Victoria' (dark pink), 'Pink Princess' (light pink) or 'Purpurea' (purple-pink). The foliage of 'Purpurea' has a purple-green tone while the leaves of 'Victoria' have a bronze hue, heightening the color of the pink flowers. They all grow 4 to 5 feet (1.2 to 1.5 m).
- Three-color weigela. For something unusual, how about 'Carnaval', which has red, pink and white flowers on the same bush. It grows 3 to 4 feet (90 to 120 cm) and flowers in June.
- Best of the variegated weigelas is 'Variegata', which has green leaves with deep yellow edges. Like all variegated forms, this thrives best in light shade. It has rose-colored flowers in June and grows 4 feet (1.2 m) high.

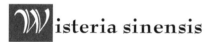isteria sinensis

Common name: Chinese wisteria

Chief characteristics

It can be a heavenly experience to sit beneath an arbor or walk through a pergola smothered with the fragrant flowers of wisteria in May. Gardeners lucky enough to have a well-trained wisteria doubtless have had many fond memories of warm evenings spent in late spring relaxing with friends beneath a canopy of the magnificent violet-blue blooms.

Location: Full sun
Type: Deciduous vine
Size: 20 feet (6 m) plus
Conditions: Fertile, well-drained soil
Flowering time: May to June
Zone: 5

There are two popular types. *Wisteria sinensis*, the Chinese wisteria, is particularly vigorous and produces soft purple clusters that can measure up to 8 inches (20 cm) long. *W. floribunda*, the Japanese wisteria, is less vigorous and less bothered by extreme cold in winter. The main difference between them is their flowering habit: the blooms on the Japanese wisteria open slowly along a cluster while the flowers on a Chinese wisteria open all at once and give a showier display. This is why the Chinese species tends to be more popular, although the Japanese wisteria has a slightly longer flowering period. Both kinds flower about the same time, from April to June.

Top cultivars of Chinese wisteria include 'Aunt Dee' (light purple), 'Caroline' (soft lavender-mauve), 'Amethyst' (light rosy purple) and 'Blue Sapphire' (blue-mauve). Top cultivars of Japanese wisteria are 'Lawrence' (deep blue), 'Pink Ice' (fragrant pink), 'Snow Showers' (dainty white-tinged lilac),' 'Longissima Alba' (white), 'Prolific' (violet-blue) and 'Rosea' (purple-pink).

Grown from seed, wisteria is notorious for taking its time to flower. You will hear people warn that new plants can take as long as 7, even 10 years, to bloom. But today most vines are grown from cuttings or grafting or layering. They are often in flower when you buy them in the pot at the nursery.

Where to plant it

You will see spectacular photographs of wisteria in full bloom covering the brick facade of old Victorian houses. In reality, wisteria is not the best choice for a climber to grow against a house. It can easily get out of hand, and the stems eventually become very woody and weighty. They twist themselves powerfully around supporting structures and can easily become a problem. Wisteria is much more suitable for growing along a sturdy pergola or over a sizable arbor. Think twice before growing one against the front of the house or over a porch entrance.

One good idea is to grow it as a standard to form a small, weeping tree. This requires diligent pruning for at least four consecutive years to get it trained properly.

How to care for it

Plant wisteria in a protected site where it will not be hit by severe frosts. It will thrive in average, moist, well-drained soil in full sun. Enrich the soil with well-rotted compost or manure at planting time and mulch well in spring. Prune to espalier and shape the plant in the early years. Once the plant is established, pruning usually comes down to cutting stems back in early spring to within a few inches (8 to 10 cm) of the previous season's growth in order to keep the vine in check. If it is still too vigorous, it can be pruned back in July, snipping back new growth almost to where it began.

Good companions

Wisteria does not leave much room for a partner, but if it is trained along one side of a pergola, arch or arbor, a rose could complement it on the other side. *Rosa* 'Félicité Perpétue', which has sensational white blooms, would be a good choice. Other top picks would be any of the following clematis cultivars: 'Madame Julia Correvon', 'Jackmanii Superba', 'Etoile Violette' and 'The President'.

For your collection

- *Wisteria sinensis* 'Black Dragon' has long trusses of almost black racemes. It is only hardy, however, to Zone 6.
- *Wisteria venusta* (silky wisteria) has fragrant white or purple flowers with silk-like hairs.
- Other climbers for growing along a pergola or over an arbor include the purple-leafed grape (*Vitis vinifera* 'Purpurea') or vigorous roses like 'Rambling Rector' (with beautiful white flowers).

*1*00 Best Plants by Type

Annuals

Heliotropium arborescens (cherry-pie plant)
Lavatera trimestris 'Mont Blanc' (annual mallow)
Nicotiana alata (flowering tobacco plant)
Pelargonium (zonal geranium)

Perennials

Adiantum aleuticum (western or five-fingered maidenhair fern)
Ajuga reptans 'Bronze Beauty' (bugleweed)
Alchemilla mollis (lady's mantle)
Aquilegia (columbine)
Artemisia schmidtiana 'Silver Mound' (wormwood)
Aster frikartii 'Monch' (Michaelmas daisy)
Astilbe arendsii 'Fanal' (false spiraea)
Astrantia major (masterwort)
Campanula persicifolia (bellflower)
Cimicifuga 'Brunette' (bugbane, snakeroot)
Coreopsis verticillata 'Moonbeam' (tickseed)
Corydalis lutea (yellow corydalis)
Crocosmia 'Lucifer' (montbretia)
Delphinium Pacific Hybrids (larkspur)
Dicentra spectabilis 'Alba' (old-fashioned bleeding heart)
Digitalis purpurea (foxglove)
Echinacea purpurea (purple coneflower)
Euphorbia griffithii 'Fireglow' (spurge)
Foeniculum vulgare 'Purpureum' (bronze fennel)
Geranium cinereum 'Ballerina' (cranesbill, hardy geranium)
Helleborus orientalis (Lenten rose)
Hemerocallis 'Stella de Oro' (daylily)
Heuchera micrantha 'Bressingham Bronze' (coral bells)
Hosta 'Frances Williams' (Frances Williams hosta)
Iris sibirica (Siberian iris)
Kniphofia (red-hot poker)
Liatris spicata (gayfeather, blazing star)
Ligularia stenocephala 'The Rocket' (ligularia)
Lupinus Russell Hybrids (Russell lupins)
Lychnis coronaria (rose campion)
Lysimachia clethroides (gooseneck loosestrife, Chinese loosestrife)
Monarda 'Gardenview Scarlet' (bee balm, bergamot)

Perennials (cont.)

Nymphaea 'James Brydon' (hardy water lily)
Ophiopogon planiscapus 'Nigrescens' (black mondo grass)
Paeonia lactiflora 'Karl Rosenfeld' (peony)
Papaver orientale 'Mrs. Perry' (oriental poppy)
Phlox paniculata 'Fujiama' (phlox)
Polemonium caeruleum 'Brise d'Anjou' (variegated Jacob's ladder)
Polygonum bistorta 'Superbum' (fleece flower, knotweed)
Primula japonica 'Miller's Crimson' (candelabra primula)
Salvia × *sylvestris* 'May Night' (perennial salvia, sage)
Scabiosa columbaria 'Butterfly Blue' (pincushion flower)
Sedum 'Autumn Joy' (stonecrop)
Stachys byzantina 'Silver Carpet' (lamb's ears)
Thymus × *citriodorus* 'Doone Valley' (creeping lemon-scented thyme)

Bulbs

Allium aflatunense (ornamental onion)
Camassia (quamash)
Lilium 'Casa Blanca' (Casa Blanca lily)
Muscari armeniacum (grape hyacinth)
Scilla (Hyacinthoides) non-scripta (English bluebell)

Ornamental Grasses

Helictotrichon sempervirens (blue oat grass)
Miscanthus sinensis 'Gracillimus' (maiden grass)
Pennisetum alopecuroides (fountain grass)

Vines and Climbers

Actinidia kolomikta (kolomikta vine)
Akebia quinata (chocolate vine)
Campsis radicans (trumpet vine)
Clematis × *jackmanii* (virgin's bower)
Hydrangea petiolaris (climbing hydrangea)
Lonicera japonica 'Halliana' (Hall's honeysuckle)
Wisteria sinensis (Chinese wisteria)

Roses

Rosa 'Ballerina' (Ballerina rose)
Rosa 'Elina' (Elina or Peaudouce rose)
Rosa 'Mary Rose' (Mary rose)
Rosa 'Morden Blush' (Parkland rose)
Rosa 'New Dawn' (New Dawn rose, everblooming Dr. W. Van Fleet)
Rosa 'Souvenir de la Malmaison' (Souvenir de la Malmaison rose)

Shrubs

Brugmansia × candida (angel's trumpet)
Buddleia davidii (butterfly bush)
Buxus microphylla koreana (Korean boxwood)
Cornus alba 'Elegantissima' (silverleaf dogwood)
Cotinus coggygria 'Royal Purple' (purple smoke bush)
Euonymus fortunei 'Emerald Gaeity' (Emerald Gaeity euonymus)
Hamamelis × intermedia 'Diane' (witch hazel)
Hibiscus syriacus 'Blue Bird' (rose of Sharon)
Hydrangea arborescens 'Annabelle' (Annabelle hydrangea)
Juniperus scopulorum 'Wichita Blue' (Wichita Blue juniper, blue column juniper)
Lavandula angustifolia (English lavender)
Philadelphus coronarius 'Aureus' (mock orange)
Potentilla fruticosa 'Abbotswood'
Rhododendron Northern Lights Series (Northern Lights azalea)
Spiraea bumalda 'Goldflame' (spiraea)
Syringa vulgaris French Hybrids (French lilacs)
Taxus × media 'Hicksii' (Hick's yew)
Viburnum plicatum 'Summer Snowflake' (summer snowflake)
Weigela florida 'Red Prince' (Red Prince weigela)

Trees

Acer palmatum 'Bloodgood' (Japanese maple)
Acer palmatum dissectum 'Crimson Queen' (laceleaf Japanese maple)
Betula utilis jacquemontii (Himalayan birch)
Elaeagnus angustifolia (Russian olive, oleaster)
Gleditsia triacanthos 'Sunburst' (thornless gold honey locust)
Magnolia × soulangiana (saucer magnolia)
Morus alba 'Pendula' (weeping mulberry)
Picea pungens 'Hoopsii' (Colorado blue spruce)
Prunus × cistena (purple-leaf sand cherry)
Styrax japonica (Japanese snowbell)
Tilia cordata 'Greenspire' (little-leaf linden, lime or basswood)

$\mathbb{T}$erms for New Gardeners

Acid soil: Soil that has a pH of less than 6.5. Sometimes called sour soil, it is ideal for growing rhododendrons, azaleas and heathers. See also pH.

Alkaline soil: The opposite of acidic soil, it has a pH of more than 7.3. Alkaline soil is also referred to as chalky, limey or sweet soil.

Annual: Plants that complete their life cycle in a single growing season.

Bare-root: A plant that has been dug up while dormant and packaged without soil around its roots. Mail orders from nurseries are mostly dispatched bare-root.

Bedding plants: Annuals, biennials and tender perennials that are "bedded out" in spring to provide temporary summer color.

Biennial: Plants that complete their life cycle in two seasons, starting from seed and establishing leaves in the first year and flowering the following year. Examples are foxgloves, wallflowers and Canterbury bells.

Cambium: The green layer of living tissue just below the woody surface of a branch. A sign that your plant is still alive.

Carpet bedding: A style of planting, popular with the early Victorians, involving the tight planting of bedding plants to create intricate floral patterns.

Compost: Dark, blackish humus formed from the decomposition of organic matter. Can be used to enrich soil or as a mulch.

Cultivar: Short for cultivated variety, this refers to a plant selected from the wild or a garden and cultivated by controlled propagation to preserve specific characteristics.

Deadhead: Removal of faded flowers in order 1) to maintain the tidy appearance of the garden; 2) to promote flower production by preventing seed development; and 3) in some cases, such as with delphiniums and lupins, to induce a second flush of flowers later in the season.

Dieback: The death of part of a shoot or branch caused by disease, water or nutrient deficiency, pest damage or incorrect pruning.

Division: A way of making more plants by dividing them into pieces, each with a root system or one or more shoots.

Dormant: Winter sleep for plants. Technically, it means there is little or no cellular activity. Plants go dormant to survive winter and save energy for the new season.

Drip line: An imaginary circle beneath a tree or shrub where water drips from the tips of the branches.

Espalier: The art of training a tree or shrub to grow flat against a wall, fence or trellis in a symmetrical pattern. It was perfected by French gardeners centuries ago.

Fastigiate: A plant whose upright-growing branches create a columnar shape.
Forcing: Getting plants to flower out of season by manipulating temperature, humidity and light.
Frost pocket: An area of the garden where cold air is trapped during winter. Only tougher, more hardy plants can survive in frost pockets.

Genus: Genus is the name for a group of closely related species, and forms the first word of a plant's botanical name: *Lonicera*, *Fuchsia* and *Cotoneaster* are examples. A plant usually has three names: genus (first), species (second), cultivar (third), as in *Lonicera periclymenum* 'Serotina'.
Grafting: Propagating by taking the stem or bud of one plant and joining it to the root or stem of another. If a bud is used, the technique is sometimes called "bud grafting" or simply "budding." Most fruit trees and roses are propagated this way.

Hardening off: Gradually acclimatizing a plant to a lower temperature in order to get it ready for planting in the garden.
Hardiness: Measure of a plant's ability to withstand extremes of cold and frost or other harsh conditions, as in hardy to −10°F/−23°C. *See also* Zones.
Heading back: Severely pruning back the main branches of a tree or shrub by a third to half.
Heeling-in: Temporarily planting a tree or shrub in a holding bed until you are ready to find a permanent home for it.
Herbaceous: Non-woody plants that die back to the ground in winter, then revive and grow again in spring.
Humus: Dark brown organic material formed from the decomposition of vegetable and certain animal matter. Humus enriches garden soil and gives it the life needed to nourish and sustain plants.
Hybrid: A new plant produced by crossing two or more different plants. Not all hybrids are improvements on the parents.

Insecticide: A chemical (liquid or powder) used to control or kill insect pests such as aphids and red spider mites.
Island bed: A flower bed, usually dominated by hardy perennials, that can be viewed from all sides.

Jardin de refuse: Polite way of describing temporary lodgings for plants you can't use, but can't bring yourself to throw away.

Juvenile foliage: New leaves that are different in their shape, size and color from the plant's more familiar adult foliage.

Knot-garden: Popular with medieval English gardeners, who liked to weave low-growing herbs or boxwood hedging into elaborate, knot-like geometric patterns, sometimes with herbs or roses.

Layering: A method of propagation in which a supple branch of a plant is bent down and anchored below ground level until roots form and the newly established plant can be safely cut away from the parent.

Leaf mold: Decomposed leaves that can be used as a mulch or dug into the soil to create useful organic matter.

Loam: The best kind of garden soil for most plants—moderately fertile, composed of clay, sand and humus, with a texture that is neither too sandy nor too heavy.

Manure tea: Water in which manure or compost has been allowed to soak to form a mild, fertilizing "tea."

Microclimate: Small area of the garden where the climate is different from the rest of the garden. When the microclimate is warmer, it means you can grow tender plants that require a climate with a higher zone rating.

Mulch: A layer of bulky organic matter usually placed around perennials, shrubs or trees to reduce moisture loss, inhibit weeds, improve soil and protect plants from frost. Good mulches include well-rotted manure, compost and leaf mold.

Native plant: A species that grows naturally in a certain location and that is not created by human cultivation.

Naturalize: Informal planting that mirrors nature's own relaxed style and design to create the impression that the plants are native.

NPK: Key plant-food ingredients of fertilizer: N for nitrogen, P for phosphorus and K for potassium. The numbers in fertilizer—for example 20-20-20—represent the percentage of each element in the mix. One way to remember what each does is to memorize "Little Red Flower" (L for leaf, nourished by nitrogen; R for roots, strengthened by phosphorus; F for fruit or flower, promoted by potassium).

Oxygenator: A submerged water plant that helps keep ponds clean indirectly by releasing oxygen into the water.

Perennial: A plant with the ability to survive winter and live on for several growing seasons.

pH: Measure (1 to 14) of acidity or alkalinity of soil. Lilacs won't thrive in acidic soil; rhododendrons dislike alkaline soil. The lower the pH, the higher the acidity.

Pinching back: A way of encouraging bushiness in a plant by using your finger and thumb to pinch off growing tips.

Pollarding: Cutting back the main branches of a tree to within inches of the trunk to create a distinct globe effect once the new branches and leaves appear.

Pricking out: Careful removal of seedlings from the original seed tray into a roomier pot or growing space.

Rhizome: A horizontally creeping underground stem from which shoots and roots develop. A good example is bearded iris.

Rootbound: What happens when a plant has been left in a container too long, allowing roots to become tangled and choked.

Species: The second word in a plant's botanical name. A category of plants that are genetically similar, sharing at least one characteristic that sets them apart from all others. *See also* Genus.

Standard: A tree or shrub that is trained to grow a straight stem clear of branches.

Stock plants: The parent plants from which cuttings are taken for propagation purposes to ensure that new plants are an exact clone.

Stress: A cry for help. Wilting and discolored foliage are two signs of stress, signals that a plant is not happy about its growing conditions. Stress can be caused by too much or too little sun, water or fertilizer.

Tanglefoot: "Tree paste" used around the trunk of a tree to make a sticky barrier against such insects as ants (which reduces damage done by aphids, mealy bugs and some scale insects), weevils, caterpillars and cutworms.

Tissue-culture: A high-tech way of propagating by "cloning" a plant, in which tiny pieces of tissue are grown in test tubes.

Top-dressing: Putting a thin layer of new soil or compost around plants or on lawns to improve the soil.

Topiary: The shaping of shrubs and trees into decorative forms.

Trace elements: The same thing as micronutrients—various minerals that plants need in small doses in order to grow.

Tuber: A fleshy root or stem (dahlia, for example) that stores nutrients for later use.

Tufa: Porous limestone rock ideal for growing alpine plants.

Umbel: A rounded, often flattened head of flowers produced at the top of a long stem. A good example is the seed/flowerhead of an angelica plant.

Underplanting: Plants that have been placed beneath taller shrubs or trees, sometimes to provide leafy groundcover or seasonal color.

Variegated: Leaves that are spotted, streaked or edged with a different color from the main one.

Vermicomposting: Making compost using worms.

Weed: 1) a plant growing in the wrong place; 2) a plant for which a useful purpose has not yet been found.

Wild garden: Informal planting style that attempts to imitate nature. Popular with avant-garde landscape architects, not with most homeowners.

X: The symbol that denotes that a plant is a hybrid between two or more species.

Xeriscaping: Method of landscaping with drought-tolerant plant material to dramatically reduce the use of water.

Zones: North America is divided into 10 climatic zones that are graded according to the average annual minimum temperatures. Zone 1 is the coldest (below $-50°F/-46°C$) and Zone 10 is the warmest ($30°$ to $40°F/-1°$ to $5°C$). Zone numbers are a useful guide in determining which plants can survive outdoors in the garden over winter.

*B*ibliography

It is difficult to compile a bibliography for a book such as this. So much has been taken in over the years of researching and writing gardening stories for *The Vancouver Sun*. The works listed here are constant sources of reference and have been particularly helpful in the compilation of *100 Best Plants*.

Aden, Paul. *The Hosta Book*. Portland, Oregon: Timber Press, 1988.

Austin, David. *English Roses*. London: Conran Octopus, 1993.

Brickell, Christopher. *Cavendish Encyclopedia of Pruning and Training*. Vancouver, B.C.: Cavendish Books, 1996.

Callaway, Dorothy J. *The World of Magnolias*. Portland, Oregon: Timber Press, 1994.

Cole, Trevor. *Gardening with Trees and Shrubs*. Vancouver, B.C.: Whitecap Books, 1996.

Cole, Trevor. *Ontario Gardener*. Vancouver, B.C.: Whitecap Books, 1991.

The Encyclopedia of Roses. Portland, Oregon: Timber Press, 1992.

Flowers by Color. Vancouver, B. C.: Raincoast Books, 1993.

The Gardener's Encyclopedia of Plants and Flowers. London: Dorling Kindersley, 1989.

Hessayon, Dr. D. G. *The Bulb Expert*. London: Transworld Publishers, 1995.

Hessayon, Dr. D. G. *The NEW Rose Expert*. London: Transworld Publishers, 1996.

Hiller's Trees and Shrubs. Holland: Hiller Nurseries, 1981.

Lancaster, Roy. *What Plant Where*. Vancouver, B.C.: Cavendish Books, 1995.

Lawson, Andrew. *The Gardener's Book of Colour*. London: Francis Lincoln, 1996.

Phillips, Roger and Martyn Rix. *Perfect Plants*. New York: Random House, 1996.

Phillips, Roger and Martyn Rix. *The Random House Book of Perennials*. New York: Random House, 1991.

Reader's Digest Encyclopedia of Garden Plants and Flowers. London: Reader's Digest, 1985.

Rees, Yvonne and Neil Sutherland. *The Water Garden*. Vancouver, B.C.: Whitecap Books, 1995.

Straley, Gerald B. *Trees of Vancouver*. Vancouver, B.C.: UBC Press, 1992.

Taylor, Patrick. *The 500 Best Garden Plants*. Portland, Oregon: Timber Press, 1993.

Van Pelt Wilson, Helen and Leonie Bell. *The Fragrant Year*. Toronto: George McLeod, 1967.

Western Garden Book. Menlo Park, California: Sunset Publishing, 1992.

Woods, Christopher. *Encyclopedia of Perennials*. New York: Facts on File, 1992.

𝓘ndex

About the Author

Steve Whysall was born in 1950 in Nottingham, England. From 1968 to 1974, he worked as a reporter and editor for various newspapers in England, including the *Leicester Mercury, Nottingham Evening Post, Bristol Evening Post* and *London Evening News.*

He married and moved to Canada in 1975. For the last seven years he has written gardening columns for *The Vancouver Sun.* Steve is also the author of *100 Best Plants for the Coastal Garden.* He lives in Burnaby, British Columbia with his wife, Loraine, their daughter, and two sons. Their English-style garden contains most of the plants mentioned in this book.

Courtesy *The Vancouver Sun*